When Sugar Ruled

Ohio University Research in International Studies

This series of publications on Africa, Latin America, Southeast Asia, and Global and Comparative Studies is designed to present significant research, translation, and opinion to area specialists and to a wide community of persons interested in world affairs. The editor seeks manuscripts of quality on any subject and can usually make a decision regarding publication within three months of receipt of the original work. Production methods generally permit a work to appear within one year of acceptance. The editor works closely with authors to produce a high-quality book. The series appears in a paperback format and is distributed worldwide. For more information, contact the executive editor at Ohio University Press, 19 Circle Drive, The Ridges, Athens, Ohio 45701.

Executive editor: Gillian Berchowitz
AREA CONSULTANTS
Africa: Diane M. Ciekawy
Latin America: Brad Jokisch, Patrick Barr-Melej, and Rafael Obregon
Southeast Asia: William H. Frederick

The Ohio University Research in International Studies series is published for the Center for International Studies by Ohio University Press. The views expressed in individual volumes are those of the authors and should not be considered to represent the policies or beliefs of the Center for International Studies, Ohio University Press, or Ohio University.

When Sugar Ruled

Economy and Society in Northwestern Argentina, Tucumán, 1876–1916

Patricia Juarez-Dappe

Ohio University Research in International Studies
Latin America Series No. 49
Ohio University Press
Athens

To obtain permission to quote, reprint, or otherwise reproduce or distribute material from Ohio
University Press publications, please contact our rights and permissions department at (740) 593-
1154 or (740) 593-4536 (fax).
www.ohioswallow.com

Printed in the United States of America
The books in the Ohio University Research in International Studies Series
are printed on acid-free paper ⊗ ™

20 19 18 17 16 15 14 13 12 11 10   5 4 3 2 1

Library of Congress Cataloging-in-Publication Data

Juarez-Dappe, Patricia Isabel, 1965–
  When sugar ruled : economy and society in northwestern Argentina, Tucumán, 1876–1916 /
Patricia Juarez-Dappe.
    p. cm. — (Ohio University research in international studies, Latin America series ; No. 49)
  Includes bibliographical references and index.
  ISBN 978-0-89680-274-2 (pb : alk. paper) — ISBN 978-0-89680-463-0 (electronic)
  1. Sugar trade—Argentina—Tucumán—History—19th century. 2. Sugar trade—Argentina—
Tucumán—History—20th century. 3. Tucumán (Argentina)—Economic conditions—19th century.
4. Tucumán (Argentina)—Economic conditions—20th century. 5. Tucumán (Argentina)—Social
conditions. 6. Tucumán (Argentina)—Politics and government. 7. Argentina—Politics and
government—1860–1910. 8. Argentina—Politics and government—1910–1943. I. Title.
  HD9114.A72J83 2010
  338.1'736109824309034—dc22
                    2009047876

To Pipo and
To my parents

Contents

List of Illustrations ix

Acknowledgments xi

Introduction: Setting the Stage 1

1. Foundations for Growth 8

2. The Sugar Industry and Tucumán's Economy 33

3. Sugarcane Planters: Patterns of Production 55

4. Sugar Labor: Field and Factory Workers 87

5. Sugar and the Province 119

Conclusion: The World That Sugar Created 143

Appendix: Census Manuscript Schedules, 1869 and 1895 153

Notes 155

Glossary 205

Bibliography 207

Index 229

Illustrations

Maps

0.1 Regions and provinces of Argentina 3

1.1 Railroad lines in Tucumán, 1895 27

2.1 Ingenios and sugarcane area, 1895 42

Figures

1.1 Rural area, 1870s 15

1.2 Tucumano carts 19

1.3 Downtown San Miguel 25

1.4 Sugarcane transport to an ingenio 29

2.1 Hacienda Esperanza, early 1870s 37

2.2 Ingenio Esperanza, 1894 40

2.3 Students of the Estación Experimental Agrícola 47

2.4 Sugarcane plantation 49

3.1 Ingenio Mercedes, 1910 57

3.2 Sugarcane plantation of Señor Attuvell 64

3.3 Colonos' houses, early 1920s 69

3.4 Sugarcane and firewood transportation 71

3.5 Sugarcane planter's family, Ingenio Trinidad, early 1920s 75

3.6 Carts loaded with sugarcane outside an ingenio 77

3.7 The end of the zafra, early 1920s 85

4.1 Workers from Santiago del Estero, October 1920 93

4.2 Hospital Ingenio Bella Vista, 1910s 97

4.3 A family of seasonal workers arriving at Ingenio Bella Vista 100

4.4 Permanent workers' houses and owner's chalet, Ingenio San
 Pablo, 1910 107

4.5   Ingenio owner's chalet, Ingenio San Pablo, 1910   107
4.6   Housing for permanent workers, Ingenio San Pablo   108
4.7   Public baths in a sugar town   110
5.1   School of Agriculture, UNT   133
5.2   Geography class, Escuela Pedagógica Sarmiento   134
5.3   Hospital Mixto, 1920   138
5.4   Government palace   141

Table

3.1   Sugarcane cultivation by size and tenure of units,
        Tucumán, 1895   65

Acknowledgments

This project could not have been completed without the encouragement and assistance of many people and organizations. At the University of California, Los Angeles, financial support from the Department of History and the Office of International Studies and Overseas Programs facilitated the funds needed for thirteen months of field research in Tucumán and Buenos Aires. A Chancellor's Dissertation Year Fellowship gave me further financial support for the completion of the doctoral dissertation on which this book is based. Postdoctoral research was made possible through a library travel grant from the Center for Latin American Studies at the University of Florida, Gainesville, and through summer grants and stipends provided by the College of Social and Behavioral Sciences and the Department of History at California State University, Northridge. Finally, a National Endowment for the Humanities Faculty Research Award enabled me to take a year off to undertake final revisions on the manuscript.

This book owes a great intellectual and personal debt to many individuals. At UCLA, I am most grateful to José Moya, my adviser. His enthusiasm and energy encouraged me to embark on this ambitious task. With patience, dedication, and the inspiration of his extensive knowledge, he provided guidance through the challenges of graduate school. I also thank Naomi Lamoreaux, William Summerhill, Kevin Terraciano, and Eric Van Young for their valuable suggestions during my years as a graduate student. I thank in particular Kenneth Sokoloff, whose enduring dedication to his students, even after their graduation, went beyond the call of duty. His invaluable intellectual guidance improved this book significantly, while his friendship offered constant support. His early passing has left an unfillable void in my life.

As I struggled to sort out the complexities of this topic, several scholars in both the United States and Argentina graciously took the time to read and discuss my research. Extensive comments from Edward Beatty, Patrick Barr-Melej, Susan Fitzpatrick-Behrens, Sofía Martos, and Ángela Vergara improved the final product in countless ways. Their friendship and constant encouragement made me even more aware that intellectual work takes place through debate and conversation. My thanks also to Donna Guy, whose insightful suggestions contributed enormously to my intellectual growth and have had an enduring and positive influence on this project. In Tucumán, I have learned much from María Celia Bravo, Daniel Campi, José Antonio Sánchez Román, and Lucía Vidal Sanz, who shared their research with me and pointed my work in new and rewarding directions. I also thank María Victoria Dappe for countless hours of conversation during Tucumán's siesta time.

I am grateful to my colleagues in the history department at CSU Northridge—Jeffrey Auerbach, Richard Horowitz, Thomas Maddux, Clementine Oliver, Michael Powelson, and Nan Yamane—for their valuable comments on various sections of the manuscript. I thank Tom Devine, Charles Macune, Miriam Neirick, and Josh Sides for their support throughout the revision process. I also thank Merry Ovnick for her guidance, extreme generosity, and kindness. To Susan Mueller and Kelly Winkleblack-Shea I owe a special debt for their assistance during difficult days and for always having a word of encouragement. Finally, I appreciate my undergraduate and graduate students at Northridge, who help me remember why I wanted to become a historian in the first place.

Special thanks to those professionals who guard the archives in Argentina today. In the Archivo Histórico de Tucumán, I particularly recognize Celina Correa Uriburu and Marcela Magliani, who played a crucial role in bringing this project to fruition. Their constant attention to my never ending requests, their patience, and their friendship made those freezing days spent at the archive not only extremely productive but, most important, a real pleasure. At the Archivo de la Legislatura de Tucumán, I acknowledge the invaluable assistance of Cristina Vilatta de Juárez. In Buenos Aires, I thank Luis Priamo for his help locating photographic materials for this book. Finally, I am forever indebted to Roberto Ferrari, who shared his collection of photographs with me, showing immense generosity and true interest in the preservation of Argentina's historic legacy.

At the Ohio University Press I am grateful to Gillian Berchowitz for her support and patience and for making this process a very enjoyable experience. I also thank Nancy Basmajian for her assistance during the copyediting process and Bob Furnish for the excellent editing and for turning my awkward prose into readable form. I thank the two anonymous readers whose comments and valuable suggestions greatly improved the manuscript. I thank the *Journal of Latin American Studies,* which has generously granted permission for use of materials originally published as part of my essay "*Cañeros* and *Colonos:* Cane Planters in Tucumán, 1876–1895."

My greatest debt is to my loved ones. I thank my siblings, Mónica and Daniel, and my friends Ericka Boltshauser, Marcela Jacobo, and Fabián Gómez, all of whom helped me in many ways and never lost faith in me. I am grateful to my parents, who early in my life taught me the importance of honesty and who have done for me far more than any daughter could reasonably expect. Finally, I thank Pipo; without his support this book would have never been finished. His love, sense of humor, wisdom and companionship make him a true partner in this project.

Except where noted, all photographs appear courtesy of the Photographic Department, Archivo General de la Nación, Buenos Aires.

Introduction

Setting the Stage

IN THE FIFTY YEARS preceding the First World War, Argentina experienced one of the highest sustained growth rates in the world. Wool for Belgian and French carpet factories, wheat for British flour mills, and beef for British consumers enabled the country's full integration into the world economy and constituted important foundations for economic expansion. By the beginning of the twentieth century, Argentina had risen from a poor and backward region into one of the wealthiest nations in the world. Between 1869 and 1914 foreign labor and capital poured into the country. Thousands of immigrants arrived and found work as sharecroppers and *peones* (farmhands), although a significant number also stayed in urban areas working in construction, transportation, meat-packing plants, and the service sector. Despite attempts by the authorities, most Europeans settled in coastal areas, some of them never leaving Buenos Aires. In 1914 half the city's population was foreign born. Not only labor but capital came into the country. Between 1880 and 1913 British investment in Argentina increased twenty times. Besides public loans and banking, British capital flowed into transportation, in particular railroads. By 1914 thousands of kilometers of tracks connected the pampas and important cities in the rest of the country with the port of Buenos Aires.

In any case, Argentina's economic miracle created a nation of contrasts. The comparative advantage of the Argentine pampas for the production of grains and meat placed the area at the forefront of this dramatic expansion. But while Buenos Aires and the pampas prospered, many provinces stagnated. During an early-twentieth-century visit, American traveler and self-declared vagabond Harry Franck confessed to have wandered the city's streets "in a semi-dazed condition" surprised to find in "the Argentine capital to-day the largest Spanish-speaking city on the globe, second only to Paris among the Latin cities of the world, equal to Philadelphia in population, resembling Chicago in extent as well as in situation, rivaling New York in many of its metropolitan features, and outdoing every city of our land in some of its civic improvements." Franck, however, highlighted the contrasts between the city and the rest of the country that resulted from "the general South American tendency to dress up the capital like an only son and trust that the rest of the country will pass unnoticed, like a flock of poor relatives or servants."[1]

However, there were some exceptions. During the last quarter of the nineteenth century, the provinces of Tucumán and Mendoza emerged as flourishing centers, in the Argentine northwest and the Cuyo region respectively.[2] The spread of viticulture gave a significant boost to Mendoza's economy, while sugar production was at the heart of Tucumán's prosperity. The main engine behind these provinces' economic expansion was Argentina's domestic market, which experienced an impressive growth during the last decades of the nineteenth century as a result of European immigration.[3] Assistance from the national authorities through modern infrastructure, increased credit, and high tariffs provided the fuel for this engine. By 1914 annual wine production was about four million liters and, although Mendoza never lost its preeminent position in Argentina's wine industry, vines were already being cultivated in three provinces: San Juan and small areas in Catamarca and La Rioja.[4] Similarly, during the last quarter of the nineteenth century Tucumán became Argentina's main sugar producer and remained in that role despite the expansion of the sugar industry to other provinces, such as Jujuy and Salta. In 1914 Tucumán produced 270,000 tons of sugar and sugarcane plantations extended over 91,000 hectares. In the words of Harry Franck, San Miguel de Tucumán had become "a town that lives, breathes, and dreams sugar." Sixty years before Franck's visit to their province, few Tucumanos could have imagined that the area was destined to become "the City of Sugar."[5]

The province of Tucumán is located in the Argentine northwest, about 1,300 kilometers from the port of Buenos Aires. The smallest province in

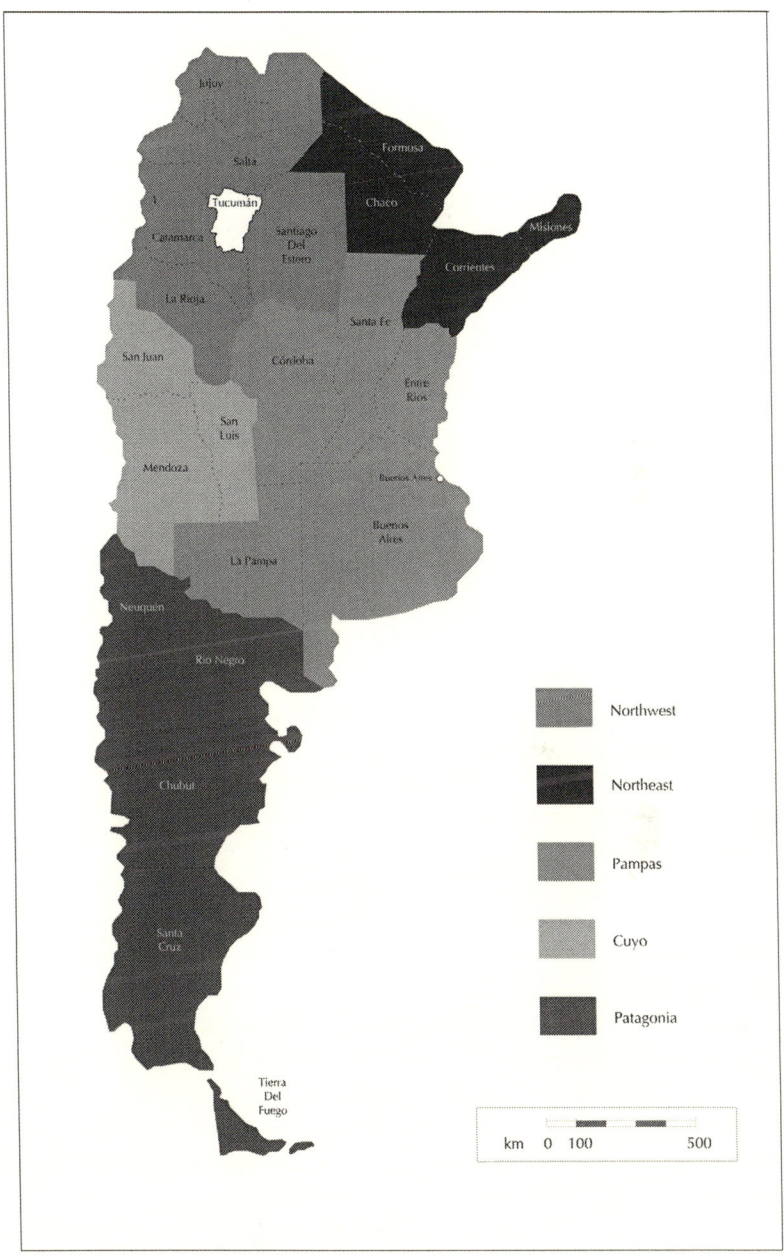

Jujuy

Salta

Formosa

Tucumán

Chaco

Santiago
Del
Estero

Misiones

Catamarca

Corrientes

La Rioja

Santa Fe

San Juan

Córdoba

Entre
Ríos

San
Luis

Mendoza

Buenos Aires C

Buenos
Aires

La Pampa

Neuquén

Río Negro

Chubut

Santa
Cruz

Tierra
Del
Fuego

Northwest

Northeast

Pampas

Cuyo

Patagonia

km   0   100   500

Map 0.1. Regions and provinces of Argentina

Argentina, its 22,000 square kilometers are crossed by rivers and streams; altitudes range from 30 to 3,000 meters. In the early 1850s Tucumán's fertile soils produced tobacco, maize, wheat, rice, sugarcane, alfalfa, and oranges. The province's economic prosperity rested not only on a diversified productive structure but also on an active local market that was complemented by trade with both domestic and foreign markets. Aside from tobacco and grains, a variety of textiles, furniture, and leather goods were transported in locally made carts to consumers throughout Argentina, Chile, and Bolivia. During those days, sugar production did not occupy a significant place in the provincial economy, as Tucumán's sugar producers still relied on primitive technology, which yielded a low-quality unrefined yellow sugar that found consumers only in the local market.

This situation started to change during the second half of the nineteenth century. Tucumano producers made investments in technology and, with the assistance of the national and provincial authorities, launched a profound transformation in sugar processing that intensified in the following decades. As a result, by the end of the century the sugar industry had achieved new preeminence in the provincial economy. Between 1876 and 1895, sugar production increased from 3,000 to 110,000 tons and the area cultivated with sugarcane expanded from 2,500 to 55,500 hectares. By 1895, Argentina had achieved self-sufficiency in sugar and the province of Tucumán emerged as the country's main sugar producer. In less than two decades sugar had moved from Tucumán's productive backyard to occupy a paramount position in the provincial economy. As Tucumán's dominant economic activity, the sugar industry was at the forefront of the transformations that took place in the province between 1876 and 1916. The industry defined the political and economic concerns of Tucumán's administrators and leading citizens. Sugar altered Tucumán's productive structure and shaped its society in profound new ways. For more than a century, the province's way of life derived from sugar and the influence of the *cañaverales* (sugarcane plantations) extended well beyond the sugar area.

This book is concerned with the changes experienced by Tucumán's economy and society as a result of sugar expansion, thus adding to the existing literature on sugar economies in Latin America and Argentina. For the Argentine case, scholars have provided in-depth analyses of specific aspects of Tucumán's sugar economy, such as sugar politics, sugarcane planters, workers, railroads, tariffs, and credit.[6] This study addresses the peculiarities of the world created by sugar production in Tucumán. By examining the province through the prism of the sugar industry, the analysis uncovers the economic and social changes that occurred in Tucumán during Argentina's golden era.

The study relies on a solid base of historical documentation, such as provincial and national reports, censuses, accounting records, congressional debates, sugar periodicals, newspapers, travelers' accounts, and other provincial publications. I have mined unused archival sources such as notarial records, civil and criminal court cases, and census manuscript schedules. During the period under consideration, Argentine authorities conducted national censuses in 1869, 1895, and 1914. Since published censuses offer only aggregate data, this analysis has relied extensively on the records of twenty-five thousand individuals and over ten thousand agricultural units obtained from the manuscript schedules corresponding to 1869 and 1895.[7] The variety of sources not only enriches the analysis by incorporating materials that have not previously been examined but also enables a more in-depth approach to the study of Tucumán's economy and society during the first four decades of sugar expansion, 1876–1916.

The time span selected satisfies both a provincial framework and a larger Argentine perspective. Since the most important questions to be answered relate to the evolution of sugar production, the four decades under consideration represent the industry's most impressive growth and its transformation into the leading and most dynamic sector of the provincial economy. The choice of 1876 provides a symbolic but convenient point of departure as it marks the arrival of the Ferrocarril Central Norte in the province that, in conjunction with other local and external factors, paved the way for the adoption of modern sugar technology and the subsequent increase in sugar output. The choice of the end point coincides with the sugarcane mosaic virus, a virulent pest that destroyed most of the province's sugarcane plantations and signaled the end of an era for Tucumán's sugar industry, as it was followed by a profound crisis of underproduction and the restructuring of the agricultural sector. From a broader national perspective, the administrations of Nicolás Avellaneda (1874–80) and the first administration of Hipólito Yrigoyen (1916–22) clearly denote two different eras in Argentine politics. The shift in the national authorities' base of support from regional elites to metropolitan middle-class consumers directly affected the fate of the industry. Through the League of Governors, Avellaneda co-opted provincial elites and opened the political game for groups outside Buenos Aires in exchange for support and cooperation. The "oligarchic regime," consolidated under Gen. Julio A. Roca, was built on that foundation. Donna Guy's analysis has uncovered the importance of the interplay of family networks, politics, and nation building in the development of Tucumán's sugar industry.[8] Four decades after Avellanada's regime, Yrigoyen's inauguration displaced those traditional groups and launched a new stage in Argentine politics in which the power of the state was used to mediate among a much broader social base.[9] By incorporating new groups into the national political arena, the rise of the Radical Party changed the country's balance of power and the position of sugar groups at both the national and provincial levels.[10]

This book should contribute to the vast literature of Argentine history albeit from a different perspective. By focusing on Tucumán's sugar industry the study attempts to construct a more richly textured analysis of modern Argentina as it shifts the analysis to a region that was not a producer of agro pastoral export commodities. The study is the result of both intellectual curiosity and a sense of personal redemption. Born into a Tucumano family and raised in Buenos Aires, I have always been amazed by the fixation of the historical literature with the Argentine capital and the coastal region. For decades, a significant majority of scholars interested in Argentine history have preferred to focus their attention on those areas, relegating the study of the Argentine "interior" to a far secondary position. The export economy, wheat and beef, patterns of land use and tenure in the pampas, European immigration, organized labor movement, and the city of Buenos Aires are some of the recurrent topics that have dominated the Argentine historiography. This imbalance is even more noticeable among English-speaking historians.[11] Since modern Argentina cannot be understood without reference to the "interior," this pampas-centrism has resulted in a limited understanding of the country's history characterized by a rather incomplete and distorted narrative of what is termed national history.

In recent years, more scholars are recognizing the importance of regions and provinces in their works and are making a concerted effort to break away from the Buenos Aires paradigm in search for a truly national history.[12] Studies on Tucumán and the sugar industry have definitely benefited from and contributed to this renaissance. For the past decade, a group of scholars have increasingly focused their attention to specific aspects of the sugar industry. Their works have opened new ambits for discussion and with them the prospect for a reevaluation of a number of interpretations not only of modern Tucumán but also modern Argentina. The classrooms of the Universidad Nacional de Tucumán and academic journals such as *Población y Sociedad* and *Travesía* have become important venues to debate and disseminate new ideas. It is my hope to partake in these efforts with this study which is part and consequence of this provincially/regionally centered intellectual renaissance.

Chapter 1

Foundations for Growth

IN THE LATE 1850s German naturalist Hermann Burmeister visited the province of Tucumán and observed, "Of all the cities in the interior, there is no doubt that San Miguel de Tucumán is the most elegant and friendliest, not only because of its location but also because of its infrastructure and population . . . a result of the vast industries that exist in the area."[1] Burmeister was not alone in his remarks. During the late 1860s and 1870s, other visitors highlighted the province's economic dynamism and the city's affluence, in particular when compared to its neighbors in the Argentine northwest. Tucumán's prosperity rested on a diversified economy characterized by a rich agropastoral sector and a large manufacturing sector. The province's population made for a strong local demand that was complemented by active trade with domestic and foreign markets. In those days the sugar industry did not occupy a significant place in the provincial economy; it contributed only 10 percent of Tucumán's total production revenues. High transportation costs not only limited the scope of Tucumán's sugar market but also made the adoption of modern technology almost impossible as it was too expensive to transport machinery from Buenos Aires to Tucumán.

The Early Years

In 1545 the discovery of silver in Upper Peru unleashed profound transformations in the economies of the region. The area became the most important mining complex in South America and quickly surpassed other silver-producing regions of the Spanish Empire, such as Zacatecas and Guanajuato. Silver production declined during the seventeenth century but revived in the following century and experienced an impressive expansion.[2] Upper Peru became South America's fastest-growing region and Potosí, the silver-mining capital of the world. Thousands of people migrated to work in the mines or to take advantage of the opportunities offered by the new economic bonanza, transforming the area into a major population center that contained at times more than one hundred thousand individuals.[3]

Remote and at a high altitude, the city of Potosí and surrounding mining areas relied for the survival of their population on goods produced in neighboring regions.[4] Hundreds of pack mules arrived regularly with foodstuffs, textiles, leather goods, furniture, and luxury goods, as well as tools, mercury, and other mining supplies. For decades, silver became the fuel that sustained the economies of the modern territories of Jujuy, Salta, Tucumán, Santiago del Estero, Catamarca, Cuyo, and Chile. In direct response to Potosí's expanding demand, a line of settlements sprouted southward to supply provisions and equipment to the mining areas. San Miguel de Tucumán was one of them. The town was founded in 1565 by Diego Villarroel, following orders from the viceroy of Lima.[5] Bounded by the Río Pueblo Viejo to the north, the Río Seco to the south, the Río Salí to the east, and the foot of the Cerro Aconquija to the west, the site chosen was more protected from Calchaquí invasions than earlier settlements such as Nieva, Cañete, and San Clemente while at the same time closer to the commercial route to Upper Peru. The city became part of the Gobernación del Tucumán (under the political jurisdiction of Lima), which encompassed the modern Argentine provinces of Córdoba, Jujuy, Salta, Tucumán, Santiago del Estero, Catamarca, and La Rioja. The founding of the town of San Miguel de Tucumán represented a major turning point, as it signaled the beginning of a more stable occupation of the region. During the late sixteenth century, people migrated and settled in Tucumán and transformed it into the most populated area in the territory that is now Argentina.[6]

The town of San Miguel did not experience significant changes until the first half of the seventeenth century. During this period, its population faced many difficulties, such as poor living conditions, lack of resources, and periodic flooding. Furthermore, native hostility rendered the commercial route through the valleys extremely dangerous. Attacks by Calchaquí groups reached a peak between 1630 and 1660 and contributed to the final relocation of the

Spanish trade route thirty kilometers to the west of its original location, leaving San Miguel isolated and in financial distress. In 1685 the city's *vecinos* (inhabitants with full citizenship rights) managed to convince the authorities in Lima to move San Miguel sixty kilometers northeast of its original site to an area known as La Toma. Located on higher ground, the new site offered protection from floods and indigenous threats as well as a more direct access to Potosí through El Camino del Perú. The city's proximity to trading routes meant new opportunities for the town's impoverished population and inaugurated a new phase in the economic history of San Miguel.[7]

During the eighteenth century, the Upper Peruvian market provided an important stimulus to San Miguel's economic development. Potosí and its adjacent mining areas depended on mules to transport mercury, silver, and provisions through the mountain passes. Mules bred in Córdoba, on their way to Salta's annual fair, passed through San Miguel. Between 1750 and the early nineteenth century, Salta, the "largest assemblage of mules in the entire world," received tens of thousands of animals annually.[8] San Miguel's fertile lands offered pastures for breeding both mules and oxen used on the carts that transported goods throughout the region. The city's inhabitants became specialized in the manufacture of those carts, which were made entirely of wood and leather. The cart industry provided an important source of provincial revenue for a large sector of the population, who were not only involved in building the carts but also in operating the convoys. Other goods, such as wool textiles, raw cotton, hides, furniture, and agricultural products, were significant sources of income for the city's inhabitants. Potosí was San Miguel's largest consumer market, although Tucumano products reached other areas as well. Maize, wheat, textiles, and furniture were traded in Cuyo and Chile, while hides and tallow reached Buenos Aires, where they were exchanged for smuggled goods that found their way into Spanish territory through the Río de la Plata.[9] Since contraband drastically reduced Spain's revenues from the colonies, the authorities attempted to reduce its negative effects with the establishment of the Aduana Seca (lit., dry customs house) in Córdoba.[10]

Limited success in controlling contraband in the region led the authorities in Spain to institute a number of reforms that altered the internal equilibrium of the Spanish Empire in South America and directly affected the fate of San Miguel. In 1776 the Spanish crown created the viceroyalty of the Río de la Plata, which enabled the port of Buenos Aires to become a lawful mediator between Potosí silver areas and Spain. The new administrative jurisdiction included Buenos Aires, Cuyo, Paraguay, Tucumán, and Upper Peru. During the second half of the eighteenth century, San Miguel's merchants maintained an active trade with the two ends of the viceroyalty as they increased their trade, especially in hides and shoe soles, with Buenos Aires but still maintained an active commerce of mules, saddles, and foodstuffs with Upper Peru.[11] Salvador de Alberdi's 1805 report indicates that while Tucumán's contacts with Potosí remained very important for the economic health of San Miguel, the local market was becoming more dependent on a wide array of European goods that arrived through the port of Buenos Aires. San Miguel's population provided an important market not only for local products but also for luxury imports, thus giving an additional stimulus to the region's economy.[12] In 1805, according to Alberdi's estimates, two thirds of Tucumán's imports came from Castile, while the area's exports reached more varied markets, such as Buenos Aires, Chile, and Upper Peru.[13]

The May Revolution, in 1810, brought an end to the colonial order and launched decades of civil strife that disrupted the region's economy profoundly. Spanish control over Upper Peru severed San Miguel's trading ties with Potosí, seriously affecting Tucumano merchants and encouraging their economic reorientation toward Buenos Aires and the Argentine littoral.[14] The declaration of independence from Spain failed to bring peace among the Argentine provinces. In the four decades following independence, the country became involved in factional struggles and civil war, and Tucumán oscillated between periods of political anarchy and stability. The situation changed for the province during the 1850s and 1860s. A relatively peaceful political climate enabled Tucumán's authorities to devote their energy to introduce important foundations for growth. Since order and stability were perceived as essential to economic modernization, the provincial government moved toward the consolidation of a strong provincial state by committing to the creation of new institutional settings that would not only legitimize their authority but also facilitate economic growth.[15] The legislature approved a new provincial statute in 1852 and a constitution in 1856. The new charter, in accordance with the 1853 national constitution, established the division of powers, guaranteed internal order, protected private property, and organized public sources of revenue. It also provided for the future sanction of a new judicial code, an electoral law, the creation of municipalities, and a public mandatory education law.

During the 1850s, Tucumán's authorities paid special attention to tax and labor legislation. Four decades of political turmoil had left public finances in disarray. In order to increase revenues, the government reformed the provincial tax structure through measures that attempted to simplify collection and prevent evasion.[16] The two taxes specifically targeted during this period were the *patentes* and the *contribución directa*.[17] Patentes dated back to the early 1820s, although their origin can be traced to colonial times. This tax consisted of a levy on the profits obtained from any economic activity, including commerce, industry, the professions, and agriculture. During the 1850s, the tax was changed several times. Originally, the levy was a fixed percentage applied equally to all activities. Over time, to increase control over taxpayers and to better reflect the changes undergone by the provincial economy, the fixed percentage was replaced by a specific rate for each activity.

The contribución directa was created in 1855 by the national government to replace the colonial tithe.[18] The new tax consisted of fixed rates on the values of real estate as well as on total amounts involved in capital transactions. During the 1860s the levy underwent successive modifications that simplified and improved its collection and reflected the increasing activity of the real estate market. According to provincial records, in 1876 patentes provided 24 percent of the total provincial income, while the contribución directa accounted for 31 percent.

Besides revisions to the tax system, during the early 1860s the government instituted a number of reforms to modernize mechanisms of tax collection. To prevent abuses and improve collection, the government appointed commissions to assess real estate values and make estimates on taxable amounts. To achieve the cooperation of taxpayers, commission members were selected from among the propertied class.[19] To guarantee a fair tax system, taxpayers could appeal the commissions' appraisals before a special jury before the tax was due. Nevertheless, these mechanisms failed to generate the anticipated outcomes, as real estate values were not updated annually to account for infrastructural improvements, commissioners were unable to verify the accuracy of tax declarations, and assessments failed to keep pace with the swift expansion of the cultivated area.[20] In any case, what these measures clearly reveal is authorities' commitment to increase their control over public revenues, inaugurating a trend that intensified during the decades of expansion of the sugar industry.

New labor legislation also occupied a significant place in the provincial authorities' agenda. Since colonial times, labor shortages had constituted a constant source of concern among Tucumán's landowners. The most acute problem, according to contemporary witnesses, was workers' tendency to run away. In an attempt to thwart a problem that not only disrupted the work routine and labor discipline but also inflicted important material losses on the propertied class, the authorities passed several pieces of legislation throughout the nineteenth century. As early as 1810, a decree authorized the use of physical punishment for those workers who escaped from their jobs. In 1823, Tucumán's *cabildo* (municipal council) penalized vagrancy and required workers to produce job certificates or other proof of employment in order to avoid incarceration or military draft. The decree also authorized the police to place vagrants in available jobs in the area, thus giving the police a new role that was to become institutionalized in the second half of the nineteenth century. Despite the government's efforts, regulations failed, as difficulties to apply the letter of the law and lack of control in the countryside rendered coercive measures largely ineffective.

In 1856 the provincial authorities made another attempt to solve the labor problem when Tucumán's legislature passed the Police Code, section 6 of which was entirely devoted to labor-related issues. Borrowing from prior legislation, that section gave the police administrative and judicial authority in labor matters.[21] Section 6 provided for the police to persecute vagrants as well as to find them an occupation. It established basic procedures for registration and penalized those registered with more than one employer. The code required workers to carry at all times a *papeleta* with their employer's name, the job's address, and the duration of the contract.[22] These job certificates were to be renewed every year. Section 6 also stated the rights and duties of both employers and employees, but it made no pretense that they were equal before the law. Workers were required to be obedient, faithful, and respectful. Employers, defined as domestic magistrates, were allowed to moderately punish workers and to detain them for twenty-four hours. After that period, the law stipulated that workers be turned over to the police, thus subjecting them to a double system of control in which both the public and private sectors reinforced each other. The code also instituted a penal principle called *hurto de servicios* (service theft), which enabled the police to consider flight a punishable offense.[23] The statute regulated workers' rights such as daily rations, wages, health care, and length of workday. Their obligations—obedience, fidelity, and respect—were established in vague terms, enabling practices that exceeded a standard working relationship. Despite the government's attempts, the 1856 regulation failed to create a stable pool of workers. During his 1869 visit to survey mining resources in Tucumán, British engineer Maj. Ignacio Rickart observed that labor in the province was scarce: "It would seem a most desirable arrangement to introduce here a number of coolies."[24] In any case, section 6 of the Police Code represented a major step toward the consolidation of coercive labor mechanisms in the province since it increased both authorities' and employers' control over workers and tightened procedures to impose labor discipline.

Institutional changes provided important foundations for growth but other factors proved to be equally important. Stressing Tucumán's rapid progress during the late 1860s, Rickart identified two additional elements that contributed to the province's prosperity, a population that "manifestly increases in number and advances in civilization" and "land [that] is comparatively cheap, and may be purchased in freehold."[25] Since colonial times, Tucumán had enjoyed a large population concentrated in a relatively small area. In 1869, according to the first national census, the province counted 108,953 inhabitants and was the second most populated in the northwest region.[26] Even more important, Tucumán's density of 1.75 people per square kilometer was the highest among its counterparts in the northwest and throughout the country second only to Buenos Aires.[27] When describing Tucumán's human and physical resources, contemporary observers praised the spirit of enterprise and economic drive of its large population but also marveled at the "pasture of the densest, richest, and most lofty kind" that justified the titles Garden of the Confederation and Italy of Argentine provinces.[28] Tucumán's fertile and well-watered plains were exceedingly well suited for a variety of crops.[29] Wheat, maize, rice, sugarcane, tobacco, alfalfa, barley, flax, legumes, vegetables, and citrus and other fruit trees were among the most common plants cultivated in large but also medium and small plots throughout the province.

As was the case in other regions in Argentina, a relatively small group of landowners concentrated large tracts of land. The group had been acquiring land since colonial times and became the main beneficiaries during the redistribution of holdings expropriated from the Jesuits after the order's expulsion in 1767.[30] Over time, their holdings increased in size as a result of marriage, purchase, or usurpation. However, at the same time, Tucumán also displayed a significant number of medium and small holdings. The group's numbers increased gradually throughout the 1700s, and the tendency accelerated during the following century, when the land market expanded, thus enabling a larger sector of the population to gain access to landownership.[31] Therefore, during the mid-nineteenth century, the province witnessed the consolidation of a group of medium and small holdings coexisting with large properties. In the 1870s contemporaries remarked Tucumán's complete absence of public lands as well as its population's widespread access to landownership.[32]

The peculiar nature of Tucumán's land tenure system is corroborated by additional evidence. In 1869 the first national census listed a total of 19,932 people engaged in primary activities in Tucumán.[33] The census reported 10,785 *labradores* (farmworkers), 6,527 *jornaleros* (day laborers) and *peones* (farmhands), 1,584 *estancieros* (ranchers), and 833 *agricultores* (farmers). Even though census figures do not provide information on property status, occupational descriptions can be used as an indication of land ownership or lack of it. While *jornalero* and *peón* were terms used for rural wage workers, *estanciero, agricultor,* and *labrador* implied direct access to land through tenancy or proprietary status.[34] In 1875, Juan Terán's survey for the National Department of Agriculture confirmed the existence of widespread access to land. According to the report, the province had a large number of

Figure 1.1. Rural area, 1870s. Rural families lived in small huts with very few possessions besides land and farm animals. *(Courtesy of Photographic Department, Archivo General de la Nación, Buenos Aires.)*

family-operated units, worked by their owners and no bigger than a couple of hectares, devoted to the production of cereals for self-consumption and of various tropical crops such as tobacco and sugarcane.[35] The group revealed a degree of prosperity not found in other areas of the Argentine northwest, as some of these units also possessed cattle and agricultural tools and its members were described as not only relatively successful and hardworking but also fiercely independent.[36]

Before the Sugar Boom

In 1853 a commission appointed by the provincial authorities estimated the total value of the goods produced in Tucumán at 1,754,250 pesos.[37] The primary and secondary sectors' participation in Tucumán's output amounted to 1,033,000 pesos and 721,250 pesos, respectively, while exports totaled 908,250 pesos. The province imported a total of 500,000 pesos in goods from other provinces and neighboring countries. The commission's report revealed a balanced and diversified economy that produced a variety of agropastoral goods and manufactures that were consumed locally as well as traded on domestic and foreign markets.

During the 1850s and 1860s, following on a trend manifested since colonial times, Tucumano farmers were still devoting most of their lands to the production of different crops and livestock. Until the early 1880s grains enjoyed a paramount position in Tucumán's agricultural sector, accounting for almost 80 percent of the province's cultivated area.[38] Maize was the most popular crop among cultivators. A traditional staple in the local diet, it did not require intensive care and was cultivated throughout the province on small and medium farms that used family labor. Since maize was consumed locally, its production expanded in response to increases in population growth. In those years, farmers also devoted their lands to other grains. For example, although not as popular as maize, wheat production grew three times between 1853 and 1880.[39] In this case, increases reflected the expansion of Tucumán's flour industry and its growing trade with foreign and domestic markets rather than changes in local demand. Between 1857 and 1877 the number of flour mills in the province—powered by steam, water, or animals—increased from eleven to sixty-nine.[40] Tucumán's lands produced other crops, such as rice, barley, and alfalfa for local consumption or to be traded with neighboring provinces. Citrus trees, in particular orange groves, surrounded the city of San Miguel as well. Locals consumed the sweet oranges and used the bitter variety for marmalades that were sold by women in small stands in the local markets. Tucumán's farmers also produced tobacco and sugarcane. Tobacco was cultivated mostly in the southern parts of the province, on family-operated plots.[41] The crop enjoyed popularity among farmers, as it required only a modest initial investment and offered quick returns. In the early 1850s, according to Belgian military geographer Alfred Marbais, the capital needed to put into production a two-hectare tobacco plantation was 4,200 pesos. That cost included land, workers, utensils, animals, taxes, and packaging materials and was reduced to one half in subsequent years. Such a plantation would yield 5,000 pesos a year.[42] Tobacco is a very delicate plant; sowing seedbeds, transplanting, pruning, and leaf-by-leaf harvesting entail total dedication and a level of expertise and dexterity not always present among cultivators. Visitors to the province pointed out that Tucumán's tobacco could compete with Brazil's only if planters devoted more time to improve its quality. They criticized producers' preference for tobacco's strength over scent and taste and their carelessness when tending the plants. Tobacco's share of the province's cultivated land remained stable during the 1870s but never exceeded 5 percent of the total cultivated area.

Another popular cash crop was sugarcane. According to contemporary witnesses, a sugarcane planter could recover the original investment made in land, machinery, and tools after one year, and sugarcane did not require the intensive care of tobacco plantations.[43] Tucumano farmers were inclined to devote part of their land to the cultivation of sugarcane because there was a captive local market, as taxes on imported sugar and high transportation costs made imported sugar too expensive. The province's trading networks with neighboring regions acted as an additional incentive to local producers, who relied on primitive technology to produce small quantities of low-quality sugar. In any case, during the 1850s the expansion of the potential market for sugar required investment in machinery that in those days was beyond the financial reach of most local entrepreneurs—this explains why during this period sugar production did not occupy a significant place in the provincial economy. According to the 1853 commission's report, sugar and rum contributed less than 10 percent of the total value of provincial output. Still, the potential importance of the crop in Tucumán's economy did not escape the attention of contemporary witnesses who predicted that, with strong government support and reduction in transportation costs, sugar production could take the lead in the province.

A significant pastoral sector complemented Tucumán's agriculture. Animal husbandry was a widespread activity, in particular in the northern parts of the province, although it never achieved the same scale as in Argentina's littoral areas. In the case of Tucumán, most cattle ranching took place on medium and small units that bred livestock for self-consumption and for the local market. According to Minister of Government Arsenio Granillo, few units owned more than five thousand head of cattle.[44] Gradually, cattle raising declined in importance, as noted by Paul Groussac, who in the early 1880s observed that agriculture's dramatic expansion had affected pastoral activities in the province in profound ways.[45] Throughout the nineteenth century animal husbandry maintained its preeminence only in some departments, such as Trancas and Graneros. Beasts of burden, in particular oxen and mules, constituted an important economic activity in those departments. Oxen carried the carts that transported Tucumano goods throughout the northwest while mules remained an important commodity in the Bolivian market. Besides being used for transportation and food, cattle provided the raw material for Tucumán's leather products, one of the many goods produced by Tucumán's diversified manufacturing sector.

The 1853 commission's report indicates the existence of a diversified and bustling manufacturing sector that contributed about 40 percent of the total value of provincial output. Textiles, shoe soles, leather products, soaps and candles, and carts and furniture were the most important manufactures in the province. Specializing in riding gear and footwear, Tucumano leather goods were traded in the littoral, Chile, and Bolivia. The tanning industry had occupied a prominent place in Tucumán's economy since the Jesuits brought it to the province during the eighteenth century. After the order's expulsion, French immigrants took over the business and invested in animals and equipment. Most of these new factories were located in the western districts of the capital city. Tanning became the most remunerative activity in the province, until sugar took the lead in the late nineteenth century. The 1875 financial crisis affected an industry already battling the effects of a scarcity of bark from the *cebil* tree, which was rich in tannin, necessary to cure the hides. The result was a reduction in the number of tanneries operating in the province.[46] Despite these difficulties, in 1882 provincial tanneries produced almost fifty thousand pieces used in saddlery (*talabartería*).[47]

Tucumán specialized not only in the production of leather goods but also in textiles. The province's needlework, knitted cloth, embroidery, tapestries, ponchos, and saddle blankets enjoyed a fine reputation throughout Argentina and received the praise of visitors such as Burmeister, who observed that textile manufacturing provided an at-home working alternative for women in both urban and rural areas. It is not possible to determine whether these women made a living from the goods they produced, supplemented their household income, or just did it as part of their domestic chores. But the German traveler offered an indication of the importance of textile production for the household economy: "Production of beautiful saddle blankets and woolen fabrics sustained many Tucumano middle-class families."[48] In any case, by midcentury Tucumán's textiles enjoyed a vast number of markets and contributed 18 percent of the output value of the provincial manufacturing sector.

Timber and furniture making occupied a significant place in Tucumán's economy during the second half of the nineteenth century as well. In 1875, Juan Terán reported that twenty-three sawmills in the province were using

Figure 1.2. Tucumano carts. Tucumán's artisans specialized in the construction of strong carts that transported goods to both local and foreign markets. Later in the century, these carts were used to carry sugarcane from the fields to the ingenio. (*Courtesy of Photographic Department, Archivo General de la Nación, Buenos Aires.*).

steam or hydraulic power.[49] Besides furniture and wood utensils, Tucumán still specialized in the manufacturing of carts that not only provided transportation but also were exported, representing another important source of provincial income.[50] Tucumán's diversified manufacturing sector as well as the excellence of its workmanship became apparent at the 1871 national exhibit in Córdoba, where the province earned gold medals for its sugar, leather, and embroidery. Silk products, indigo, sugar, and wooden products received silver medals. Finally, ponchos and rum collected bronze medals.[51]

Tucumano goods were consumed locally as well as traded in domestic and foreign markets. Since colonial times, a dense population concentrated in a small territory created an important local market. In 1778, Tucumán's twenty thousand inhabitants consumed more than half of the goods produced in the area.[52] This situation continued during the mid-1850s. The 1853 commission's report estimated that Tucumán's eighty thousand inhabitants consumed over 60 percent of the agropastoral products and almost 30 percent of the manufactures produced in the province. Besides the local market, the report revealed the importance of Tucumán's trading networks as exports to neighboring provinces, Chile and Bolivia contributed more than half of the total value of provincial output. Notwithstanding the restrictions posed by long distances, poorly maintained and unsafe roads, and high transportation costs, cartloads of leather goods, textiles, and other manufactures arrived to Bolivia, Chile, and Buenos Aires.[53]

The destination of Tucumano goods, in particular manufactures, indicates not only the survival of colonial trading networks but also the increasing importance of the national market, as 82 percent of the export values in 1853 came from trade with other provinces.[54] The report does not offer specific information on the final destination for Tucumán's goods, but additional evidence suggests that a large part of provincial manufactures were dispatched to Cuyo as well as to the port city of Rosario, a trend that intensified during the late 1870s, with the arrival of the railroad in the province.[55] Within the primary sector, maize and tobacco were the only crops exported. However, while most maize remained in Argentina, likely in neighboring provinces, Tucumán's tobacco was consumed more widely, as it was exported to Bolivia and Chile.[56] As for the pastoral sector, cattle on the hoof were exported to neighboring provinces, while mules and oxen were traded mostly in Bolivia. Since Tucumán could not provide for all its population's needs, the province's hides, textiles, and tobacco paid for a large number of imports, such as fine linens, iron roller mills, fine wine, beer, medicines, and barrels.[57]

Tucumán's diversified economy and widespread markets provided provincial entrepreneurs with opportunities to invest in a wide range of activities including agriculture, animal husbandry, manufacturing, and commerce. Such was the case of Esteban Gutiérrez, whose estate inventory after his death, in 1862, indicates that he was involved in a number of different activities, as it included barrels for sugar, rum, and honey, plantations with fruit trees, a small warehouse to store tobacco, livestock for consumption and beasts of burden, sugarcane-processing machinery, carts for transportation, agricultural tools, firewood, water rights, and real estate.[58] As Gutiérrez's case illustrates, the opportunities offered by the provincial economy created an environment that rewarded investment flexibility. Provincial entrepreneurs diversified their estates in an attempt to minimize risks and actively pursued the consolidation of mercantile relationships with the littoral areas while maintaining old colonial trading routes.

Personal connections and informal credit mechanisms assisted Tucumanos in fulfilling their increasing capital needs.[59] The Nougués family epitomizes this business strategy. In 1817, Juan Nougués arrived in Tucumán from France. In 1826 he purchased part of the former Jesuits' estates with capital he had accumulated from the tanning business. The French entrepreneur devoted those lands to cultivating some of the sugarcane that Obispo José Eusebio Colombres had distributed in 1821 as well as to cereals such as maize, wheat, rice, and barley. He installed a flour mill to grind his grains. Nougués also raised livestock and installed a modern sawmill to process the wood obtained from neighboring forests he owned. During the 1830s the family business continued to grow. By 1840 they owned four *estancias*, one of them, San Pablo, almost completely devoted to the production of sugar. The *ingenio* (sugar mill) administered after 1865 by Juan Luis Nougués, became during the 1880s one of the most important in the province.[60]

During the 1860s, British travelers M. G. and E. T. Mulhall visited Tucumán and, after surveying the province's political institutions, economic structure, and people's industriousness, finally concluded that the "whole town presents an aspect of progress and prosperity not found in other regions."[61] However, Tucumán's prosperity was more apparent in the Capital Department than in the rest of the province. According to the first national census, in 1869 the capital was home to 33 percent of the province's population who had declared an occupation. Half the department's working population was employed in the secondary sector, 30 percent in the service sector, and 20 percent in the primary sector.[62] The occupational pattern of Capital Department reveals a diversified and dynamic economy during the 1850s and 1860s. Secondary activities predominated, in particular leather and textile manufacturing, with high employment among the adult population. Timber was still an important activity, as judged by the number of workers engaged in furniture and cart making. Within the primary sector, peons and day workers constituted a clear majority, although the evidence indicates the existence of a significant group of landholders.

A sample of census manuscript schedules corresponding to Capital Department provides additional insight into the department's occupational structure.[63] Of the 7,644 residents surveyed, 4,556 (59.6 percent) were over fourteen years old. There was remarkable labor participation among the working-age group since 3,769 (82.7 percent) declared an occupation.[64] The schedules indicate a clear division between the sexes in various occupations.[65] Tucumán's well-diversified economy allowed women to be engaged in a vast number of activities. The sample indicates that rates of female employment were high, since 73.3 percent of women over fourteen declared an occupation, predominantly in manufacturing and service activities.[66] Tucumán's female artisans contributed significantly to the province's livelihood and the goods they produced were traded regionally and internationally.[67] Women constituted 64 percent of the population engaged in the manufacturing sector and enjoyed a clear majority in the areas of textiles, clothing, and cigar making, representing more than 95 percent of the workers employed in those activities.[68] Within the service sector, female laborers accounted for 53 percent and revealed a clear preeminence in domestic activities, in particular household servants, laundresses, cooks, and ironers. Males predominated in the primary sector (94 percent) and their participation in the secondary sector was limited to the tanning and furniture industries, where they represented almost 100 percent of the workers. Finally, men made up almost 100 percent of the workers in the liberal professions, mostly lawyers, and 83 percent of those engaged in commercial activities.

Capital Department enjoyed not only diversified and high employment rates but also a steady population growth. Between 1869 and 1874, the department increased its share of the total provincial population from 36 to 44 percent.[69] A large number of employment opportunities transformed

San Miguel into an important urban center in the Argentine northwest and attracted individuals from neighboring provinces. The significant number of migrants living in Tucumán during this period attests to the economic dynamism of the city. In 1869, 9 percent of Tucumán's population came from other provinces, the largest percentage in the Argentine northwest. Almost half the migrants chose San Miguel as their final destination and accounted for 12 percent of the population of Capital Department.[70] Searching for jobs, hundreds of people traveled to Tucumán, in particular Santiagueños and Catamarqueños, who represented almost 80 percent of the nonlocals residing in the province.[71] Census returns uncover important disparities among migrant workers in terms of their labor choices and literacy levels, clearly indicating that the province's prosperity and diversified economy offered opportunities for a broad range of individuals. In the sample, 19.6 percent of the population over fourteen was not from Tucumán. There was high employment among this group; 84 percent declared an occupation. Almost 38 percent found employment in the agropastoral sector (mostly as peons), 29 percent in the manufacturing sector, and 33 percent in the service sector. While Catamarqueños and Santiagueños had high illiteracy rates and predominated in the primary sector, Cordobeses and Salteños were engaged in commerce and service activities and were, as a group, more literate than people coming from other provinces. Therefore, as early as the 1860s, Tucumán's economic prosperity attracted migrants from neighboring provinces, anticipating a trend that would acquire new intensity during the last decades of the century as a result of sugar expansion. In contrast, only a few foreigners chose Tucumán as their final destination. According to official figures, in 1869 fewer than four hundred foreigners resided in the province and most of them lived in Capital Department. Of the seventy-three foreign individuals in the sample, sixty-five reported an occupation, mostly in the primary and secondary sectors.

Tucumán's economic dynamism did not escape the attention of contemporary visitors, in particular those visiting the city of San Miguel. Writing in 1880, Vicente Quesada recalled an "affluence . . . apparent in the clothes of peasants, bourgeois, and the working class" and contrasted it with Salta, where everything had the "color and decay of old things."[72] During this period, as was the case for most of Argentina's "secondary cities," San Miguel became Tucumán's "oasis of modernity," as it concentrated the province's political and administrative functions and became its intellectual and cultural center.[73] As the most important trading center in the province, the city was also the main site for commercial houses and businesses. With a population of over seventeen thousand, San Miguel was the largest urban center in the Argentine northwest. During this period, the city underwent important infrastructural improvements, such as better pavement; kerosene street lighting; construction of public schools, a public hospital and a new cemetery; and remodeled public buildings.[74] Private construction accelerated as well. According to a witness, a "construction fever" invaded the provincial elite, whose houses were demolished and rebuilt under the direction of European architects.[75] These new buildings were made with brick and lime mortar and had two stories and terrace roofs, not unlike those seen in Buenos Aires. They housed the most powerful families in the province and future sugar barons, such as Juan Manuel Méndez, Wenceslao Posse, and Juan Crisóstomo Méndez.[76]

However, infrastructure and housing improvements benefited mostly downtown San Miguel. In 1865 the poorer sectors of society lived in "miserably dirty mud-and-straw hovels" in most of the suburbs, with their narrow, dirty, poorly paved streets and unreliable lighting.[77] The suburbs also lacked security; the city's night watchmen patrolled only a few blocks in the downtown area. Regularly, vast areas in the suburbs experienced "dreadful floods" that caused material and human losses.[78] Arsenio Granillo recalled that the 1863 flood had almost reached San Miguel's downtown and that such floods had previously occurred in the province.[79] Furthermore, most tanneries and primitive sugar factories were located in the city's outskirts, especially in the northern and western neighborhoods, adding to the already bad living conditions in the more populous sectors. These problems only intensified with the constant arrival of workers in search of jobs.

Tucumán's bustling and diversified economy was more remarkable when weighed against that of its neighbors. In 1866 the British-owned Ferrocarril Central Argentino (Central Argentine Railway) commissioned engineer Pompeyo Moneta to survey the area between Córdoba and Jujuy "to find the best, shortest, and least expensive route for a line between Buenos Aires and Salta."[80] The report included information on soil fertility, commercial traffic, natural features, and productive activities in the area. Moneta's estimates of production and population for Tucumán, Salta, and Catamarca placed Tucumán's per capita output above the other two provinces.[81] Moneta indicated that the area offered potentially high profits for the construction of a

Figure 1.3. Downtown San Miguel. During the 1870s the municipal authorities increased investments in infrastructure to improve San Miguel's downtown areas. *(Photo by Angel Paganell, courtesy of private collection of Roberto Ferrari.)*

railroad line but advised against it because of the obstacles that the region's topography could pose to construction.[82] The potential benefits of a railroad line in the area did not escape the attention of other contemporary observers. For example, in 1870, Ignacio Rickart predicted that the province would "indeed be a rich and important territory" once the railroad arrived.[83] In the absence of private investors' interest, it was the national authorities who undertook the task of building the line.[84]

Railroads and Tariffs

Improved communications between Buenos Aires and the Argentine northwest had been a priority in the national government's agenda since the early 1850s. In 1863, President Bartolomé Mitre (1862–68) summarized the two main objectives behind the railroad programs elaborated by the Argentine government during the second half of the nineteenth century: "[Railroads] will bring wealth where there is poverty and order where there is anarchy."[85] Economic considerations guided the concessions granted for the construction of the Central Argentino and Ferrocarril del Sud lines.[86] Political priorities guided the national government's interest in railroad construction to Cuyo and the Argentine northwest. The railroad's layout identified critical components of the national political coalitions of the time. Tucumán's location made the province an important military stronghold and the ideal region to establish a stable center of support for the authorities in Buenos Aires.[87] However, besides political priorities, the project indicated the government's awareness of Tucumán's economic importance in the northwest. Tucumán's diversified productive structure, strong merchant community, and well-organized trading networks offered an additional incentive for the modernization of the transportation system. Furthermore, originally planned to continue to Salta and Bolivia, the project clearly revealed an attempt to maintain or revive colonial trading networks while reinforcing the area's existing links with the emerging economic littoral axis.

The Ferrocarril Central Norte was inaugurated in 1876 and extended from Tucumán to Córdoba. The line penetrated Tucumán from its southeast side, at Estación La Madrid. Following a south-north direction, the railroad passed along the departments of Graneros, Río Chico, Chicligasta, Monteros, Famaillá, and Capital. The line monopolized Tucumán's railroad traffic for more than a decade and provided a fast, safe, and cost-effective route for passengers and cargo traveling between Tucumán and the littoral. However, with only six stations within provincial boundaries, the line failed to provide door-to-door service to the existing ingenios. Ox and mule carts remained the main means to transport machinery and sugar to and from the railroad stations.[88]

The obstacles posed by the absence of a more comprehensive railroad network within the province, and in particular one that provided service to the western region, became quickly apparent to the provincial authorities. These problems were overcome in 1888 with the Ferrocarril Noroeste Argentino, a line extending from La Madrid station, point of entry of the Central Norte, to San Miguel de Tucumán. Tracks crossed the province's main sugar areas and attended to the specific necessities of the ingenios, albeit those located in the western areas of the province. The Central Norte connected Tucumán to Córdoba. From that point the Central Argentino provided transportation to Rosario, thus facilitating communications between the Argentine northwest and the littoral. The line operated on narrow-gauge tracks that required the expensive and inconvenient unloading

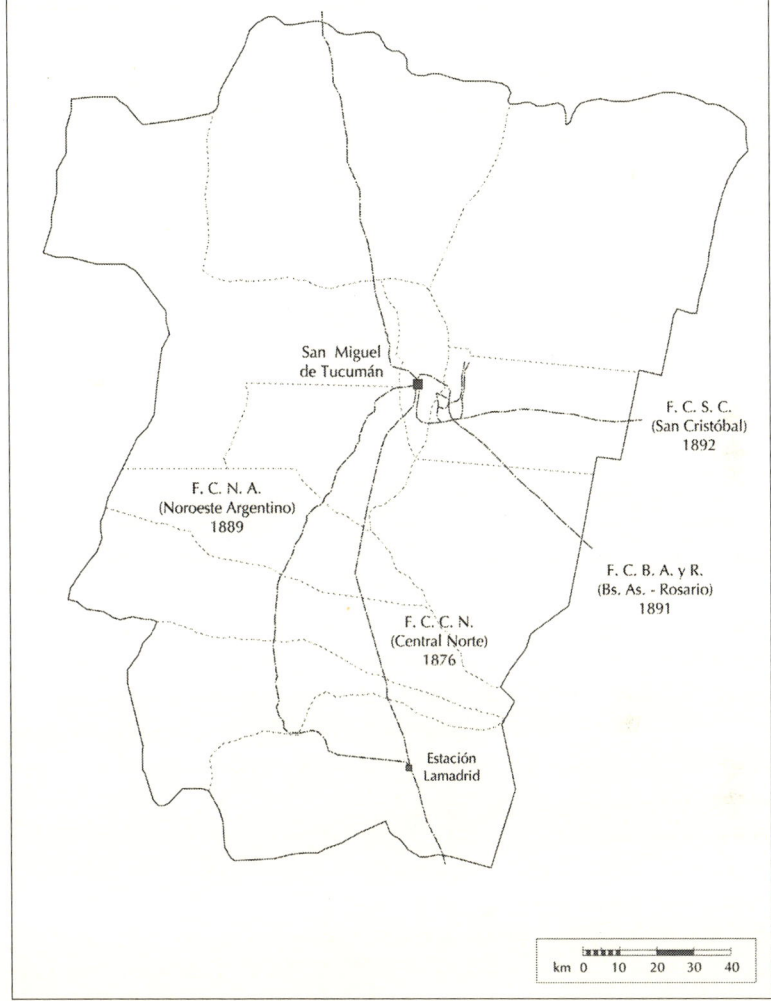

San Miguel
de Tucumán

F. C. S. C.
(San Cristóbal)
1892

F. C. N. A.
(Noroeste Argentino)
1889

F. C. B. A. y R.
(Bs. As. - Rosario)
1891

F. C. C. N.
(Central Norte)
1876

Estación
Lamadrid

km 0   10   20   30   40

Map 1.1. Railroad lines in Tucumán, 1895

and loading of cargo to the broad-gauge Central Argentino.[89] In an attempt
to surmount this obstacle, the Ferrocarril Buenos Aires y Rosario opened
for service in 1891 and offered an important advantage over the Central
Norte, as it established a direct route from San Miguel to Buenos Aires
using the broad gauge. The line also served the needs of those ingenios located in the eastern areas of the province. A fourth line, the French-owned

Ferrocarril San Cristóbal, started operations in 1892. Its tracks penetrated the province from the department of Cruz Alta and ran parallel to the Buenos Aires y Rosario.[90] In 1892 a newspaper reported that "an express line departing from Abraham Medina's ingenio consisting of thirty carts carrying three thousand bags of sugar reached Buenos Aires in twenty four hours, the fastest trip done by Argentine railroads to this time."[91] By then, four different railroad companies in Tucumán, totaling almost 650 kilometers of track, provided transportation between the province and the rest of the country.[92]

Railroads constituted an essential component in the impressive growth experienced by Tucumán's sugar industry and its subsequent path to leadership in the provincial economy.[93] Tucumán's location required modern transportation to haul the machinery and ship the sugar. Railroads consolidated Tucumán's economic reorientation toward the littoral, thus facilitating the arrival of technology and, more important, increasing the potential market for its sugar. By creating a railroad network that met the specific needs of local producers, they expanded the area under sugarcane cultivation and consolidated the crop's preeminence in the province. The national government assumed the initial risk and paved the way for private companies to invest in the region. Railroad investment accelerated sugar expansion. In turn, the industry's promising future was the reason behind the railroad revolution of the 1880s. Lines built between 1888 and 1892 perceived the economic potential of Tucumán's sugar industry and responded to the opportunities offered by an industry that revealed an increasingly dominant role in the economy. Of the thirty-five ingenios operating in Tucumán in 1895, more than half were founded after 1876 and none was farther than thirty kilometers from one, two, or even three lines.[94] As in other sugar economies in Latin America, railroads accelerated an already existing process and later sustained it by providing for its specific needs.[95]

Safer and cheaper transportation encouraged and enabled industrialists to adopt modern technology, thus increasing sugar production. By 1895, Argentina had achieved self-sufficiency in sugar and Tucumán contributed 80 percent of the sugar consumed in the country. However, the industry required additional government involvement to protect domestic sugars from cheap imported ones. As Miguel Nougués observed in the late nineteenth century, "If Argentina stops protecting its sugars the country will be divided in two. Buenos Aires, Santa Fe, Entre Ríos, Corrientes, and parts of Córdoba will

Figure 1.4. Sugarcane transport to an ingenio. Railroads enabled sugar producers to obtain sugarcane from remote plantations. *(Courtesy of Photographic Department, Archivo General de la Nación, Buenos Aires.)*

have no problems sustaining their economies with agricultural and pastoral products, but Tucumán will be ruined and its neighbors Catamarca, La Rioja, Santiago del Estero and Jujuy, whose populations benefit from Tucumán's prosperity, will fall into the utmost misery."[96] The authorities responded with high tariffs and a bounty system that guaranteed the preeminence of Tucumán's sugar on the national market.

The use of tariffs was not new in Argentina. Since independence, Argentina's authorities had relied on the collection of customs duties as a main source of revenue and a mechanism to balance public finances. Therefore, when the European crisis of 1873 interrupted the flow of capital from abroad, leading to a fall in public income and affecting the government's ability to service the foreign debt, it came as no surprise that the legislature passed a new customs law that increased duties on a large number of imported articles, including sugars. This in turn encouraged increases in local production.[97] During the 1880s the national government adopted a more vigorous stance to assist the sugar industry through several revisions to tariff schedules that increased the effective rate of protection for domestic sugars.[98] Besides tariffs, domestic sugars experienced implicit protection as a result of currency depreciation.[99] In addition, since sugar duties did not reflect the fall in world prices, the effective rate of protection was even higher.[100]

Tariffs protected Tucumán's sugar industry and guaranteed local producers full control over an expanding domestic market, thus creating an environment conducive to the industry's expansion.[101] However, they failed to offer a safeguard against unsold stocks and their depressive effects on prices, a situation that producers faced in 1896 as two consecutive large crops left 139,000 tons of unsold sugar on the market. A year later, the national government offered additional protection in the form of bounties that were expected to eliminate the depressing pressure of excess stocks on domestic prices.[102] While initially government action provided invaluable assistance for the expansion of an infant industry, bounties aimed at rescuing an already mature industry facing a crisis of overproduction. Sugar tariffs were not modified, although the government introduced a new classification system for refined and unrefined sugars more consistent with international standards but that still protected the interests of Argentine sugar producers.[103]

Bounties compensated for low prices and high shipping costs, but the conditions of the international sugar market limited their potential positive effects. Sugar producers faced the difficult task of finding outlets for their sugar in an already saturated and extremely protected international market.[104] The situation worsened during the early 1900s as new international conditions rendered bounties futile.[105] The Brussels Treaty changed the conditions of the sugar international market and forced the Argentine government to implement new policies. In 1904 the national congress eliminated bounties and production taxes on sugar but maintained duties on imported sugar.[106] Consumer demands to reduce protection to the industry intensified after 1904. In 1912 the national congress approved the Saavedra Lamas Law. The new legislation did not eliminate sugar duties but established a gradual descending scale. Starting in 1913 the duty on both types of sugar would decrease annually until it reached seven cents for one kilogram of refined and five cents for one kilogram of unrefined sugar by 1921. The law established penalties on imports of bountied sugar and authorized the national government to intervene in the domestic market by reducing import duties to control domestic prices.[107] Therefore, as late as 1912, although in a much more cautious way, the national government was still responding to the interests of sugar industrialists, showing its commitment to protect the sugar industry.

Not surprisingly, the new legislation was received with skepticism by those defending orthodox free-trade policies but with much optimism among sugar interests, as the daily newspaper *El Orden* observed when examining the bill, "the Saavedra Lamas Law eliminates the uncertainty surrounding Tucumán's economic future to guarantee a new potential, a foundation for its development."[108] Clearly, protective policies became indispensable for guaranteeing the industry's expansion. High tariffs enabled Tucumán's sugar expansion, as they eliminated foreign competition in the domestic market, while export bounties had the potential of making Argentine sugar prices more competitive in foreign markets.[109]

DURING THE 1850s and 1860s, Tucumán emerged as the most prosperous province in the Argentine northwest. Its fertile soils and a large population with widespread access to land contributed to the development of a diversified economy that rested on a large range of agropastoral and manufacturing products. The province's population made for a strong local market that was complemented by active trade with domestic and foreign markets. Local merchants shipped cartloads of maize, tobacco, cattle, hides, textiles, and furniture to neighboring provinces, as well as to Cuyo, Rosario, Buenos Aires, Bolivia, and Chile. Even though decades of civil war could not completely break colonial networks, trade patterns during the 1850s and 1860s indicated the consolidation of the shift toward the Atlantic and the increasing importance of the littoral markets for Tucumán's commodities. Tucumano entrepreneurs took advantage of the situation and diversified their investment portfolios, devoting capital to different economic activities, including sugar production. In those days, the expansion of the sugar industry faced serious obstacles, as high transportation costs limited the area under cultivation and prevented technological modernization while imported sugars supplied the needs of consumers in the littoral areas. In the last quarter of the nineteenth century, the national and provincial governments came to the industry's assistance with investments in railroads and protectionist policies such as tariffs and bounties. Initially a politically motivated decision, the railroad revolution became one of the most important transformative forces of Tucumán's economy. By facilitating communication with the littoral areas, the tracks opened new markets for Tucumán's sugar and enabled technological modernization. Similarly, tariffs and bounties encouraged sugar production by protecting domestic sugar from the volatility of the international market and enabling local producers to maintain a captive domestic market despite high production costs. Direct government intervention provided a degree of predictability and stability that encouraged further investments in the industry. As a result, the sugar industry expanded dramatically.

Chapter 2

The Sugar Industry and Tucumán's Economy

DURING THE LAST DECADES of the nineteenth century, at the same time Argentina consolidated its position in the international market as a producer of beef and grains, Tucumán's economy experienced important transformations. Describing the province in those days, Harry Franck observed, "Toward the end of the last century the northern part of the republic 'went sugar crazy' and burned whole forests of orange-trees in order to plant cane."[1] Sugar production jumped from 3,000 tons in 1876 to 109,253 tons in 1895. Correspondingly, the area cultivated in sugarcane increased from 2,487 hectares to 55,453 hectares.[2] After decades of relying on imports from Cuba and Brazil, in 1895 Argentina achieved self-sufficiency in sugar and Tucumán emerged as the country's main producer. The province accounted for 93 percent of the area cultivated with sugarcane and produced more than 80 percent of all the sugar consumed in the country. The industry's expansion had profound and long-lasting consequences for the provincial economy.

The Industry's Beginnings

Sugarcane arrived in Tucumán during the late sixteenth century but remained a marginal crop for more than a century. During those early years, farmers cultivated the plant in small plots in the departments of Capital and Chicligasta and relied on primitive technology to produce modest quantities of rum and hard candies, mostly for self-consumption. It was the Jesuits who undertook sugar production on a larger scale in their mission San José de Lules around the early eighteenth century.[3] After the order's expulsion, in 1767, the main driving force behind sugar manufacturing was lost for several decades until the efforts of Obispo José Eusebio Colombres reinvigorated interest in sugar. In the early 1820s the priest installed two wooden mills (*trapiches*) and distributed sugarcane among planters in the area. Colombres made sugar nectar (*miel de caña*), sugar tablets (*canchacas*), and small amounts of yellow sugar, which were consumed in Santiago del Estero, Salta, and Catamarca.[4] Soon after, in an attempt to diversify their investments and boost profits without incurring great financial risks, more local producers started planting small plots with sugarcane, in combination with other crops such as maize, wheat, and rice.

Besides increasing the area planted with sugarcane, during the late 1820s and early 1830s Tucumano entrepreneurs invested in primitive and inexpensive milling technology, such as wooden mills, copper pans, and rudimentary milling facilities. Protective legislation, such as the 1834 provincial law that established levies on imported sugar, in conjunction with high transportation costs and Tucumán's active trading network with its neighbors, secured a small market for the nascent sugar industry. In 1845 Governor Celedonio Gutiérrez was already referring to the industry as a "promising venture" for Tucumán.[5] However, the industry's primitive production methods limited its potential market. Consumers in the littoral areas preferred white sugar to the varieties produced in Tucumán, which were not only of lower quality and spoiled faster but also denser and more difficult to transport. It became clear to producers that in order to reach a larger consumer market, Tucumán's sugar industry would need to adopt modern processing technology to both increase output and produce a better-quality sugar.

Traditional sugar manufacture consisted of three main operations: grinding, boiling, and purging. After the sugarcane was brought to the mills, workers fed the stalks into wooden-roller mills that extracted the juice. The liquid was then transferred through a wooden trough to a linear series of iron cauldrons arranged over several furnaces in the boiling room (*fondo*). The juice was first heated to just below boiling so that impurities (*cachaza*) could be skimmed off. After the first heating, the liquid was transferred to progressively smaller containers, where the heating process continued. Finally, the liquid was poured into the smallest container (*templero*), where the sugar master knew by smell, touch, and appearance when the syrup was ready. After the thick mixture of molasses and sugar crystals reached the so-called striking point (*punto de azúcar*), it was transferred to a copper cooler and from there the syrup was poured into conical clay molds (*hormas*) in the pouring house. There it was stirred continuously with a wooden spatula until it nearly solidified. After a couple of days, the remaining liquid, containing molasses and impurities, drained out through holes in the bottoms of the molds. In ten or twelve days, the open top of the mold was covered with mud so that the water could percolate through the molds and thus facilitate the process of liquid drainage. This mudding operation was repeated three times, once every twenty days. Once the liquid had completely drained off, the cone of sugar was removed from the mold and the yellow sugar removed with a knife. Tucumán produced two types of unrefined sugar, a yellow product that deteriorated fast and a white sugar of higher quality that lasted longer. Besides sugar, ingenios also produced sugar by-products, such as hard candies made of boiled sugar (*alfeñiques*), sugar tablets, and sugar syrup.

The incorporation of modern technology started in Tucumán during the late 1850s and affected all three stages of sugar manufacture.[6] Iron rollers replaced the wooden ones and increased mills' crushing capability. Hydraulic power provided a more even and stronger pressure on the cane, thus offering twice the extractive capacity of an animal-powered mill. Higher extractive power put a heavy demand on the traditional boiling and purging stages. New vacuum pans lowered the boiling point of the juice and saved fuel. And large centrifuges separated the molasses from the syrup much faster than the old draining system. The resulting sugar was not only drier (and thus lighter, reducing transportation costs) but of better quality. But because of the risks involved and the large sums of capital required, the adoption of modern technology occurred gradually.

The first major attempt to introduce new machinery in Tucumán's ingenios took place in 1858. Baltasar Aguirre, in partnership with Argentine president Justo José de Urquiza, invested in water-powered iron-roller mills, vacuum pans, filters, a centrifuge, and steam boilers for his ingenio in El Alto, in Capital Department. Aguirre also built an irrigation canal and an aqueduct to irrigate the area as well as to guarantee the necessary waterpower for the mill. During the first year, the ingenio produced a very small quantity of sugar and syrup. Soon enough, Aguirre discovered that his estimate of high returns by the third year of operation would require additional investment and an expertise he did not possess. A succession of bad harvests, technological problems, political turmoil, and bad management resulted in the collapse of the enterprise. Aguirre's lands were repossessed by his creditors and most of the machinery was purchased by the Méndez brothers, owners of Ingenio Concepción.[7]

But Aguirre's failure discouraged investment in the industry for only a few years. During the late 1860s and early 1870s, industrialists renewed their interest in modern sugar-processing machinery. Patterns of investment among sugar producers varied significantly. After his visit to Wenceslao Posse's Hacienda Esperanza, Ignacio Rickart praised it as an example of a highly capitalized sugar mill relying on modern machinery. However, he bemoaned the fact that only a few ingenios had incorporated the new technology: "The sugar growers who [do not have the new machines] are obliged to follow the old system," which was cumbersome and less profitable, since it "required a very large amount of house accommodation and apparatus, as well as considerable capital to enable the sugar maker to wait for the completion of the process and realize his profits."[8]

Two years later Arsenio Granillo left a detailed list of the ingenios operating in the province that illustrates Rickart's point but also indicates that more ingenios were expanding and undergoing significant technological change. In 1871, of the forty-six operating ingenios in Tucumán, 60 percent were using iron-roller mills and hydraulic power, while 25 percent had already adopted centrifugal machines and employed steam power.[9] The adoption of new technologies was accompanied by an increase in the number of operating ingenios. Between 1872 and 1877 the number of mills in the province jumped from forty-six to eighty-two.[10]

The process of modernization did not affect all ingenios equally, although the adoption of modern technology had long-lasting effects on the future organization of the industry. Modest plantations were able to incorporate only hydraulic power while bigger planters, with access to more capital, were able to buy vacuum pans and centrifuges. The coexistence of old and modern technologies had direct consequences on ingenios' sugar output and the quality of the final product. Not surprisingly, there was a clear correspondence between plantation size and technology. Almost 75 percent of the ingenios using iron mills and 100 percent of the ingenios relying on steam-powered centrifuges owned more than twenty cultivated *cuadras* (forty-one hectares) each.[11]

Figure 2.1. Hacienda Esperanza, early 1870s. Initially Hacienda Esperanza relied on primitive technology for the manufacture of sugar. *(Photograph by Angel Paganelli, courtesy of private collection of Roberto Ferrari.)*

Technological modernization and the increase in cultivated area resulted in a significant rise in sugar output. In 1853, according to official reports, the province's total area planted in sugarcane did not exceed 200 hectares, and sugar production amounted to less than 300 tons.[12] By 1876 the total area planted in cane had expanded to 2,400 hectares. Correspondingly, sugar production had increased to 3,000 tons and its share of the provincial economy significantly improved. In 1853 sugar accounted for only 10 percent of the value of Tucumán's output, clearly behind the value of cereals, tobacco, hides, and saddle blankets. More than a decade later, sugar was responsible for 36 percent of total output values.[13] Despite sugar's increasing participation, in the 1870s the province still had a diversified economy. Cereals, hides, and tobacco maintained their preeminent positions, a clear indication that new investments in the sugar industry resulted from the flexible investment strategy of Tucumán's entrepreneurs, which attempted to diversify into potentially profitable activities rather than shift into sugar specialization.

This flexible behavior becomes apparent in the contract signed between the García brothers in 1874. According to its stipulations, the two brothers created a partnership to raise livestock and produce sugar in the department of Cruz Alta. Sugarcane cultivation did not occupy a preeminent position in the agreement, although the partners' choice to devote part of their capital to sugar production indicates that Tucumán's entrepreneurs, aware of the potential returns, were investing more capital in sugarcane plantations and sugar-processing machinery. Three years later the partnership was renewed under the same conditions.[14] By 1883, however, both partners were devoted exclusively to the production of sugar, revealing a pattern of specialized investment that, as demonstrated by José Antonio Sánchez Román, characterized most sugar industrialists during the late nineteenth century, in contrast to patterns observed in other parts of the country.[15] In any case, contemporary witnesses observed that during the early 1870s Tucumán still preserved its diversified economy.[16] In 1874 the area cultivated with sugarcane represented only 5 percent of the total cultivated land in the province, while cereals—in particular maize and wheat—maintained their preeminence, accounting for 70 percent.

Therefore, during the 1860s and 1870s, in their pursuit to maximize profits, provincial entrepreneurs added sugar to their already diversified range of investments. Sugar production was preferred to other crops, such as tobacco, as it offered a viable and profitable alternative to Tucumán's entrepreneurs. Tucumán's sugar enjoyed a larger domestic market than tobacco as low-quality sugar could compete with foreign imports, particularly Brazilian sugars.[17] Furthermore, Tucumán's landlocked position, coupled with poor transportation between coastal areas and the Argentine northwest, created a formidable obstacle for imported sugars to reach northern Argentina. Tucumán's sugar was consumed in Santiago del Estero, Catamarca, La Rioja, Córdoba, Salta, Mendoza, and San Juan, but the expansion experienced by domestic demand, as revealed by the fivefold increase of sugar imports between 1853 and 1875, indicated to Tucumán's producers the potential that the national market had for the local industry. At the same time, the growth of cereal production in the littoral and the construction of modern tanning facilities in Buenos Aires seriously limited the range of commodities that Tucumán could sell in the nascent national market. While the national authorities were searching for political alliances in the Argentine interior to consolidate their power, sugar offered a point of convergence between national and provincial interests. Discussing the early years of Tucumán's sugar industry, British traveler John Foster Fraser observed, "Tucumán sugar, however, could not in those days compete, either in quality or price, with that which came from other countries. It was, therefore, decided to give encouragement to Argentine sugar growing by a tariff on sugar which came from across [the] sea."[18] Modern transportation, capital sources, and a protected domestic market had a pivotal role in the dramatic expansion experienced by Tucumán's sugar industry in the four decades that extend from the last quarter of the nineteenth century to the early twentieth century.

Four Decades of Growth

In 1876, Tucumán contributed 12 percent of the sugar consumed in Argentina. Two decades later, domestic demand had increased threefold and by then the province was processing more than 80 percent of the sugar consumed in the domestic market. A significant increase in the area cultivated in sugarcane and the adoption of modern technology accounted for the impressive expansion of Tucumán's industry during the decades that followed the arrival of the railroad to the province. In his 1881 report, Paul Groussac estimated that ingenios had invested a total of 1.2 million pesos in new sugar machinery in the five years that followed the arrival of the Ferrocarril Central Norte in the province.[19] That year a British traveler reported that most mills had already adopted the new sugar technology, including diffusers, clarifiers, evaporators, centrifuges, and vacuum pans.[20] In 1882, 80 percent of Tucumán's ingenios used steam power, a significant increase from the early 1870s, when only 10 percent of the machinery relied on it.[21]

The railroad revolution led to a technological revolution in Tucumán's sugar industry, although at the expense of other economic activities. During the 1880s, investments in other areas declined. The number of flour mills experienced a substantial decrease. Similarly, by the end of the decade the number of working tanneries was less than half of those operating in 1874. Entrepreneurs who had previously invested in manufacturing and commerce shifted to sugar production or expanded their sugar-processing plans, as did Ingenio Esperanza.

The adoption of new technologies took place in different fashion, depending on each ingenio. As a result of high cost, some ingenios proceeded gradually in introducing new machinery over a period of several decades.[22] For example, Ingenio Concepción, founded in 1835 by Juan José García, started with traditional wooden-roller mills powered by animals. During the

Figure 2.2. Ingenio Esperanza, 1894. During the last quarter of the nineteenth century, the ingenio greatly increased its processing capacity by investing in modern machinery. *(Courtesy of Photographic Department, Archivo General de la Nación, Buenos Aires.)*

late 1850s, the ingenio shifted to water power. In 1870 the Méndez brothers took over the ingenio and made further investments on iron-roller mills, vacuum pans, and one centrifuge.[23] A second wave of technological investments took place during the second half the 1880s, when Alfredo Guzmán purchased the ingenio and tripled its milling capacity through the adoption of roller mills with more crushing power. The new owner also incorporated additional centrifuges, vacuum pans, and a modernized boiling room. At the same time, the ingenio embarked on the construction of an irrigation system and increased the area cultivated in sugarcane, although the mill never stopped relying on outside cane suppliers.[24] By 1895, Concepción was fourth in the province in sugar output and the following year it was the first ingenio to install a refinery.[25]

In other cases, the adoption of modern technology took place all at once. This was the case of Ingenio Lules. In 1879, Clodomiro Hileret and Juan Dermit created a partnership to operate an ingenio. The ingenio started with an initial investment of 35,000 pesos, shared equally between both partners.

Dermit contributed land, animals, buildings, and planted sugarcane; Hileret supplied most of the capital. The arrangement stipulated that the proceeds corresponding to the first three years were to be reinvested in machinery and land.[26] Located in Lules, the mill initially consisted of a main brick building and two adjacent warehouses. Most of the sugar machinery was purchased from the French company Fives-Lille, which provided a favorable payment plan that enabled the ingenio to acquire all the modern technology at once. The ingenio relied on both hydraulic and steam power in order to avoid work stoppages in case of drought. It also incorporated iron-roller mills with powerful crushing capacity, centrifuges, and vacuum pans. In 1881, Ingenio Lules could produce 850 tons of sugar and its distillery had a capacity to produce 1,700 barrels of rum.[27] Even though the contract stipulated a ten-year commitment, the partnership was dissolved in 1881 when Dermit canceled the arrangement. He received a total of 130,000 pesos as payment for his share in the company, a clear indication of the significant investments made in technology by both partners in such short period of time.[28]

In 1895, according to official figures, Tucumán concentrated almost 80 percent of Argentina's sugar machinery.[29] The province's mills could crush 63,000 tons of sugarcane per day, enough to produce 4,250 tons of sugar.[30] However, as smaller ingenios found it impossible to access the capital needed for the purchase of expensive machinery, not everybody was able to invest in modern technology, and Tucumán's sugar industry experienced a significant shakeout. By the early 1880s the number of operating ingenios had dropped to less than half the 1877 figure. In 1881, Groussac pointed out that few wooden-roller mills were still grinding and that, in most cases, those planters had abandoned the sugar business or had become sugarcane providers for bigger ingenios.[31]

Technological modernization not only increased sugar output but also improved the quality of the final product. During the early years, Tucumán's ingenios produced unrefined sugar, mostly consumed in the northwest region, as the Argentine littoral with its large immigrant population preferred the whiter variety of sugar. To reach the main consumer market, the industry needed to produce refined sugar. After several failed attempts in the early 1880s, in 1889 a group led by Ernesto Tornquist opened the first sugar refinery in Rosario.[32] Tornquist's success resulted from his personal connections and credentials as an accomplished businessman as well as from the coalition that supported the project.[33] For the first five years of its operation,

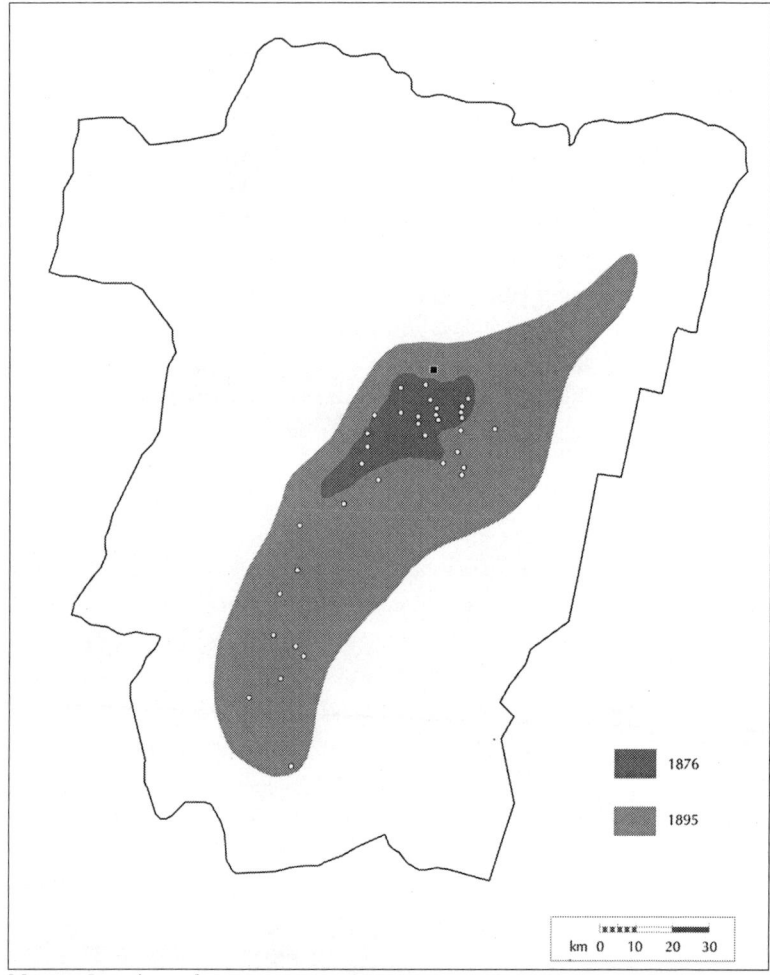

Map 2.1. Ingenios and sugarcane area, 1895

the facility refined half the sugar consumed in the country.[34] During the late 1890s and 1900s, Ingenios Concepción, Bella Vista, and Lastenia opened refineries. By 1920 Argentina had a total of six refineries, and Rosario's refinery had lost preeminence to its competitors in Tucumán.[35]

The adoption of modern technology increased ingenios' demands for raw materials. Between 1876 and 1895 the land planted in sugarcane in the province increased from 2,487 hectares to 55,453 hectares.[36] Sugarcane cultivation took over new areas in the province, displacing other crops and economic activities. In 1881, Capital Department concentrated 82 percent of Tucumán's operating mills, 73 percent of all land cultivated in sugarcane, and 79 percent of the province's planters. In 1895 only 50 percent of Tucumán's ingenios, cultivated area, and planters were located in that department.[37] Throughout this period, Famaillá increased the area cultivated in sugarcane, while departments such as Río Chico, Chicligasta, Graneros, and Monteros became cane producers as well, thus contributing to Tucumán's consolidation as the most important sugar producer in the country.

Attracted by the prospect of high profits, other provinces—Jujuy, Salta, Santiago del Estero, Chaco, Santa Fe, Misiones, Corrientes, and Formosa— were drawn into sugarcane cultivation during the late 1880s and early 1890s and contributed to the impressive expansion of the Argentine sugar industry.[38] After a timid start, the 1880s witnessed a rise in sugar production in Santa Fe, Corrientes, Misiones, and Santiago del Estero. Santa Fe's two modern ingenios produced 1,066 tons of sugar in 1892. Nevertheless, sugar production in that province could not compete with cereal agriculture and never attained preeminence. In contrast, Misiones had a tradition in the manufacturing of sugar that dated back to colonial times, when the Jesuits made small amounts of sugar, syrup, and candies in their missions. That province's tropical climate offered better conditions for sugarcane cultivation than the temperate climate of Santa Fe. In 1895, the ingenios in Misiones produced 800 tons of sugar. In the case of Corrientes, the province's only ingenio was founded in the early 1880s and could process only a couple of hundred tons of sugar each year. In Santiago del Estero, where sugar production had begun around the same time as in Tucumán, Pedro San Germés, a local businessman, made significant capital investments to modernize his Ingenio Contreras. By 1889 the province had seven modern ingenios that produced approximately 1,200 tons of sugar and 3,000 barrels of rum annually. Plantations in Santiago supplied only part of the sugarcane needed by ingenios. San Germés visited Tucumán and arranged for planters in the province to supply the raw material for Santiago's factories periodically.[39] However, dry weather, infertile soils, and lack of capital led to the gradual deterioration of the industry in the province and by 1905 only one ingenio was still working.

During the 1890s, Formosa, Salta, Chaco, and Jujuy started sugar production as well. Formosa's sugar industry was short lived. In 1895 the province's two ingenios produced only 130 tons of sugar. Output reached its highest point in 1914, with 430 tons, and declined steadily afterward as a result of unsuitable soils and lack of investment. Chaco experienced a similar pattern of initial boom and steady decline, although sugar output was higher than Formosa's. Its cultivated area grew rapidly following 1895 but dropped by the 1910s. At its peak of production, during the early 1900s, the province's three ingenios together could produce 3,600 tons of sugar annually. Sugar production in Salta and Jujuy dated from colonial times, although it was not until the 1910s that these provinces experienced a significant increase in production.[40] In both areas, sugar was produced in vertically integrated ingenios. Since the eighteenth century, Salta had manufactured small amounts of sugar and rum for the local market. In 1888, the province produced 270 tons of sugar. As a result of significant investments in modern technology, cane cultivation and sugar production increased gradually and steadily, reaching 1,290 tons in 1914. Similarly, Jujuy's sugar industry started as early as the eighteenth century. Despite the obstacles posed by the lack of good transportation systems, the province's ingenios invested in modern machinery during the late 1870s. In conjunction with technological innovation, Jujuy's cultivated area grew steadily between 1875 and 1914. During the second decade of the twentieth century, Jujuy consolidated its position as the second-largest producer in the country and participated with almost 10 percent in the total area cultivated with sugarcane in the country. As in other areas in Latin America, the need to obtain full control over water resources resulted in the concentration of land in the hands of the large ingenios in these two provinces. Jujuy's large ingenios not only cultivated and processed their own sugarcane but also took over the commercialization of sugar, thus leading to a high degree of capital concentration not found in other sugar areas in Argentina.[41]

The incorporation of new sugar producers was disparate and unstable and had consequences for the future development of Tucumán's sugar industry. Throughout this period, provinces other than Tucumán contributed roughly between 10 and 20 percent of the total national sugar output. Therefore, although these producers never undermined Tucumán's position as the country's main sugar supplier, by increasing stocks they created additional pressures on the local market. During the last decade of the nineteenth century, Argentina's sugar production increased from 49,321 to 117,209 tons. Production kept expanding and by 1908 the country's total sugar output had reached 160,597 tons.[42] The expansion of sugar production to other areas contributed to the impressive growth experienced by Argentina's sugar industry and was a response to the important rise in domestic consumption and the profitable investment opportunities offered by the industry. Between 1876 and 1894 sugar consumption grew from 20,000 tons to 75,000 tons.[43] But as quickly as the domestic market expanded, sugar production expanded even faster. In 1895, Tucumán produced 109,253 tons of sugar—an amount that, added to the 20,747 tons produced by other provinces, far exceeded domestic demand. Large amounts of sugar piled up in ingenios' storehouses and resulted in a dramatic drop in prices and the first in a series of crises of overproduction, which revealed the dangers involved in excessive specialization and government protection.

The 1895 crisis inaugurated a new era for the sugar industry characterized by price instability, violent fluctuations in sugar output and cultivated area, and lack of balance between demand and supply. In 1896 a second bumper crop left 139,000 tons of unsold sugar on the market, provoking a dramatic drop in prices. In two years, sugar prices declined almost by half while sugarcane prices stood at one-fourth of pre-1895 levels. Not surprisingly, the area cultivated in sugarcane in Tucumán experienced a significant reduction. "Rescuer frosts," as they were called by contemporaries, resulted in an even more significant decrease in sugarcane cultivation and sugar output. After a small recovery during the last two years of the century, prices plummeted once again and reached their lowest point in 1903.[44] During the following decade prices remained relatively stable, while cultivated area and sugar output increased steadily. In 1913 sugar output again exceeded demand and the industry faced a significant decline in prices. Once again, nature came to the rescue of the industry. The sugarcane mosaic virus infected Tucumán's crops in 1915, leading to a significant drop in sugarcane production and then to a price recovery that started around 1916.

Sugar industrialists faced the post-1895 era by increasing pressure on national authorities for additional protective measures but also with the incorporation of modern technology, although at a much slower pace, and changes in firm organization. Since the last years of the nineteenth century, Tucumán witnessed the founding of new and important ingenios, such as La Florida in 1895, Aguilares in 1902, and San Antonio in 1910. By 1914 the number of operating ingenios in the province had declined, although the industry's crushing capacity had increased significantly. Increases in the number of vacuum pans and centrifuges, in addition to the switch to steam, electric, and internal combustion engines, resulted in a considerable rise in sugar output. While thirty-one ingenios in 1895 milled 2.0 million tons of sugarcane, by 1914, twenty-seven ingenios were milling 2.7 million tons. Tucumán's sugar production jumped from 109,000 tons in 1895 to 270,000 tons in 1914.[45]

Industrial modernization during this period took place in conjunction with changes in firm organization.[46] Many ingenios adopted a modern corporate form that increased firm size, fostered concentration of capital, and raised productivity, thus enabling them to confront crises of overproduction more efficiently.[47] For example, Guzmán y Compañia, Compañía Azucarera Wenceslao Posse, and Ingenio Luján abandoned the traditional family-operated firm structure. At the same time, a new sugar company, the Compañía Azucarera Tucumana (CAT), emerged and became the largest sugar corporation in Tucumán.[48] Initially, the company owned Ingenios Nueva Baviera, La Florida, and La Trinidad. By 1901 the CAT had purchased Ingenios Lastenia and San Andrés.[49] The CAT not only owned large ingenios in the province but also shared board members with Rosario's refinery, which gave it an advantage in the refining business. Furthermore, its members had political ties in Buenos Aires and Tucumán and were important sugar wholesalers. Besides technological modernization, the company expanded its landholdings, although it never achieved vertical integration.[50] In 1914 the CAT's production represented almost one-fourth of the province's total sugar output.[51]

More plant capacity resulted in a larger demand for raw material. Between 1895 and 1914 the number of sugarcane planters in Tucumán increased significantly, while the area cultivated in sugarcane almost doubled, reaching 90,848 hectares.[52] Besides increases in cultivated area, the agricultural sector experienced other important changes during the first decades of the twentieth century. Since the industry's early years, producers had grown the Creole cane (*caña criolla*) in two of its varieties—*morada* and *rayada*. The 1900s witnessed official attempts to promote research on alternative varieties with higher sucrose content and more suitable to Tucumán's climate. In the early 1910s, studies done at the Estación Experimental Agrícola (Agricultural Experimental Farm) determined that one of these, the Java variety, was the most appropriate for conditions in Tucumán since it was frost resistant, matured faster, and had higher sucrose content.[53]

The provincial authorities distributed seeds of the new variety to planters in the province. However, the shift required a large investment that neither

Figure 2.3. Students of the Estación Experimental Agrícola. Researchers tested more than two hundred varieties of sugarcane at the school's experimental ingenio to determine the best varieties for the local climate. *(Courtesy of Photographic Department, Archivo General de la Nación, Buenos Aires.)*

ingenios nor planters were willing or able to make at that point. In 1915 bad weather and the mosaic disease affected Tucumán's plantations and resulted in a 60 percent reduction in the province's sugarcane cultivated area. The following year severe frosts gave another blow to the industry. Provincial sugar production dropped 55 percent, and the amount of land under cultivation decreased by 42 percent. If a better prospective yield was not incentive enough for planters and ingenio owners to switch to the Java variety, the 1916 frosts provided convincing arguments for the urgency for change. The new variety's introduction started in 1916 but it was several years before the process was complete.[54]

During the last decades of the nineteenth century, Tucumán's sugar industry experienced dramatic growth. By 1895 it had become the most active sector in the provincial economy. In response to the new demand for raw materials, thousands of farmers switched to sugarcane, abandoning traditional crops and changing Tucumán's agricultural sector in profound ways. The effects that sugar expansion had on the provincial economy did not escape the attention of the press. In 1884 *El Orden* warned, "Articles of first necessity come from other areas: cattle from Córdoba and Entre Ríos, flour from Santa Fe and San Juan, rice from Carolina, and even maize! which is imported from Santa Fe, while all our industrial activity remains concentrated in the sugar industry."[55]

Sugar Expansion and Changes in Tucumán's Economy

The impressive growth experienced by the sugar industry had important consequences for Tucumán's agrarian structure. A bewildered observer noted in the early twentieth century that "virtually the entire province of Tucumán is covered with sugarcane and orange trees. The rivalry between these two products has been acute for decades, now one now the other usurping the center of the stage."[56] Between 1876 and 1916 Tucumán's total cultivated area experienced a dramatic increase and sugarcane was the engine behind it.[57] In four decades, the land planted in the crop in the province expanded from 2,300 to 91,000 hectares. The expansion of cultivated land affected the province unevenly. The process of sugarcane dispersion into new areas that had started in the 1880s intensified during the early 1890s. Traditional sugar producers, such as the departments of Famaillá, Cruz Alta, Río Chico, and Capital, more than doubled their cultivated area. The departments of Monteros, Leales, Burruyacu, and Chicligasta experienced significant growth in cultivated area as well. In contrast, marginal sugarcane producers, such as Graneros, Trancas, and Tafí, experienced only moderate increases in their cultivated land.

The expansion in sugarcane cultivation resulted from the incorporation of new lands but also was made at the expense of other crops, especially wheat, tobacco, and, to a lesser extent, maize. In 1874 wheat fields extended over almost 14,000 hectares in Tucumán.[58] By 1914 the province had only 670 hectares planted in the grain. Tobacco growing also declined steadily, from 2,700 hectares in 1895 to 650 hectares in 1914.[59] In 1895, Tucumán's minister of finance reported that tobacco and wheat, important sources of provincial wealth in the past, had been "abandoned by planters who became delirious with the profits offered by sugarcane cultivation."[60] However, the reduction in land planted in wheat and tobacco was also due to the emergence of an important wheat belt in the littoral and of better-quality tobacco in the northeast, against which Tucumán farmers could not compete.

Figure 2.4. Sugarcane plantation. Supervised by the overseer, workers cut and clean the cane before loading it into carts. *(Courtesy of Photographic Department, Archivo General de la Nación, Buenos Aires.)*

The fate of maize and alfalfa was somehow different. Maize, a very popular staple in Tucumanos' diet, was cultivated throughout the province and, before the sugar craze, occupied a preeminent place in the provincial agrarian sector. Despite sugarcane expansion, the grain maintained its position and even experienced a significant increase from the mid-1870s until the late 1890s. Between 1874 and 1895 the area cultivated in maize grew 50 percent in absolute terms, although the grain's share of total cultivated area declined from 43 to 31 percent. That downward trend slowed in the first decade of the twentieth century. By 1914, the area cultivated with maize had increased 10 percent in absolute terms, but it had lost its position relative to sugarcane, since it accounted for only 26 percent of the total cultivated area.[61] The only crop that experienced a steady increase during this period, besides sugarcane, was alfalfa. Used as fodder in both sugar and nonsugar areas, the plant grew steadily and was able to maintain a fairly constant share of Tucumán's total cultivated area. In four decades Tucumán's agrarian sector traded diversification for specialization in sugarcane. By 1914, 91,000 hectares of sugarcane made up 70 percent of the province's total cultivated land.

However, despite increasing specialization, a number of variables led to disparate patterns of land use in the province. The analysis of the manuscript schedules of the 1895 national census offers a snapshot of Tucumán's agricultural sector during the peak of the sugar boom and provides a thorough understanding of the effects of sugar expansion in the provincial agrarian structure.[62] Census manuscript schedules list a total of 10,470 agricultural units, of which 70.5 percent were managed by their owners, 27 percent by tenants and sharecroppers, and 1.5 percent by *colonos* (cane planters who leased out ingenio's land). The share of each group in the total cultivated area renders similar results: 69.4 percent of the cultivated land was worked by owners, 27.8 percent by tenants and sharecroppers, and 2.8 percent by colonos. The significant number of owners and their participation in the total cultivated area of the province indicates the persistence of a pattern of widespread ownership that, higher than the national average, had characterized Tucumán's land tenure before the sugar boom.[63] Therefore, as the evidence clearly indicates, sugar expansion in Tucumán did not produce massive land dispossession, as was the case in other sugar economies in Latin America. Small and medium planters were able to maintain their holdings, although they revealed different patterns of land use than those of large holdings.

Census manuscript schedules reveal that holdings of ten hectares or less accounted for 74.4 percent of the units listed by the census and held 12.1 percent of the total arable land. These small units farmed 24.4 percent of Tucumán's cultivated area. Among this segment, maize had a paramount position, since it accounted for 67.8 percent of the group's total cultivated area, while sugarcane occupied only 17 percent. The group contributed only 7.5 percent of the total area cultivated in sugarcane in the province. Holdings between 11 hectares and 100 hectares constituted 22.5 percent of the units surveyed and held 24.6 percent of Tucumán's arable land. The group accounted for 34.6 percent of the total area cultivated in the province and farmed 32 percent of Tucumán's sugarcane land. In this segment, there is a tendency to increase the area planted in sugarcane, which took over 52 percent of the total area cultivated by the group. Still, in 1895 this segment of medium-size owners maintained a rather diversified pattern of land use. The group devoted 36 percent of their cultivated land to maize and 6 percent to alfalfa.

The evidence clearly indicates that specialization in sugarcane occurred in larger units. The segment between 101 and 500 hectares represented only 2.6 percent of the total units recorded and owned 19.3 percent of Tucumán's arable land. This group farmed 26 percent of Tucumán's cultivated area.

The group devoted 81 percent of its cultivated lands to sugarcane and only 17 percent to maize and alfalfa. Their contribution to the total sugarcane area reached 37.5 percent. Units over 500 hectares constituted only 0.5 percent of the holdings surveyed in 1895, although they contained 44 percent of Tucumán's arable land. The group held 15 percent of the total cultivated area and accounted for 23 percent of the total sugarcane area in Tucumán. Within this group, 83 percent of the cultivated land was devoted to sugarcane and 12 percent to maize and alfalfa.

Therefore, patterns of land use varied depending on the size of the landholding. The expansion of sugarcane cultivation affected in particular mid-size and large owners, who became specialized in sugarcane cultivation at the expense of other crops, especially grains. In contrast, holdings smaller than ten hectares maintained a more diversified pattern of land use and devoted only part of their holdings to sugarcane. Small holdings were not exempted from the sugar craze, although they did maintain their adherence to food staples and thus devoted a larger share of their lands to maize than to sugarcane. This group contributed more than half the area cultivated with maize in the province in 1895. The significant participation of smallholders in the production of maize attests to that group's rational behavior when making planting decisions. Their choice offered a potential increase in revenues by devoting parts of their holdings to the cash crop but without losing the autonomy guaranteed by the cultivation of maize. Published data from the 1908 Argentine Agricultural and Pastoral Census confirms that this pattern persisted and that small units were still supplying the largest share of grains in the province during the late 1900s.[64] Patterns of land tenure and use varied among departments depending on the share of sugarcane in the total cultivated area. Sugar departments, defined as those that devoted more than 30 percent of their cultivated land to sugarcane, had a slightly higher number of owners and more land concentration than nonsugar departments.

In 1914, when sugarcane had reached most departments in the province (with the exception of Trancas), patterns of land use and tenure for the entire province resembled those that had characterized sugar departments in 1895. The expansion of sugarcane in Tucumán did not provoke profound modifications in land tenure patterns, although the evidence indicates that the province did experience an intensification of land concentration during the first decades of the twentieth century. Between 1895 and 1914 the number of smallholdings declined, and by 1914 they accounted for only 64 percent of the agricultural units in the province. Smallholders' participation in the total arable land in the province declined to 7.2 percent. The reduction in the number of small units directly correlated with the decrease in the area cultivated in maize. In contrast, holdings between 11 and 100 hectares experienced a significant increase, accounting for 32.2 percent of the total units recorded in the province. The next larger category, 101 to 500 hectares, also experienced an increase, accounting for 3.2 percent of all units surveyed. Units larger than 501 hectares accounted for 0.6 percent of the total units listed but accounted for 56.2 percent of the province's arable land.[65]

The transformation that was taking place in the agrarian sector had a parallel in Tucumán's occupational structure. Between 1869 and 1895 the industry's expansion created new labor possibilities and transformed provincial occupational patterns in profound and permanent ways.[66] In 1895 the population that declared an occupation experienced a significant increase in absolute terms. However, census data reveal a decline in the share of the adult population listed with an occupation.[67] While in 1869 more than half of Tucumán's adults declared an occupation, in 1895 only 42 percent were listed as having employment.[68] The balanced occupational pattern that had characterized the province until the early 1870s underwent significant changes, paralleling the province's specialization in sugar production. Not surprisingly, the population listed in the primary sector experienced a steep increase both in absolute and relative terms, and the sector became the most important source for employment in the province, accounting for more than half the workers listed with an occupation. The expansion of agricultural activities is illustrated in the growth of the category of jornalero, which increased more than threefold between 1869 and 1895. The service sector moved to second place, although the increase experienced by that sector was not as impressive as that of primary activities.[69]

Sugar expansion coincided with the decline of traditional cottage industries in the province. Domestic textile production could not compete with cheap textiles from Great Britain, and the adoption of cigarette-rolling machines and soap and candle factories in Buenos Aires dealt a profound blow to Tucumán's manufacturing sector.[70] The sugar industry was unable to compensate for the loss of jobs that resulted from the decline in manufactures. Therefore, secondary activities lost their preeminence and by 1895 they came in last place, accounting for only 21.5 percent of the population listed with an occupation. The dramatic contraction experienced by the secondary sector between 1869 and 1895 affected particularly female employment. Aggregate data from 1895 indicate that only one-third of the working population was female.[71] Furthermore, women represented 79 percent of those listed in the new census category "no-occupation."[72] The evidence indicates that during the last decades of the nineteenth century, female workers moved toward the service sector, choosing occupations such as cook, laundress, ironer, and seamstress.[73]

The expansion of the sugar industry provoked important changes in the occupational structure of the province. Sugar expansion must have created more labor opportunities for males, but it seriously hampered female employment. The limited number of occupations for women in the sugar industry could not compensate for the loss of jobs in the manufacturing sector, thus forcing female workers out of the labor pool and increasing their economic dependence on the male head of the family.[74] In 1913, John Foster Fraser visited Argentina. By then Tucumán had consolidated its role as the country's sugar bowl. The industry was the most active sector in the provincial economy and its expansion affected Tucumán's productive structure profoundly, replacing its diversified economy and altering patterns of occupation. Fraser visited Tucumán at the peak of the harvest season and insightfully described the position of sugar as well as the consequences of sugar expansion in the provincial economy: "Tucumán became a veritable El Dorado. . . . The advance in the sugar industry in Argentina during the last dozen years has been nothing short of amazing. While fortunes were being created in the cultivation of the sugarcane, orchards, orange crops, pasturage, and arable land were either being transformed or neglected."[75]

IN 1903 Carlos Pellegrini wrote, "Tucumán suffers from sugarcane indigestion. . . . What can we do? Cure the indigestion eliminating the excess because as long as [sugarcane] flourishes, provoking our misfortune, the problem will remain, despite agreements, trusts, bounties, and all other clever ameliorative measures."[76] In this statement, Pellegrini perceptively pointed to the changes experienced by Tucumán's economy during the last decades of the nineteenth century. Between 1876 and 1895 sugar production consolidated its position in Tucumán and changed the provincial economy profoundly. The impressive growth experienced by the industry provoked long-lasting consequences for the provincial economy as sugar specialization replaced

Tucumán's diversified agrarian sector. Industrialists made significant investments in modern processing machinery, while farmers cultivated thousands of hectares in sugarcane. The expansion of sugarcane cultivation in Tucumán altered patterns of land use profoundly, in particular among medium and large planters, who became specialized in sugarcane cultivation at the expense of other crops, especially grains. The evidence indicates that the larger the plot, the more it became specialized in sugarcane, although the largest contribution of sugarcane did not come from units over 500 hectares but from those between 101 and 500 hectares. Smaller holdings were not exempted from the sugarcane craze, although they maintained their adherence to food staples, and devoted a larger share of their lands to maize. In this case, the opposite occurred, as the smaller the plot, the less specialized it became in sugarcane. Therefore even though hectares of sugarcane took over land previously planted with cereals and tobacco, monoculture was more apparent in units over 100 hectares. Small holdings maintained a more diversified pattern of cultivation that combined subsistence farming with sugarcane planting. The industry's dramatic expansion did not result in massive land dispossession but rather facilitated the incorporation of thousands of independent planters into the sugar economy.

Chapter 3

Sugarcane Planters
Patterns of Production

SPECIALIZATION IN SUGAR quickly replaced Tucumán's diversified productive structure, although it did not provoke profound modifications in
Tucumán's land tenure patterns. Changes in methods of sugar manufacturing appeared in conjunction with a division between the industrial and
agricultural stages of production. Rather than opting for vertical integration,
ingenios took advantage of preexisting patterns of landownership and relied
on large, medium, and small growers for a large share of their raw material.
Small and medium farmers, who had previously produced only for self-
consumption and the local market, adapted successfully to the requirements
of the nascent industry and remained an essential component in the development of the sugar economy. The incorporation of thousands of farmers into
the sugar economy changed Tucumán's rural society. As French geographer
Pierre Denis observed in the late 1910s, "The most original feature of the organization of the sugar industry at Tucumán is the maintenance of a class of
independent cultivators, the *cañeros,* side by side with the large enterprises.
This survival of small and medium properties is a fact to which we find no
parallel in the other sugar districts of tropical America."[1]

The Organization of Production

During the last decades of the nineteenth century, the sugar industry consolidated its role in the provincial economy. The adoption of modern technology

increased ingenios' processing capacity and hence their demands for raw materials. Unlike Jujuy's ingenios, which were vertically integrated, Tucumán's ingenios met higher sugarcane demands through different strategies that combined self-supply with purchases from outside growers, thus enabling them to guarantee an adequate and stable provision of raw materials.[2] Sections of ingenios' lands were placed under direct production of salaried personnel hired by the mill or were allocated to sugarcane planters, known as *colonos,* who agreed to cultivate those holdings and sell the cane to the ingenio. Besides obtaining raw materials from their own lands, ingenios also purchased sugarcane from outside growers, or cañeros, independent planters with plots of varying sizes, either owned or rented, located near the mills. According to Antonio Correa's 1897 report, cañeros produced 38 percent of the sugarcane processed in the province, while the colonos produced 36 percent.[3]

Since colonial times, there were many independent planters in Tucumán devoted to the cultivation of cereals and other crops both for self-subsistence and to be traded in local and domestic markets. The existence of a large pool of independent planters in the province facilitated ingenio owners' decision to resort to outside suppliers, but other reasons also accounted for their not choosing vertical integration. Contemporary observers noted that ingenios lacked the capital needed to embark on sugarcane agriculture, as the incorporation of modern technology had required large investments that depleted their already limited resources.[4] There is no doubt that limited access to capital must have prevented some ingenios to engage in direct sugarcane production, in particular those that did not own large tracts of land, such as Ingenio Santa Lucía or Ingenio Caspinchango.[5] However, these factors failed to explain Ingenio Concepción's or Ingenio Santa Ana's decision to resort to outside suppliers, as both companies owned large tracts of land and had the financial resources to invest in plantations.

Rather than being unable to place all their lands into production, most ingenios chose not to do so, for a number of reasons. Outside growers gave them the possibility to disperse production risks and therefore concentrate more resources on the modernization of the mill. Additionally, outside suppliers released ingenios from the costs of organizing and monitoring field labor during harvest time, a factor that acquires more significance in Tucumán, a province that experienced significant problems in order to guarantee the stability of its workforce. However, extreme dependence on one source of supply could have increased ingenios' vulnerability. Therefore, instead of resorting to a

Figure 3.1. Ingenio Mercedes, 1910. View from the owners' chalet of permanent workers' housing, colonias, and the ingenio's facilities. *(Courtesy of Photographic Department, Archivo General de la Nación, Buenos Aires.)*

single supplier, ingenios combined self-production and contractual arrangements with a diverse pool of outside growers that included both cañeros and colonos. Most important, ingenios maintained a high degree of control over production through the establishment of individual agreements with planters that stipulated, among other considerations, quality and specific delivery conditions within a strict timeline.[6]

Ingenios' needs coincided with those of planters, which explains the group's enthusiastic participation in the sugar business. The increasing demand that followed technological innovation offered potentially high and rapid returns on the investment. According to Paul Groussac, in 1882 the cost of planting one hectare of sugarcane amounted to 500 pesos. The harvested cane could be sold for 540 pesos.[7] Therefore, the planter could recover the initial capital invested after the first year. Between 1880 and 1894 sugarcane prices increased rapidly, thus making the investment even more attractive to planters. A rational choice to maximize benefits guided the shift of thousands of farmers to sugarcane planting. In 1892, Edward Mulhall offered an interesting estimate of the cash value of one acre of sugarcane relative to that of other crops. Sugarcane yielded around 188 pesos per hectare, tobacco and rice 123 pesos, sundries around 54 pesos, and grains only 25 pesos per hectare.[8] This situation did not change after the 1895 crisis of overproduction. According to Correa's report, during the last years of the nineteenth century sugarcane cultivation was still more profitable than any other crop, and when faced with the possibility to plant tobacco, maize, or rice, planters still chose sugarcane.[9] Although agricultural costs and yields varied depending on the location of the plot, high returns and increasing demand encouraged thousands of farmers to shift to sugarcane, reinforcing a process that had announced itself timidly before the adoption of modern technology.[10]

The incorporation of independent planters into sugarcane cultivation started gradually in the early 1870s and accelerated during the last decades of the nineteenth century. The Méndez brothers must have been among the first industrialists to resort to outside suppliers, since their sugarcane plantations barely exceeded 100 hectares when they began to incorporate iron mills and centrifuges in their factories.[11] In his 1875 report, Juan Terán estimated that a total of 160 independent planters were supplying the existing mills with sugarcane. In those early days, their contribution was still marginal, since the ingenios' plantations exceeded 1,900 hectares, whereas the planters' accounted for only 300 hectares.[12] During the 1880s thousands of farmers started sugarcane cultivation. In 1883 the *Boletín nacional de agricultura* reported a total of 670 planters.[13] By 1895 their numbers had expanded to almost 2,700.[14] In 1902, Emilio Lahitte observed that immediately after the 1895 crisis ingenios experienced a slight increase in their share of farmed lands, which accounted for 61 percent of the province's land cultivated in sugarcane.[15] The trend reversed soon after and the number of independent growers resumed its increase. The system created in the 1880s remained almost unaltered during the following decades, although the evidence indicates that the number of outside growers increased over time. Between 1895 and 1914 the number of sugarcane holdings increased to 4,684, and planters accounted for almost 40,000 hectares of sugarcane, 41 percent of the total cultivated area in the province.[16] As the evidence clearly indicates, Tucumano farmers successfully adjusted to the demands of the nascent industry and became a part of the expanding sugar economy as outside suppliers.

Planters' increasing participation in sugarcane cultivation should not obscure the fact that ingenios' landholdings expanded in the province, in particular since the late nineteenth century. It is difficult to gauge the growth of ingenio holdings in the province before 1888 since provincial reports, such as those of Juan Manuel Terán and Eduardo Quintero, are based on patente tax records that taxed only land under production, which was systematically

underreported. In 1888 mills owned 53,036 hectares. By 1895 their holdings had increased to 144,266 hectares. By 1914 the mills' lands extended
over 223,517 hectares. These figures are consistent with other reports from
the period that point to the fast expansion of ingenios' plantations, in
particular after the 1895 crisis. In 1903 *El Orden* reported that two hundred
small cañeros lost their lands to the surrounding mills.[17] In 1909 the same
newspaper concluded that the CAT had expanded its plantations at the expense of small cañeros from the area.[18]

Popular culture criticized ingenios' land concentration policies as well. In
1909 the public and the media acclaimed the stage play *Cañas y trapiches*.
The play offers a glimpse into sugarcane planters' lives and their relations
with ingenios. The protagonists are sugarcane planter Salustio, who lives
on his farm with his wife and his daughter, Ercilia, who is engaged to Luis,
son of the mill owner Leoncio. In the opening scene, Leoncio announces a
visit to Salustio's home and the planter assumes the purpose is to discuss
wedding plans. However, during his visit Leoncio notifies the planter that
the company in Buenos Aires has decided to demand the repayment of the
planter's debts. Salustio owes the ingenio a large sum that he has received in
the form of cash advances before the beginning of the harvest. A few scenes
later it becomes clear that the ingenio has rejected a significant amount of
the sugarcane delivered by Salustio, which prevents him from honoring his
debts. For that reason, his farm is seized and later bought by Luis, who also
breaks up his engagement with Ercilia after dishonoring her. The family is
left with no other option than to leave for the city in search of a better future.
During his farewell speech, Leoncio refers to the planters' unfortunate situation, the evil scales, the ingenios' steady encroachment over their lands, and
the group's gradual loss of position in the sugar economy. He says, "Planters
are leaving as the trapiches are swallowing us."[19] In any case, in Tucumán
the ingenios' land concentration did not result in dispossession among small
farmers. Tucumán's preexisting patterns of landownership offered ingenios
the possibility of dispersing investment risks between the agricultural and
manufacturing sectors without losing complete control over the provision of
raw material. Therefore, sugar specialization did not result in the disappearance
of small and medium farmers but rather reinforced the existence of a large
and socially differentiated planter group. As *El Orden* pointed out in 1890,
"Sugar fever has infected everyone. Poor and rich, big and small, smart and
dumb, they all have started planting sugarcane."[20]

Sugarcane Planters, a Heterogeneous Crowd

During the last quarter of the nineteenth century, thousands of Tucumano farmers who owned or leased plots of land of different sizes shifted to sugarcane planting and became the suppliers for large ingenios in the area. Despite their shared interest in sugarcane cultivation, the group was far from homogeneous. For example, in 1893 *El Orden* published a report listing the tools and belongings of two planters from Colonia Sosa who were involved in a bitter dispute with Abraham Medina, the owner of Ingenio San Vicente. The inventory illustrates the significant disparities that existed among sugarcane planters in the province, since while one colono's possessions totaled 1,000 pesos, his neighbor's amounted to 7,300 pesos.[21] Besides material possessions, Tucumán's sugarcane growers were characterized by important differences in their origin, the size of their landholdings, patterns of land use and tenure, and living conditions. These differences in turn resulted in the development of distinct relationships with ingenios and with fellow planters.

A chief disparity resulted from the group members' diverse socioeconomic background and the different paths chosen to become sugarcane suppliers. In 1882, Paul Groussac pointed out that the industry's modernization had left behind ingenio owners who could not afford to pay for the new technology and, instead of abandoning sugar production, became outside sugarcane suppliers for the modernized mills.[22] This was likely the case of Leoncio Herrera, who, according to Arsenio Granillo's 1871 report, owned twelve hectares planted in sugarcane as well as a small wooden-roller mill.[23] During the 1880s, Herrera was involved in a number of different business transactions and sugarcane planting was still part of his investment portfolio.[24] To expand his small plot, in 1883 he signed a lease on a fifty-hectare property in Famaillá Department. The contract required Herrera to cultivate and maintain a sugarcane plantation on the property for the duration of ten harvests. Afterward the property was to revert to its owner.[25] A decade later the planter was still in business as a supplier for Ingenio El Manantial. According to the contractual arrangement with the ingenio, Herrera committed for the 1894 harvest forty hectares planted in sugarcane for which he would receive a share of the sugar produced.[26] Herrera's case is a clear illustration of a small ingenio owner turned sugarcane planter. His story, however, provides an explanation for the origin of only a small segment of cañeros.

The small and medium cañeros, who predominated numerically in the industry, came from a different pool of individuals. Attracted by the industry's expansion and its profitability, farmers who had previously devoted their lands to cereals or tobacco switched to sugarcane and became suppliers of ingenios located near their plantations. However, it is significant that these farmers acted with caution and did not turn all their lands to sugarcane planting. For example the 1882 contract between José Posse and Benjamín Ledesma created a partnership for the cultivation of sugarcane and other "crops that the administrator considers convenient." In this case, sugarcane and sugar production occupied an important position, but both partners acted with caution and did not place all their lands into sugarcane cultivation at once.[27] As late as 1890 planters were still maintaining a relatively diversified pattern of land use, as indicated by the arrangement made between Manuel Palacio and his brother, Gerónimo, in which only those plots located closer to the ingenio were the ones cultivated with cane.[28] Planters' shift to sugarcane cultivation was gradual and responded to actual increases in demand, as illustrated by Fernando Giacometti, who during the 1880s devoted his lands to both tobacco and sugarcane. In 1890 the planter signed a contract with Ingenio La Florida that, among other provisions, required the elimination of his tobacco plantation while providing for additional years to increase the amount of land cultivated with sugarcane. It was not until the planter was able to secure a buyer for his cane that he decided to specialize in one crop.[29]

Besides finding buyers, planters had to face other difficulties that placed significant limitations on their ability to become sugarcane suppliers. Sugarcane planting offered high and relatively fast returns on the initial investment but required an important outlay of capital not readily available to everybody. In 1888, Governor Lídoro Quinteros enumerated the problems facing the agricultural sector in the province and proposed the establishment of systems to guarantee the access to credit to "protect and assist the small planter in our countryside as a way to guarantee suppliers for the sugar industry."[30] Whether to start or to increase the size of a plantation, partnerships between capitalists and sugarcane planters became one mechanism frequently used by farmers to participate in the sugarcane business by gaining access to capital sources without losing control over production.[31] In some of these arrangements one partner acted as investor and the other took over the plantation's administration. This was the case of Miguel Segundo Peñalba and Carlos Ferreyra's agreement to expand an existing sugarcane plantation on Peñalba's land. According to the agreement, Ferreyra was appointed administrator and contributed a small amount of money to the partnership. In this case, however, Ferreyra's most important contribution was a preexisting contract with Ingenio Santa Bárbara that secured a buyer for the partners.[32] In other cases one partner supplied not only labor but also a small amount of capital to the partnership. This was the case of the agreement between Narcisa de Villafañe, who contributed the land planted in sugarcane, a small irrigation canal, and agricultural tools, and Ramón de la Vega, who provided some capital and his labor to the eight-year partnership.[33]

Sometimes partners gathered resources to start sugarcane cultivation in previously unused lands. This was the case of the partnership established between Nino Urbani and Juan Muzzarelli, who contributed equal amounts to start planting sugarcane in lands that both partners had recently purchased. Muzzarelli took over the administration of the plantation and received compensation for his labor. The agreement was established for a period of eight years, and one clause in the contract allowed for the incorporation of more lands should the expansion of the venture require it.[34] This was likely the case in the contract signed six months later between Muzzarelli and Antonio Casanova, which provided for the cultivation of sugarcane in lands owned by Casanova. Muzzarelli remained the administrator of the plantation and the profits of the partnership were to be equally divided between both partners.[35] In other instances, arrangements were made by planters with debts and in need of immediate access to cash. For example, in 1881 Clodomiro Usandivaras and Tomás Ríos established an eight-year partnership to plant and sell sugarcane. One partner contributed land that was already planted in sugarcane, machinery, tools, and his work, while the other invested a large sum and paid off his partner's outstanding debts.[36] This arrangement enabled Ríos to keep his plantation and provided an opportunity for Usandivaras to enter the sugar business. A year later, both partners expanded their business through a similar agreement with another planter who contributed the land and his work in return for the capital needed to keep his plantation running.[37]

The specific length of partnerships varied significantly, although most of them exceeded five years. Long-term partnerships allowed planters to enter the business gradually and, as explicitly stated in many contracts, depending on the evolution of the economy, expand their investment either by increasing the size of the plantation or by investing in milling technology. This initial caution reflects not only the unpredictability that characterized the early years of sugar expansion but also planters' rational economic behavior, which responded to market incentives. For example, in 1883, Lorenzo Grant and Enrique Lassart included in their agreement a provision stipulating that the ten-year planting operation was to evolve into one devoted to sugar making when "the partners feel it is the appropriate time to do so."[38]

Modern transportation, increasing demand, high prices for sugar, and improved labor recruitment mechanisms acted as powerful magnets for groups outside agriculture to participate in sugarcane cultivation. For example, in 1882, Manuel Navarro rented lands from Clementino Colombres and signed a contract with Eduardo Escudero to cultivate sugarcane. According to the contract stipulations, Escudero contributed the capital needed to start the plantation and Navarro, the rented lands and his labor.[39] Urban professionals became interested in the agricultural business as well. Such was the case of Zenón Cortadellas, an attorney from San Miguel de Tucumán, who in 1884 leased a plantation for eight years in order to personally manage it.[40] In some cases, urban professionals became only financial partners in the sugar venture. This was the case of the partnership established between Ángel López and Dr. Agustín López. According to the agreement, Dr. López contributed land and capital while Ángel participated as the administrator of the plantation. The importance ascribed to supervisory work was reflected in the distribution of the profits between both partners, as the administrator received a larger share of the total revenue obtained from the sale of the cane.[41] Outsiders' interest in sugarcane planting did not decrease over time. The 1895 census manuscript schedules report some names associated with liberal professions—such as Alurralde, Rodríguez Marquina, and Sal—as cane planters.[42] Furthermore, during the early 1900s Pedro Alurralde observed that lawyers and doctors were still participating in the profitable business of sugarcane cultivation as cañeros or colonos. According to the author, easy transportation from the city of San Miguel to rural areas facilitated urbanites' daily commute from the city to the countryside.[43]

Not only Tucumanos participated in sugarcane cultivation. The evidence indicates a few cases of businessmen from other provinces such as Buenos Aires and Mendoza who made investments in plantations through representatives, adding one more component to the heterogeneity of the sugarcane

Figure 3.2. Sugarcane plantation of Señor Attuvell. The planter, in a dark suit, supervises the harvest. *(Courtesy of Photographic Department, Archivo General de la Nación, Buenos Aires.)*

planters. Such was the contract signed in 1882 between Mendocinos Felix Aguinaga and Federico Moreno and Gerardo Constanti from Tucumán. According to the agreement, the two Mendocino partners contributed 80 percent of the capital to the society, while Constanti supplied the remaining 20 percent and was in charge of running the plantation. The partnership was established for eight years with the possibility of renewal, and profits were to be distributed equally among the three partners at the end of every year.[44] A similar arrangement was made between Zacarías Tapia from Tucumán and three investors from Buenos Aires. In this case, one representative of the Porteño (native or inhabitant of the city of Buenos Aires) group traveled to Tucumán just to establish the partnership. Tapia remained in charge of the plantation's administration and received, in addition to a share of the profits, monetary compensation for his services.[45]

Besides the different paths they chose to become sugarcane suppliers, planters also exhibited important disparities in tenure arrangements and patterns of land use. The analysis of 1895 census manuscript schedules yields a thorough picture of the diverse social universe that characterized sugarcane planting in Tucumán.[46] In 1895, census manuscript schedules for Tucumán reported 2,733 units totaling 55,484 hectares planted in sugarcane.[47] A significant number of these units, 78 percent, were managed by

TABLE 3.1

Cultivated hectares (units) with sugarcane by size and tenure, 1895

Hectares	Owners	Tenants	Sharecroppers	Colonos
0–10	3,582 (1,108)	499 (180)	117 (32)	16 (5)
11–100	10,427 (850)	4,353 (194)	181 (16)	2,602 (57)
101–500	10,733 (132)	2,595 (26)	251 (3)	6,995 (69)
501–	11,459 (34)	10 (1)	132 (2)	1,189 (9)
Total	36,201 (2,124)	7,457 (401)	681 (53)	10,802 (140)

Sources: My own elaboration based on census manuscript schedules of the Segundo Censo Nacional, Censo Económico y Social, Sección Agricultura, Boletín 27, Vols. 3–4, Fols. 46–133.
Note: The table does not include information on the units that did not disclose tenure arrangement.

their owners and accounted for 65.7 percent of the sugarcane cultivated in the province. The rest of the land was worked by tenants, sharecroppers, and colonos. Tenants and sharecroppers worked 16.7 percent of Tucumán's sugar plantations and contributed 14.7 percent of the sugarcane cultivation in the province. In both cases planters leased land for a specific period of time, ranging from three to ten years, on condition that they grow sugarcane on at least part of the property. Contracts varied but in most cases landowners provided tools, temporary housing, animals, concessions over water and firewood, and even workers. According to most arrangements, the tenant was required to tend the plantation but also to perform other tasks, such as fence, canal, and building renovation. This was the case of the contract signed between the Viaña brothers and the Zelada brothers in 1888. The property was enclosed by a wire fence and included land planted in sugarcane, fruit, and alfalfa, an aqueduct, two houses, a pen, and agricultural tools. The tenants were expected to maintain the crops and care for the property. One clause prohibited the sublease of the property or any of its parts. The arrangement was for three years and the rent was a fixed sum, to be paid in cash in advance at the beginning of each year.[48]

In other cases, when arrangements were for longer periods, the stipulated rent was not a fixed sum. This was the case of the contract signed between Mauricia Herrera de Villagra and Fidel Álvarez in 1880. The six-year arrangement was for the lease of a portion of Villagra's property and rent was to double after the second year. Since the rented land was not yet planted in sugarcane, this clause gave the tenant the possibility to set up the plantation and time to recover the initial investment, but it also indicated the landowner's expectation that sugarcane prices would continue to increase during the 1880s.[49] Besides tools, houses, water, and land, some tenants also received workers as part of their arrangement. In these cases they were required to take over workers' debts and to pay for their salaries and sustenance, as illustrated in the contract between José Monteros and Alfredo Bousquet in 1885, which established very specific requirements on how to deal with peons' debts and care for them.[50] In most cases, improvements made to the property reverted to the owner at no additional cost, as stipulated in the three-year contract between Gerónimo Palacio and Aquiles Lucca. The arrangement provided for the tenant to care for the property's house and aqueduct and to support the costs incurred in any additional required maintenance.[51] However, whenever properties needed significant improvements or required large investments, tenants were compensated. Such was the arrangement between Severo Carbonetti and Antonio Lancivica that stipulated the tenant should be reimbursed for the costs of wire fences and additional improvements made on the property. Tenants were expected to return the land planted in sugarcane.[52]

Contracts did not necessarily contain provisions for the sale of the cane unless the landowner had a previous arrangement with an ingenio. This was the case of the agreement between Pedro Marañón and Juan Simón, who was required to honor Marañón's contract with Ingenio Santa Bárbara during the first harvest. After the first year, the planter was allowed to sell the crop to the ingenio of his choice.[53] In very few cases, contracts gave the landowner priority in the purchase of the cane. For example, in the contract between Clementino Colombres and Manuel Navarro, one clause established that the tenant had to sell the sugarcane to Colombres, provided his was the best offer.[54] Nevertheless, in most cases tenants had the right to choose the buyer for their sugarcane, although distance from the plantation to the ingenio must have significantly limited that choice.

Tenancy agreements allowed those individuals without direct access to land to become sugarcane planters. Contractual arrangements guaranteed both parties' rights and duties and provided for mediation in case of conflict. Still, tenants were in a relatively vulnerable position, as most contracts included strict eviction clauses. Such was the case in the contract between Colombres and Navarro, which provided for the eviction of preexisting tenants on the property to increase the size of the sugarcane fields. Contracts always included clear stipulations of the penalties for noncompliance, late payment, or property loss, as indicated by the agreement between José Díaz and Manuel Lander, which provided for the creation of an outside commission to assess potential problems and to determine the need to annul the agreement.[55]

Sharecropping was an alternative for those without significant capital resources to participate in sugarcane cultivation. In some cases, owners provided tools and seeds. For example, in 1885 Emidio Posse leased thirty hectares to Pedro Arancibia for ten years. The planter was required to plant sugarcane with seed provided by Posse and paid as rent one cent per arroba of sugarcane sold, with no requirements that the cane be sold to any particular ingenio.[56] Arrangements provided for the cultivation not only of sugarcane but also of other crops. For example as part of the arrangement between Leandro Guerra and Ramón Gómez, Guerra was required to plant sugarcane, rice, maize, and tobacco. Except for sugarcane, there was no stipulation on the area to be planted in each crop. The contract established different shares of payment depending on the crop; one-fourth of the rice, sugarcane, and tobacco was required and one-third of the maize. Maize's importance in Tucumanos' diet may account for its larger share. The remaining provisions of the contract are similar to those of a regular tenancy agreement.[57]

Despite internal disparities found in contractual arrangements, tenancy and sharecropping offered an option to participate in sugarcane cultivation to those individuals who did not own land. At the same time, since all contracts required planters to return the property planted in sugarcane, they provided landowners with an alternative to start a plantation or to expand an existing one without the need to incur additional expenses. For tenants, fixed rents must have acted as an incentive to increase production in order to maximize profits. However, fixed rents failed to reflect variations in sugarcane prices, thus intensifying tenants' financial burden during periods of low prices. Furthermore, these arrangements failed to provide a secure buyer for the cane, which increased their vulnerability during times of overproduction. Landowners maintained control over parts of their property since they never gave up all their water rights and in many cases reserved the use of buildings and pastures on the property. In some instances, contracts gave owners the right to cancel the agreement at any time after the first harvest. To reduce their extreme dependence on one crop, tenants and sharecroppers—especially those working on small and midsize properties— followed patterns of land use similar to those of small owners, reserving at least part of the property for the production of other crops. One significant disparity was in the size of the plots cultivated by each group. While almost half the properties managed by tenants were in the midsize range (11–100 hectares), the vast majority of sharecroppers tended plots smaller than ten hectares.[58] It is not possible to assess the degree to which this group had access to landownership after a few years of working the land, although some contracts included priority sale clauses.

Farmers with some capital but without land could also participate in the sugar business as colonos. Mills divided their lands and allotted them to colonos, who were obligated to plant, care for, and sell the sugarcane to the mill.[59] These lands, called *colonias,* were located close to the ingenios as was the case of the colonias in Ingenio Santa Ana, created the same year the mill started operation.[60] During the late 1910s, Colonia Santa Catalina and Lules, the two largest colonias of Ingenio Santa Ana had almost 9,000 hectares planted in sugarcane.[61] According to an official report, colonias represented the response of ingenio owners to the increase experienced by sugarcane prices during the 1880s.[62] *Colonato* arrangements enabled ingenio owners to exercise quality control while securing a steady supply of sugarcane without incurring additional expenses. Furthermore, colonos allowed mills to disperse investment risks while maintaining almost complete control over the production of the raw material. A colonia's share in the mill's sugarcane supply varied over time and depended on the size and number of colonias owned by the ingenio.[63] In 1895 manuscript census returns reported a total of 140 colonos, mostly concentrated in the departments of Cruz Alta, Río Chico, and Famaillá. The group tended 5 percent of the province's sugarcane holdings, although their participation in the total area planted in sugarcane was almost 20 percent. Colonos' holdings were larger than tenants' since almost half the units extended between 101 and 500 hectares.[64] In his 1889 report on the sugar industry, chief of statistics Paulino Rodríguez Marquina observed that colonos paid a small fixed rent for the property.[65] However, contracts and letters from colonos suggest that in most cases the land was granted without any rental payment required.

Limited by their own personal situation, which varied from that of small capitalists who personally worked the land to individuals with only managerial roles, colonos followed different strategies to become sugarcane planters. In some cases, cañeros with existing sale agreements took over additional lands owned by the ingenio and near their own plantations, thus expanding

Figure 3.3. Colonos' Houses, early 1920s. Houses varied significantly among ingenios, from very basic huts to the more modern facilities shown here. *(Courtesy of Photographic Department, Archivo General de la Nación, Buenos Aires.)*

their own holdings through colonato agreements. So it was with Honorio Alurralde, who in 1885 signed an agreement with Ingenio Caspichango for the sale of sugarcane produced on his plantation and on an additional plot owned by the ingenio that he received in colonato for as many years as the sales contract lasted.[66] Ingenios set up different systems and material incentives to attract colonos to the ingenio. For instance, between November 1890 and February 1891, Ingenio La Florida resorted to newspaper advertisements to recruit colonos who were only required to provide workers into the arrangement.[67] Prospective colonos used newspapers to offer their services as well. In 1893, *El Orden* published an announcement from a family offering to tend, as colonos, plots planted in sugarcane or tobacco.[68] In most cases, colonos were granted not only land but housing, which provided an additional incentive for families to settle in the area. For example, the contract between Abraham Medina and his colonos stipulated that besides land, seeds, and water rights, each family should receive a brick house with two rooms and a porch. During court proceedings against Medina, colonos complained that despite contract stipulations they lived in "miserable huts, like those used by peons."[69]

Colonato arrangements usually contained very specific stipulations. The land agreement consisted of a concession of a plot of land over a period of time that included careful instructions on when and what to plant as well as how to care for the crop and the land. The contract between Ingenio San Vicente and Arturo Romero, a rather typical colonato contract, granted Romero 160 hectares of land. The arrangement required that Romero plant a minimum of eighty hectares in sugarcane, leaving the rest of the land to be planted in other crops. Over the total eight-year period that the contract was to last, Romero was granted four years to plant the cane. In most cases, colonos received sugarcane seeds from the ingenio. For example, in the contract between Ingenio Santa Lucía and Sisto López, the ingenio provided the sugarcane to start the plantation but the colono was in charge of all expenses incurred in planting and harvesting. According to the agreement, López received sixty hectares for a period of eight years and was granted three years to complete the cultivation of the plot. If the colono failed to do so, the ingenio had the right to take over the unused lands and place them under the direct production of the ingenio or rent them out to another colono.[70]

Whenever colonos received land already cultivated, contracts contained detailed instructions on soil care and maintenance.[71] Agreements included clauses that accounted for weather-related setbacks, as in the arrangement between Ingenio Santa Lucía and José Moreno that stipulated different prices paid for sugarcane affected by frost or drought.[72] Water and pasture rights were included in contracts as well. For example, the agreement between Ingenio Bella Vista and Clodomiro Pereira provided for the colono's use of pastures that belonged to the ingenio. The contract also established a detailed schedule for irrigation rights that gave the colono full access to the ingenio's water on specific days of each month.[73] Ingenios always reserved priority rights over water. For example the contract between Ingenio Amalia and Gustavo Malhberg included a clause requiring the colono to share his quota of water in the event the mill ran out of water for its plantations.[74] Besides water rights, contracts contained stipulations on the use of other resources such as wood and construction materials, as in the agreement between Ingenio Santa Lucía and Melitón Ceballos that provided for the ingenio to cut and transport the firewood to be used by the colono and gave him permission to use tools and construction materials that belonged to the ingenio.[75]

Colonato contracts included sale stipulations as well. In nearly all cases, colonos were required to sell all their sugarcane to the ingenio; only under extraordinary circumstances were they allowed to sell to other ingenios. For example, Gustavo Malhberg's contract with Ingenio Amalia stipulated that the colono could sell his cane to other ingenios only if the mill stopped working, and then only until repairs were completed. As part of the sale agreement, contracts allowed for substantial price reductions in the case of lower-quality sugarcane. In cases of negligence or noncompliance by colonos, contracts

Figure 3.4. Sugarcane and firewood transportation. Carts loaded with sugarcane and wood, waiting to be hauled to the ingenio. *(Courtesy of Photographic Department, Archivo General de la Nación, Buenos Aires.)*

enabled mills to fine planters or terminate the agreement and evict the colono with no right to compensation. For example, the contract between Juan Robaletti and Ingenio Mercedes established a forty-month period to plant the uncultivated part of the land granted in colonato. Should Robaletti fail to meet the deadline, the contract established a steep fine for each uncultivated hectare and the land reverted to the ingenio's control.[76]

Credit was an important part of the arrangement between ingenios and colonos, as many planters depended on ingenios' financial assistance for day-to-day expenses, in particular during harvest. Contracts included clauses specifying interest rates and very detailed payment schedules, as indicated by several of the agreements between Ingenio Santa Lucía and its colonos. In such cases, interest rates were always above 10 percent and the contracts clearly stipulated repayment conditions and penalties for noncompliance.[77] Antonio Correa pointed out that high interest rates included in contract provisions, coupled with additional abuses committed by mills, severely affected colonos, who, after settling their debts, had to look for other jobs to survive during the slack season.[78]

Besides supplying sugarcane to the ingenio, colonos fulfilled an important role in Tucumán's labor-hungry sugar economy. They were expected to share their workers with the mill as well as to personally provide additional services that ranged from routine maintenance to the construction of housing facilities. The contract between Ingenio Santa Lucía and Domingo Cuello included a clause that stipulated that half the colono's workers remain in the ingenio after the contract was over.[79] In other cases, the ingenio was allowed to borrow workers from the colono, as in the arrangement between Abraham Medina and the colonos from his Colonia Sosa. In this case, the ingenio was expected to feed and provide housing for the workers while under its employment.[80] Even though some contracts stipulated the duties and payment for additional services, in most cases they were part of the colonato agreement and not remunerated, as with improvements made on the land or building renovations, which always reverted to the mill without any compensation to the colono. For example, as part of his arrangement with Ingenio Santa Lucía, Melitón Ceballos was expected to repair and maintain the fence surrounding the plantation as well as to perform other repairs on set days every month.[81]

Not only did outside growers display disparate socioeconomic backgrounds and patterns of land tenure but the size of their holdings and patterns of land use varied significantly. Contemporary observers and statistical records verify this peculiar aspect of Tucumán's agriculture. Even as early as 1875, Terán's report indicated the existence of large holdings in conjunction with a group of very small planters. Unfortunately, the report does not offer information on the size of individual holdings. Rodríguez Marquina's 1888 analysis of the sugar industry presents a similar problem. Even though the author recorded the number of planters by category, the report included the total hectares cultivated without distinguishing individually by planter.[82] The analysis of the 1895 manuscript schedules overcomes these limitations and provides insight into sugarcane planters' patterns of land use (see chapter 2).[83] The evidence indicates the existence of a large number of small units planted in sugarcane, although they accounted for only a small share of all provincial land devoted to cane. Small planters made the rational choice to shift to the crop with the highest return but reserved at least one-third of their plots for other traditional crops, mostly those for their self-subsistence, thus guaranteeing certain degree of independence for themselves and their families. A significantly large share of sugarcane was cultivated in units over ten hectares. Larger units became specialized in sugarcane; more than 80 percent of their total cultivated area was devoted to the crop, at the expense of grains and alfalfa.

However, it was not only origin, size, and patterns of land use and tenure that differed among sugarcane planters. There were also significant disparities in living conditions.[84] In the late 1890s, Antonio Correa observed that "sugarcane was cultivated by individuals from all social classes, from the rich landowner to the modest farmer, who sometimes owned or sometimes rented his small piece of land."[85] Large cañeros and colonos resided most of the year in San Miguel de Tucumán. To this category must have belonged planters such as Rafael Amaya and Nicanor Posse. Amaya was a wealthy colono who, according to one witness, drove "his car to the colony but [did] not evade the hard tasks of sugarcane planting."[86] Posse was a cañero and a member of the provincial elite with close family ties to Ingenio Esperanza and a plot of land of over 600 hectares in Cruz Alta. Large planters' material possessions guaranteed them a comfortable existence, similar to the one enjoyed by elites in other regions of Argentina. This privileged group lived in large two-story houses made of brick and lime mortar, adorned with patios and arches. Their daily routines consisted of visits to the church and the market, walks in the plaza after sunset (to avoid the blazing sun), drinks with friends at any of the many downtown cafes to discuss the economy and politics, and weekly performances offered at the city's theaters.

The large majority of sugarcane planters owned smaller plots of land and shared almost nothing in common with the large cañeros and colonos. Census manuscripts and other sources also indicate significant variation in terms of material possessions among small and medium sugarcane planters, making it difficult to generalize. For example, the testaments of Rafael Escobar and Ramón Rosa Juárez clearly reveal a disparity in material goods that must have had a direct impact on each planter's living conditions. Rafael Escobar, a midsize cañero, died in 1888 and bequeathed two houses; two plantations in Cruz Alta totaling eighty-five hectares, ten of which were planted in sugarcane; and a large number of silver utensils, furniture, clothes, and some jewelry.[87] In contrast, Ramón Rosa Juárez's assets consisted of one ten-hectare plot planted in fruit trees and only five hectares of sugarcane. After his death in 1887, the latter cañero left to his heirs a house, some furniture, few clothes, and one piece of silver. In this case, many of the goods were described as old and broken, a reflection of the planter's less-privileged position than his neighbor's.[88]

Still there were some common elements among small and medium planters. The evidence suggests that most owned horses and other farm animals, farming tools, and some personal possessions such as furniture and durable household supplies.[89] In general, their residences were in the countryside, close to the plantation.[90] Even though they lived in close proximity to fieldworkers, they enjoyed stronger and more comfortable dwellings than peons did.[91]

Contemporaries referred to planters' residences as *casas habitación* (dwelling houses), a term that indicates a clear difference from workers' ranchos, which were smaller and consisted of one room only. Of course, it could also be argued that this distinction may not reflect actual disparities but just subtleties in the use of language. Yet, additional evidence seems to indicate that there were indeed material differences. For example, photographs of sugarcane planters' dwellings depict one-story structures with arched galleries, several rooms, and tiled roofs.[92] Sugarcane contracts also describe the houses as having two or more rooms and a gallery, a clear distinction from the descriptions by contemporary observers of peons' single-room accommodations.

It is likely that living conditions for sugarcane planters with one- or two-hectare plantations remained closer to those of permanent field- or mill-workers. This was the case of José Ávila, a very small planter who owned five hectares of land with less than one hectare planted in sugarcane. The testament's inventory listed very few material possessions, which, according to the notary, "did not exist anymore since his sister had already taken care of them," and makes no mention of a house. A few *fanegas* of maize and the plot of land account for almost a third of the total value of Ávila's goods, which totaled only 127.12 pesos.[93]

Clearly, sugarcane planters were a heterogeneous lot. Despite their differences, the incorporation of thousands of small and medium planters in Tucumán's economy represents a distinctive case in Latin America and resulted in the emergence of a complex rural society. Sugar expansion did not provoke profound modifications in Tucumán's land tenure patterns and enabled small, medium, and large holders to participate in sugar production, thus extending the potential benefits of the sugar economy to a larger sector of rural society. Ingenios took advantage of preexisting patterns of landownership and relied on thousands of farmers for the provision of their sugarcane. Their incorporation in the sugar economy was achieved by the establishment of contractual arrangements. Rather than being a transitional solution, contracts became the norm in Tucumán. Terms varied depending on economic factors such as the type of agreement, size of the plantation, and financial capability of the sugarcane grower as well as on noneconomic, factors such as family connections and political ties. As Pierre Denis pointed out, "It is only the more important cañeros who have the privilege of selling by the truckload, or selling to distant works. The small growers are compelled to deal with the local ingenio."[94]

Figure 3.5. Sugarcane planter's family, Ingenio Trinidad, early 1920s. *(Courtesy of Photographic Department, Archivo General de la Nación, Buenos Aires.)*

Ingenios and Sugarcane Planters

A sales contract stipulated the conditions under which sugarcane planters participated in the sugar business and regulated the relations between the industrial and agricultural sectors. In general, it consisted of a mutual agreement between a planter and an ingenio to sell a determined quantity of sugarcane for a specific price over a certain period of time. The length of partnerships varied widely, from one to ten years. During the industry's early years, contracts were usually signed more than six months before the harvest. These early arrangements applied predominantly to small planters, who depended on ingenios' assistance for the capital required to meet planting and harvesting expenses. By means of early contracts, small planters secured a market for their sugarcane but at a fixed price, which most of the time did not reflect changes in market conditions. One way to avoid this problem was through share payments. For example, in his 1893 contract with Ingenio El Manantial, Dalmiro Mur established a five-year commitment to deliver two hundred thousand arrobas of sugarcane. The first year, the ingenio guaranteed the planter a fixed price of eighteen cents per arroba, whereas for subsequent years the contract stipulated a share payment of three arrobas of sugar per one hundred arrobas of sugarcane to be paid either in sugar or its cash equivalent.[95] Share payments were not extremely popular and were more common among small and medium planters and colonos. According to *Revista azucarera,* in the case of share payments, cañeros always received higher shares than colonos.[96]

Large planters were in a much better position to negotiate more favorable terms, so they not only obtained cash for their crop but also could afford to wait longer to sign their contracts and bargain for better terms. However, this strategy did not always prove to be successful. For example, in September 1884, *El Orden* reported that factories were not accepting sugarcane at prices higher than six cents per arroba, whereas a month before the price paid was eight cents. The paper observed that several large planters in the southern parts of the province who had waited too long to sell their sugarcane had been affected by the situation.[97] After the 1895 crisis the market became more volatile and unpredictable, which was reflected in contractual arrangements. In general, late-nineteenth- and early-twentieth-century contracts maintained similar land, delivery, and sale stipulations. However they responded to market instability by including clauses that gave ingenios the right to terminate the agreement without compensation to the planter and reduced the average length of a contract to one or two years.[98] Furthermore, new contracts modified payment conditions and required that planters pay for new taxes imposed on the industry.[99]

Sugarcane deteriorates rapidly after cutting; delays in delivery and grinding have a direct impact on sucrose content. It is not surprising then that contracts carefully stipulated delivery conditions. Such was the agreement between Fernando Giacometti and the Méndez brothers, which gave the planter no more than two days for delivery after the cane was harvested. The contract also contained stipulations on price reductions that were proportional to decline in sucrose content.[100] Delivery stipulations enabled mills to maintain control over important aspects of coordination. For example, Dalmiro Mur's 1893 contract determined that the mill would schedule harvest and delivery times.[101] In this case, the mill assumed responsibility for transporting the sugarcane. In the arrangement between Ingenio Azucarera Argentina and Isidoro and Juan Gómez, the ingenio was obligated to secure seven freight cars to transport Gómez's sugarcane daily. Once the sugarcane

Figure 3.6. Carts loaded with sugarcane outside an ingenio, waiting to be weighed. *(Courtesy of Photographic Department, Archivo General de la Nación, Buenos Aires.)*

arrived at the railroad station, the ingenio assumed full responsibility for any inconvenience associated with delays in transportation.[102]

Large planters enjoyed direct access to railroad transportation, which enabled them to engage in contracts with mills located farther away. In these cases, ingenios were required to notify planters of the milling schedule in advance, as shown by the contract signed in 1883 between Ingenio San Vicente and Arturo Romero, which provided for the planter to be notified of delivery ten days in advance.[103] Finally, in order for ingenios to maintain a steady flow of sugarcane, contracts included minimum daily amounts to be delivered by the planter and stipulated that deliveries were not to be interrupted once they had started unless there was a problem with the machinery. For example, the contract between Carlos Vega and Ingenio Amalia included stipulations on the daily quantity of sugarcane that the planter was required to deliver to the ingenio.[104]

Arrangements also included provisions for sugarcane freshness and planting procedures. The contract signed in 1888 between ingenio owner Justino

Posse and Ismael Gutiérrez instructed the planter on how to prepare the fields before planting.[105] Specific clauses enabled ingenios to reject sugarcane of lower quality, although contracts did not establish clear mechanisms to determine sucrose content. According to *El Orden,* refusal to accept sugarcane became a common practice by ingenios, especially during periods of overproduction.[106] In some cases, contracts stipulated lower prices for sugarcane that had experienced frost or otherwise had not been properly cared for. For example, the arrangement between Ingenio Cruz Alta and Juan Muzzarelli determined different prices for cane exposed to frost and high winds or that had not been adequately irrigated.[107] Contracts established an exclusive relationship between partners. Only under exceptional circumstances could planters sell their cane to other ingenios. The contract between Ingenio San Vicente and Arturo Romero determined that the ingenio could interrupt milling for twenty days for routine maintenance or machinery problems. The arrangement enabled Romero to sell his cane to another ingenio, but only if it failed to start milling after that period, yet the planter still required the ingenio's authorization.[108]

Since many planters depended on ingenios for money up front to finance their expenses, contracts often provided for cash advances. Credit stipulations were similar in most cases, although interest rates varied widely. Planters received cash advances in several installments before the harvest, and reimbursement was not expected until the harvest was over. Interest rates fluctuated between 6 and 12 percent annually, depending on the length of the contract.[109] Dalmiro Mur's long-term contract carried an annual interest rate of 9 percent, whereas Leoncio Herrera's one-year contract set it at 12 percent; both contracts were signed in the same year. Loans were secured on property and sometimes cosigners were required to underwrite the contract, as in Fernando Giacometti's agreement with the Méndez brothers. Here the lenders did not charge interest rates but the planter was required to use all his assets as collateral.[110] Planters' financial needs placed them in a very vulnerable position; in case they were unable to pay back the debt, ingenios could foreclose on their property or pressure them into renewing their contracts. For example, in 1883 Mercedes Zavalía renewed the sales contract her late husband had signed with Ingenio La Trinidad in order to pay debts he had left behind. The agreement offered the planter an additional cash advance at a low interest rate but stipulated a fixed price for the sugarcane she produced for the three years that the contract was to last.[111]

The implementation of contractual relations in the countryside represents one way in which innovation was promoted by the sugar industry. The establishment of contracts expanded capitalist relations in Tucumán's countryside. By means of contracts, planters secured a market for their sugarcane but at the expense of surrendering some of the control over the productive process. There were, however, differences among planters, as cañeros were in a position to bargain more effectively over the terms of their contracts than colonos. Contracts not only enabled mills to guarantee a steady supply of sugarcane without incurring large expenses but also accorded them more control over specific aspects of production. Contracts reduced the possibility of interruptions in delivery on the planters' part and guaranteed a stable supply of sugarcane during the peak grinding season. As Alan Dye has convincingly argued for Cuban sugar, hold-up threats become particularly acute during the grinding season and the incorporation of specific contract stipulations gave mills control over coordination and operating decisions, thus providing one important mechanism to attenuate their potentially dangerous consequences on ingenios' grinding operations.[112]

Contractual agreements sanctioned ingenios and planters' mutually dependent relationship but could not prevent the emergence of conflicts between both groups. In 1893, *El Orden* followed a dispute between the owner of Ingenio San Vicente, Abraham Medina, and twelve colonos in Colonia Sosa.[113] According to newspaper reports, in December 1892 Medina and his henchmen assaulted and tried to force the planters off the colonia's lands. The mill owner claimed that colonos had failed to fulfill their contracts, neglected to pay workers, and squandered cash advances.[114] Shortly thereafter he sent eviction notices and made his overseers confiscate colonos' farm animals and tools. Since the colonos refused to leave the property, in January Medina forcefully evicted them and seized their belongings. The colonos appealed to the authorities and accused the mill owner of using physical violence, failing to supply sufficient water, and not paying for the delivered sugarcane and borrowed labor. At the same time, the group launched a relentless media campaign in which they described their miserable living and working conditions and denounced the brutality and complicit participation of the authorities during eviction procedures.[115] After several months, the court ruled in the colonos' favor and forced Medina to submit to mediation, thus marking a significant turning point in the case.[116] On May 15, 1893, in the case of Abraham Medina versus the colono Alejandro San Martín, the ingenio owner was required to return the planter's belongings as well as to indemnify him for damages incurred to San Martín's possessions. A year later, a civil judge endorsed the resolution, thus giving legal sanction to the ruling and securing a very important victory for sugarcane planters' rights.[117]

Rather than an isolated incident, the dispute between Medina and his colonos illustrated some of the problems faced by sugarcane planters in Tucumán as well as the different strategies pursued by the group to minimize threats to their survival and to reassert their rights. Disagreements revolved around a number of circumstances that emerged mostly during the harvest, such as failure to fulfill specific contract provisions, misuse of water rights, and mishandling of sugarcane weighing procedures.[118] In 1895, *El Orden* observed, "The precarious position of the planter originates in his relations with ingenios . . . sugar industrialists have eschewed the friendly way and have imposed themselves on planters as superiors."[119] Contracts offered a tool that protected planters against abuse and opened a legal channel for grievances. Because of the nature of sugarcane handling and the slowness of Tucumán's judicial system, sales contracts as well as tenancy and colonato arrangements included clauses that provided for mediation in case of conflict. Mechanisms to select commission members varied from contract to contract but in most cases they allowed for both parties to select agents to represent them. It is difficult to assess the number of grievances solved through the use of mediators, as those disputes never made it to court. In any case, when mediators failed to facilitate an acceptable solution to the conflict, planters resorted to the civil court, as illustrated by Benedicto Robles's lawsuit against Ingenio Bella Vista for failing to pay for the sugarcane he had delivered on time.[120]

Some of the conflicts confronting planters and ingenio owners resulted from the intensification of problems that had plagued the province before the sugar boom, as was the case with disputes over water rights.[121] Sugarcane requires a plentiful supply of water and good drainage systems.[122] The adoption of modern technology and the expansion of the area cultivated in sugarcane thus intensified the demand for water. To guarantee a stable and constant supply, ingenio owners and large planters in Tucumán undertook significant irrigation investments, but without much coordination. For example, when building an aqueduct to irrigate his sugarcane plantation, Francisco Daporte cut through Carmen Delgado's property, rendering her pasture lands useless and threatening to flood the entire area.[123] Lack of planning resulted in a very unsystematic irrigation system and an extremely unequal distribution of water that brought planters into conflict with ingenio owners daily.[124] These problems intensified during times of drought. Until the 1880s the government intervened indirectly in water regulation by appointing landowners to serve on ad hoc commissions that regulated water use and distribution. However, the absence of more comprehensive legislation on water use doomed this solution to failure.

To prevent abuses and fill the void left by lack of legislation, contracts very clearly stipulated each party's water share as well as their responsibilities to maintain and repair aqueducts and canals. In many instances, and to avoid extreme dependence on ingenios' water resources, planters purchased water from other farmers. The planters Romualdo Mora and Zacarías de la Zerda, for instance, agreed to build an aqueduct and shared irrigation rights to supply their sugarcane plantations.[125] Still, planters were unable to prevent ingenios from monopolizing control of water resources, and disputes over water abounded. Faced with the possibility of losing their crops, planters resorted to a wide range of strategies, from direct violence to litigation in court. In a lawsuit between Miguel del Castillo and Abraham Medina, Castillo alleged that Medina stole property from him and failed to guarantee access to the ingenio's water, thus jeopardizing his harvest. The judge ruled in favor of Castillo and compelled Medina to indemnify the colono for his losses.[126] When legal action failed, however, planters resorted to more direct strategies, such as water theft or the obstruction or destruction of aqueducts and canals. Contemporary observers noted that many of Tucumán's ingenios protected their water sources with armed guards, further indication of planters' threat to ingenios' water supplies.[127]

Besides direct action, sugarcane planters engaged the authorities and the media to protect their water rights. In 1896, *El Orden* observed that "disorder, confusion, and injustice" characterized water distribution in the province and demanded immediate measures.[128] In response to these demands, in 1897 the provincial government approved the first Irrigation Code. According to the law, water was a public resource and thus it was the government's duty to supervise and guarantee its fair distribution. The code's main purpose was to provide equal access to water rights for all the groups involved in any agricultural production, and sugarcane production in particular. It established the obligation to register the number of hectares under irrigation, created a quota system for the distribution of water, granted both permanent and temporary concessions, limited the size of new concessions, established rules for cleaning and maintaining the canals and aqueducts, and imposed a new tax to improve the provincial irrigation system. Although the code did not eliminate tensions between both groups in matters of irrigation, it did allow for a more balanced distribution of water among planters and ingenios in the province. It was in Tucumán's authorities' interest not only to secure a harmonious relation between the groups responsible for the growth and development of the province's mother industry but also to protect what they perceived as the most vulnerable group, the small sugarcane planters.[129]

The government could intervene only in those areas that were considered a public service, such as water rights. Planters were in a much more vulnerable position in their daily dealings with ingenio owners. For example, at the time of sugarcane delivery, employees hired by ingenios were responsible for weighing the sugarcane and recording the information on the mill's ledger. Upon downloading, planters obtained a receipt that stated the number of cartloads delivered as well as their weight and the amount owed the planter. Receipts were redeemable at the end of either the month or the harvest, depending on the arrangement between planter and ingenio. This procedure was usually clearly stipulated in contracts, but since scales were supervised by the ingenio's employees, planters had little control over weighing issues. Therefore, dubious weighing procedures set off countless disputes between planters and mill owners. Contemporary sources agreed that scales were set to underweigh, around 30 to 50 percent of a load.[130] In 1885, as part of a campaign to protect planters' rights, *El Orden* demanded more government control to prevent further abuses committed by *basculeros* (scale operators) and their "evil scales."[131]

The provincial authorities did not intervene until the early twentieth century, leaving planters with no other option but litigation or more direct action. For example, in 1894 a group of planters sued Ernesto Bazet, an employee of Ingenio Lastenia, for fraudulent manipulation of the scale. According to the complainants, the basculero purposely set the scale to underweigh their sugarcane loads. After a long trial, involving an extraordinary number of witnesses and an in-depth investigation, Bazet was found guilty and sentenced to eight months in prison. It was an important victory for planters' rights.[132] In 1897, when the industry was suffering from the first crisis of overproduction, *El Orden* reported that ingenios were still resorting to fixed scales to defraud planters and demanded that the authorities take action against those "high-society speculators."[133] In 1903 the government decreed that two scale inspectors supervise sugarcane weighing procedures, and although the real motivation behind this regulation was to prevent tax evasion, it did assist planters by increasing their control over ingenios' scales.[134]

Cañeros and colonos also resorted to extralegal means in their dealings with ingenios. To counter ingenios' weight manipulation, planters added stones, sticks, or pieces of iron to the loads of cane they delivered. Even though it is difficult to assess the regularity of this strategy, the evidence seems to indicate it was common. When Ingenio San Pablo accused Pedro Suárez of sabotaging the mill, the peon argued, "This isn't the first time sugarcane has arrived at the mill with stones and sticks added to increase the weight."[135] In other cases, planters bribed basculeros to record a higher delivery weight. Basculero Eusebio Gramajo was sued by Ingenio La Trinidad in 1897 for manipulating delivery weights to favor planters.[136] Occasionally, planters resorted to more violent means, such as destruction of an ingenio's property. Luis Barbarino set fire to the sugarcane he had sold to Ingenio Mercedes, which represented a significant financial loss to the mill.[137] In some cases these conflicts escalated into direct confrontation and physical violence. In 1894 a dispute that had started as a result of weighing irregularities turned violent and led the administrator of Ingenio Industria Argentina to shoot a disgruntled planter who had threatened him with a knife. The planter was not mortally wounded and the judge decided in favor of the administrator, who, according to witnesses, had acted in self-defense.[138]

Throughout these conflicts, the local press proved to be very receptive to planters' pleas, offered them a space to voice their concerns and express their grievances, and became an advocate for their rights. *El Orden* published numerous editorials on planters' behalf and described planters as a hardworking "privileged and superior caste." The group was perceived as the main engine behind the sugar industry, the backbone of the most modern economic sector in the province. Portrayals of planters as exemplary individuals abounded. For example, as part of a campaign in defense of the planters, in August 1895, *El Orden* published a series of articles entitled *La defensa del cañero*, which highlighted the importance of the group to the development of the province's mother industry and demanded more active participation from the government to protect them from abuses committed by ingenios.[139] Planters were perceived as pawns in the ingenios' power game and as the most vulnerable group in the sugar economy, as they lacked the power to negotiate sugarcane prices and most of the time depended on ingenios' willingness to fulfill contracts, which explains the media's constant support for the group.[140] For example, on several occasions *El Orden* denounced the use of forceful evictions and the expropriation of planters' assets to cancel debts, which left planters homeless and in deep poverty.[141] The positive contributions of planters to the province went beyond the economic realm, as indicated by an editorial published in 1893 that described the effects of colonias in the countryside as "democratic, just, and equitable."[142] Contemporary observers and public officials also shared the press's view of planters as an extremely vulnerable group victimized by ingenio owners. As observed by Antonio Correa in 1897, despite the significance of sugarcane planters for the successful operation of ingenios, "the mill owner . . . is indeed a cruel tyrant that sometimes does not even consider norms of reciprocity and culture."[143]

In any case, rather than being powerless victims, in their disputes with ingenios, planters carefully evaluated their possibilities and often challenged abuses with direct action. The group resorted to a variety of strategies to minimize threats to their survival, although they never questioned the principles on which the system was founded. Planters knew their contractual rights and used the legal system to get protection, but they also actively sought the support of the provincial press and the authorities. The press offered an important venue in which planters could voice their demands, while Tucumán's government responded to their pleas by passing legislation that tried to guarantee the well-balanced development of the most important source of provincial income.

WHEN EXAMINING the consequences of the 1895 crisis, Tucumán's minister of public finance demanded from the government more assistance to independent planters, as "their participation in the provincial economy as an element of production, wealth, order, civilization, and patriotism is indispensable."[144] During the late 1870s and 1880s, Tucumán's sugar industry went through a process of rapid technological modernization and industrial concentration that in turn led to a division between the industrial and agricultural stages of production. Rather than opting for vertical integration, ingenios took advantage of preexisting patterns of landownership and resorted to outside growers to supply a significant share of their sugarcane needs. Therefore, the penetration of capitalist relations of production in rural Tucumán did not result in massive land dispossession but, much to the contrary, reinforced Tucumán's presugar land tenure pattern.

Figure 3.7. The end of the zafra, early 1920s. Planters and workers together celebrate a successful harvest season. *(Courtesy of Photographic Department, Archivo General de la Nación, Buenos Aires.)*

The vulnerability of an industry that was born during extremely volatile international conditions explains Tucumán's organization of production. Ingenio owners made the rational choice of obtaining part of their raw material from outside growers in order to reduce costs as well as to disperse the risks of investment among a larger number of individuals. Contractual arrangements secured ingenio owners a significant degree of control over production without the need to invest in the agricultural sector. It was this division between the agricultural and industrial sectors that ensured the reproduction and expansion of the industry. Protectionist policies, coupled with increasing demands for sugarcane, made small and medium plantations, with their proportionately higher costs of production, economically viable. Therefore, even though these smaller family-operated farms might have not been able to keep unit costs below world prices, active government participation guaranteed the group's survival.

In direct response to market incentives, many small, medium, and large farmers gradually shifted to sugarcane planting. Outside cane growers became central to the growth of Tucumán's modern sugar industry during its early years and remained a permanent feature in sugar production throughout the twentieth century. The incorporation of thousands of planters into sugarcane cultivation provoked profound changes in Tucumán's rural society by creating a new rural sector that benefited from the sugar boom. However, since the organization of sugar production reinforced the existence of a socially heterogeneous planter group, it also hindered, for many decades to follow, the consolidation of a coalition able to present its sectorial demands to mill owners or to the authorities as a unified group.[145] Growth in sugar production required increased labor. Ingenios and planters employed skilled and unskilled workers and were equally confronted by the problem of labor shortages. At the same time, attracted by the possibilities offered by the sugar boom, thousands of men, women, and children arrived from neighboring provinces to work in the harvest. Their arrival provoked additional changes in Tucumán's rural society.

Chapter 4

Sugar Labor
Field and Factory Workers

GROWTH IN SUGAR PRODUCTION required comparable additions to labor. Contemporary accounts differ in their estimates on the total workers engaged in sugar production, although they all agree that during the harvest their numbers reached many thousands. Harry Franck observed during his visit to Tucumán's sugar areas, "Thousands of workmen of many races are scattered among the horseman-high plants which stretch to the horizon in every direction, slashing off the canes at the ground . . . and tossing them with graceful easy gesture upon piles often several meters away."[1] Since the nature of sugarcane cultivation attracted only a few immigrants, sugar industrialists and planters had to meet the industry's intensive labor requirements with native migrants. Tucumán's authorities and sugar producers partook in the construction of a stable and disciplined labor pool. A body of legislation systematized mechanisms of control and provided the legal framework that sustained the diverse strategies developed by ingenio owners and planters to fulfill their labor needs. Thousands of workers, mainly from the neighboring provinces of Santiago del Estero and Catamarca, made the journey to Tucumán's sugar areas sometime around late May or early June and remained in the region until the harvest was over.

New Labor Needs, Legislation, and Recruitment

Sugar production is a labor-intensive activity that depends on the seasonal availability of large numbers of workers to toil in the fields and ingenios. The impressive expansion experienced by Tucumán's sugar industry put a heavy strain on a province already experiencing difficulties in guaranteeing a stable labor force.[2] During the last decades of the nineteenth century, ingenio owners and planters urged provincial authorities to take the necessary steps to solve the labor problems that they perceived prevented the industry's further development.[3] Tucumán's legislators came to the industry's rescue with a body of legislation that combined preventive and coercive measures in order to secure a large, disciplined, and stable pool of workers. The labor provisions of the 1856 Police Code included monitoring and restricting workers' activities (see chapter 1). The code provided an initial step toward the consolidation of a disciplined workforce and paved the way for the two pieces of labor legislation that responded more directly to the industry's acute labor needs, the 1877 Police Code and the 1888 Servants' Law.

In 1877, Tucumán's legislators made important changes to the Police Code, including ones that facilitated the consolidation of a more stable working force in the province. Legislators perceived unemployment as a problem that threatened public order and gave the police broad jurisdiction over control, enforcement, registration, and distribution of papeletas. Among its most important revisions, the new law incorporated a definition of vagrant, which included anyone without a "trade, profession, salary, occupation, or any licit means for survival . . . who chose not to work or who, with insufficient means for survival, engaged in gambling or loitering."[4] The vagueness of phrases such as "insufficient means for survival" acquires special significance in a province with so many smallholders. Purposely broad, this definition enabled the authorities to apply the law to a larger group of individuals who, if unable to prove they had an occupation, could be potentially recruited to work in the sugar industry or become subject to incarceration or forced labor.[5]

The code's revisions provided additional mechanisms to secure the availability of sugarcane harvesters by requiring the renewal of work certificates, or papeletas, in June, at the beginning of harvest season. To keep workers' in their jobs, the new code also required written permits to leave. Additionally, it authorized the police to relocate unemployed individuals to districts experiencing labor shortages, usually those departments engaged in sugar production. To prevent employers from hiring laborers with unfulfilled contractual agreements, the law required workers to produce a certificate of release and established limitations on cash advances employers could give.[6]

The code remained in force for more than a decade and was complemented by other legislation aimed specifically at assisting the sugar industry, such as a decree in 1879 that exempted those working in sugar production from the military draft.[7]

The 1877 code attempted to limit workers' mobility but also to increase the pool of available workers. However, mechanisms of registration were barely modified, thus rendering many of the code's prescriptions useless. Sugar producers and the media joined forces and increased their demands for the provincial authorities to pass labor legislation that responded more directly to the needs of the industry. In 1881, Eudoro Avellaneda and Juan Méndez, both names associated with the sugar industry, presented a bill that provided for stricter mechanisms to register workers and included new procedures to issue papeletas.[8] The provincial legislature rejected the bill and for several more years the authorities failed to address producers' demands. It was not until 1888 that the government finally responded to sugar industrialists' pleas and passed the Servants' Law (ley de conchabo), thus inaugurating a new period in Tucumán's labor legislation.[9]

The 1888 Servants' Law, the first labor code enacted in the province, systematized mechanisms of control and regulated the lives of thousands of men, women, and children in and outside Tucumán until its abrogation, in 1896.[10] It indicated a new attitude toward the "labor problem" with the sanction of a law intended to address it specifically. The code confirmed the police's monitoring role over labor issues, although it expanded their prerogatives by extending their jurisdiction to the supervision of hiring procedures, discipline of workers, and screening of absenteeism. The law drew some of its provisions from the 1881 bill and tightened mechanisms of registration by requiring the authorities to produce three different sets of records, one for registered workers, another for runaways, and another for workers on leave. To increase control over workers, the new work certificates contained more detailed information on the worker and the job than what had been required by the 1877 code.

The 1888 Servants' Law revealed the government's commitment to protect and promote the sugar industry. It responded to the specific demands of sugar producers by increasing the pool of potential workers, as it authorized children under fourteen years old "to be registered [to work] by their parents or tutors with the intervention of the police."[11] The potential application of the law to minors illustrates one important aspect of Tucumán's sugar industry, with its reliance on migrant families, whose children now became potential laborers. Another indication of the importance acquired by seasonal labor in the industry was the stipulation that indebted workers repay their debts with services instead of cash, a clear attempt to ensure their permanence in the area. The law included provisions that reflected the variety of tasks required by sugar production by providing for a wide array of situations, from skilled labor to unskilled piecework. It allowed for extended workdays during the harvest and prescribed punishments for those who failed to show up for work or ran away. It maintained the dawn-to-dusk workday and increased employers' control over workers' leisure time by including specific mandates on overtime. Complementary laws penalizing excessive partying, coupled with ingenio owners' direct control over cantinas, clearly aimed at limiting workers' possibilities to socialize and develop any sense of community that could potentially challenge the stability and discipline of the labor force. The Servants' Law responded to sugar interests by providing for coercive mechanisms that created a stable and disciplined workforce, although it also included some progressive provisions, since it banned corporal punishment, guaranteed workers' rations in case of sickness, and required witnesses whenever contracts were signed.[12]

Public contribution to the mitigation of labor shortages was not limited to the enactment of legislation. In 1878, Julio Roca offered Tucumán governor Domingo Martínez Muñecas a contingent of indigenous people from southern Argentina to work in the sugar industry. According to Roca, the province provided a distant and "civilized" setting that would favor the assimilation of indigenous groups into the new nation by subjecting them "to the work that regenerates and to the life and example of other habits to modify theirs, deprived of their useless language [and] to transform them into civilized and productive forces." He concluded that this arrangement would be beneficial for the sugar industry, by "substituting those lazy and stupid Indians in Tucumán [Matacos] with the Pampas and Ranqueles, who despite being below the moral and civilized level of the gauchos, are still smarter and stronger."[13]

In 1879 a group of five hundred indigenous people arrived in the province. A commission consisting of government officials and ingenio owners drafted a standard labor contract that required employers to supply food, lodging, and clothing. The two-year arrangement justified lower wages for the indigenous workers on the grounds that they would be receiving training on the job. Salaries would be paid at the end of the first year, although in order to keep workers on the plantation a special stipulation allowed employers to withhold payments until the end of the two-year arrangement.[14] To prevent abuses, the contract also stipulated regular visits of public officials to sugar areas. The evidence, however, indicates that those visits did little to guarantee the well-being of the workers. For example, during a scheduled visit to Ingenio El Colmenar, the *defensor de pobres y menores* (public defender of children and the poor) found that out of fifty-one individuals, thirteen had died and thirty had left the ingenio. Those who remained on the premises were terrified by the abuses committed by the foreman and complained of deficient medical care and insufficient rations.

During the early 1880s more groups arrived from Chaco but their small numbers failed to satisfy the ever-increasing demand for labor in the sugar industry. Reports about indigenous people during this period revealed that they were not only running away but also offering armed resistance, thus, in the eyes of ingenio owners, becoming a source of social instability in the area. For example, in 1885 a group of indigenous workers entered the premises of Ingenio Amalia by force and refused to leave. When the authorities arrived, the group attacked them with bows and arrows and only after several hours of struggle and the deaths of two workers were they defeated.[15] In response to this episode, Governor Santiago Gallo wrote to the national minister of war complaining that indigenous workers were causing numerous disturbances in sugar areas and requested that further groups be better "distributed" among ingenios.[16] The letter clearly indicated the government's attempt to prevent the concentration of indigenous workers in one area in order to limit the possibilities of active resistance or flight that could have encouraged the creation of runaway communities. By the end of the decade the number of indigenous people brought to work in sugar production in Tucumán decreased, and although it is not clear when the last group arrived in the province, the last report dated back to 1888.

The decline in the number of indigenous workers did not pose a problem for the industry, as by the early 1880s sugar producers were already relying on alternative sources of labor that offered a more dependable and "civilized" workforce. Ingenio owners put into practice recruitment mechanisms that attracted thousands of workers from neighboring provinces and guaranteed the availability of labor during the harvest. Every year independent contractors (*conchabadores*) visited sugar areas before the harvest to learn about ingenios' labor needs.[17] Contractors signed agreements with each ingenio's administrator that stipulated the number of workers to be recruited, job duration, responsibilities, and commissions. As part of the agreement, contractors received a lump sum to cover workers' cash advances, transportation, food, and the cost of licenses and legal fees.[18] Subsequently, they traveled to the neighboring provinces of Santiago del Estero and Catamarca, where they directly recruited workers or relied on overseers and subcontractors to transport them from the hinterlands to the railroad station where the final arrangement was made.

In the presence of the judge or the police, workers received cash advances and signed what was termed a contract but resembled more a promissory note. The written arrangement contained the amount advanced, the length of the job, and the worker's wage. Contracts lacked stipulations for working conditions, tasks, length of workday, method of payment, or additional benefits, such as rations or housing. Contracts' coercive aspects did not escape the attention of contemporary observers. Emile Daireaux, a French traveler who visited the province during the 1880s, observed that working agreements contained many complicated conditions that originated in the Spanish encomienda and that combined slavery with free wage labor.[19] Recruiters received authorization from ingenios to make changes to the written contract or to incorporate oral agreements into the existing written notices. The contract between Ingenio Nueva Baviera and Tristán Herrera authorized the recruiter to raise the advances paid to "trusted workers" up to 50 percent over the originally stipulated sum and provided for higher cash advances to those individuals who had worked for the ingenio in the past.[20] Contractors collected a finder's fee for each worker recruited, which in some instances was paid in full after the job was completed; in other cases, as in the contract between Nueva Baviera and Herrera, it was paid as a monthly commission for each worker that remained in the ingenio.[21] This provision allowed ingenio owners to pass on to the recruiter at least part of the responsibility for keeping workers on the job and indicated the difficulties involved in guaranteeing the stability of the workforce in sugar areas.

As a result of this system of recruitment, neighboring provinces experienced a significant loss of their adult male population. The authorities of Catamarca and Santiago del Estero tried to prevent the exodus of workers by creating mechanisms intended to limit workers' mobility. For example, in 1884, Tucumán's industrialists denounced Catamarca's government for

Figure 4.1. Workers from Santiago del Estero, October 1920. Workers from Santiago del Estero and Catamarca made the annual journey to work as sugarcane cutters. These Santiagueño families are getting ready to return home. *(Courtesy of Photographic Department, Archivo General de la Nación, Buenos Aires.)*

the obstacles that the provincial authorities had imposed on those laborers attempting to leave for Tucumán.[22] In 1894, Santiago del Estero's legislature presented a project to raise the fees for passports. The project was never approved but it worried mill owners, who complained incessantly to the authorities.[23] Nevertheless, it was depressed wages and lack of job opportunities in their provinces, in conjunction with higher salaries in the sugar areas, that accounted for the seasonal departure of workers from Catamarca and Santiago del Estero to Tucumán.[24] Migrant workers resisted total proletarianization by adapting to a seasonal labor pattern that enabled them to work for a few months in Tucumán and then return to their hometowns. According to contemporary witnesses, Santiagueños and Catamarqueños were able to save enough from their wages in the sugar industry to supplement their income during the rest of the year, thus guaranteeing their survival and that of their families.

Private recruitment ensured the availability of workers in sugar areas during the peak season. However, the industry required additional mechanisms to guarantee their obedience and stability. Tucumán's legislation provided an adequate and comprehensive legal framework that facilitated the implementation of the different strategies used by sugar producers to secure discipline in the workplace. Labor stipulations were framed within a discourse that emphasized the need to guarantee an obedient workforce. The letter of the law defined employers as domestic magistrates, thus granting them the right to monitor workers' behavior within their domains. The evidence indicates that corporal punishment, or the threat of it, was constantly used in the ingenio. In 1887, *El Orden* reported that natives working in Ingenio San Pablo were punished by the administrator and treated like "black slaves in Brazil."[25] British traveler Mark Jefferson, who visited the area and worked in Ingenio La Providencia between 1886 and 1889, recalled that in 1888 a peon was punished with fifty lashes and was left all night in the stocks for running away.[26] The 1888 Servants' Law banned corporal punishment but it preserved employers' rights to detain workers and failed to specify either a maximum period for detention or the reasons that warranted detention. The prohibition against corporal punishment did nothing to eliminate its actual use to discipline workers, as indicated by Ceferino Carrizo, who in 1895 accused the ingenio's overseer of whipping him with a thick metal wire for his alleged attempt to sabotage the mill.[27] Punishment was used regularly not only with field and factory workers but also with any individual who violated the rules of the ingenio. For example, in 1891 *El Orden* reported that Ingenio Bella Vista's owner detained a planter in an "ad hoc facility" when he failed to pay back money he owed the mill.[28] Workers were still punished as late as 1913, as denounced by *El Orden* in an editorial that condemned corporal punishment and other abuses in sugar areas.[29]

To increase control over workers, ingenios resorted to surveillance and private security systems that complemented provincial legislation. Many ingenios supported small police stations on their premises and hired *rondines,* watchmen that patrolled the mill and surrounding areas, particularly at night, to guard the mill and keep workers from running away.[30] Under the threat of dismissal, the Servants' Law compelled workers to help employers subdue revolts and maintain peace in the workplace. The evidence seems to indicate that ingenio owners regularly relied on workers' assistance. For example, in 1893, during a dispute with his colonos, Abraham Medina brought his overseers and peons to forcefully evict the colonos.[31] In this case, Medina acted in connivance with local authorities. Indeed, assistance from local police was indispensable in successfully controlling workers. Ingenio owners guaranteed cooperation by becoming involved in the selection of police personnel or by directly appointing friends and relatives. Such was the case of Roque Pondal Jr., who was the police chief of Los García and had jurisdiction over the area where his father's ingenio was located. In 1894, Pondal was involved in a dispute with a sugarcane planter who accused the police chief of abuse of power. According to court proceedings, Pondal had intervened in a disagreement between the planter and the ingenio's administrator and had placed the planter under arrest for no apparent reason. Since the conflict had escalated into a violent confrontation between planter and administrator, the accusation against Pondal was not pursued any further, although the police chief's actions revealed that ingenios resorted to arbitrary mechanisms of social control to guarantee the discipline of those individuals living within their areas of influence.[32]

In their goals to discipline the working force, both public and private mechanisms of control complemented one another. Labor legislation favored the consolidation of private systems of control. The use of coercion embodied the propertied groups' common perception of workers as uncivilized and, above all, unreliable, as well as their inherent right to control them. Coercion was perceived as a preventive against idleness and as a necessary step to facilitate the introduction of a factory work routine into workers' lives. Therefore, its use was considered by the government and sugar groups as an indispensable aspect in the process of building a modern workforce. No one expressed this idea better than Paulino Rodríguez Marquina, who defined the Servants' Law as "tyrannical but necessary for peons to acquire traits other than the corrupt and unsightly ones they currently posses."[33]

Tucumán's sugar production depended not only on a large and disciplined workforce but on workers remaining in sugar areas during the harvest. Regulations and punishment could guarantee the former, but only to a certain extent. Industrialists resorted to a number of additional mechanisms to secure a stable pool of workers when most needed, during the peak season. At the time of hiring, workers received cash advances.[34] Upon the contract's termination, the worker, if unable to pay back the debt, was forced to stay on the job for another season, thus, as a contemporary observer noted, transforming them into perpetual debtors of their employers.[35] Even though in a context of chronic labor shortages, cash advances could easily become market incentive mechanisms, debt cannot be examined without reference to the political context and the existing legislation. Until its abrogation in 1896, Tucumán's Servants' Law reinforced the coercive nature of cash advances by allowing mill owners to require payment in services and providing for the police to go after and detain those who failed to fulfill their obligations with employers.[36] Besides cash advances, ingenios offered other material incentives, such as small and rudimentary dwellings located in the immediacies of the ingenios. The arrival of thousands of individuals every season put significant stress on the region's supply of housing. The provision of houses was an effective mechanism to control workers and keep them on the job, especially for those who migrated with their families or who had no personal networks in the area. The importance of housing as a mechanism of control became clear during the 1904 sugar strike. Four days into the strike, Ingenio San Miguel's workers were evicted from the company houses. According to a contemporary report, entire families had no alternative but to "return by foot to Santiago because they lacked other resources."[37]

As an additional incentive for workers to stay, these communities included schools and basic medical facilities. Although, as Jefferson points out, "the care of men became only a matter of business, [since] a sick man could not work. . . . Remedies were administered on the spot, and the offer of them had occasionally the effect of persuading the man that perhaps he might as well go to work."[38] Nevertheless, in a province plagued with bad roads and insufficient hospitals, accessible basic medical care and education in close proximity to workers' living quarters must have played a significant role in tying workers to the job and guaranteeing labor stability in sugar areas. Finally, ingenio owners also provided for their workers' entertainment through outdoor activities and celebrations. In 1890 the new owners of Ingenio La Trinidad organized a celebration to honor the patron saint of the ingenio a few days before the beginning of the harvest season. The event was attended by scores of workers and consisted of a religious service and a banquet for all the guests. According to a witness, the celebration showed the ingenio owner's desire to reward some of his loyal workers and encourage others to follow their example through a ceremony that in reality "demonstrated the principle of social regeneration, which makes everyone equal in the face of a task to be accomplished."[39]

Since its beginnings, Tucumán's sugar industry faced chronic labor shortages. The intensive nature of sugarcane cutting and sugar processing

Figure 4.2. Hospital Ingenio Bella Vista, 1910s. *(Courtesy of Photographic Department, Archivo General de la Nación, Buenos Aires.)*

required a large and stable pool of workers. A body of legislation provided a legal framework that sustained the different strategies developed by sugar producers to fulfill the needs of the industry. As Daniel Campi has pointed out, the consolidation of a capitalist labor market in Tucumán went through a transitional period in which coercive mechanisms coexisted with material incentives.[40] The combined strategies implemented by public and private groups resulted in a significant increase in the number of workers engaged in sugar production during the last quarter of the nineteenth century. Rodríguez Marquina estimated that in 1889 the sugar industry employed 12,734 individuals. By 1895, according to other official estimates, that number had jumped to 23,000.[41] In their analysis of population growth in Argentina, 1895 census commissioners noted that "the littoral provinces' physical and topographic conditions ensure them a high rate of population growth, whereas only one in the north—Tucumán—has achieved a high rate, as a result of the great expansion of the sugar industry."[42] Every year, thousands of individuals from Santiago del Estero and Catamarca made the sojourn to Tucumán's sugar areas to work in the sugarcane fields or sugar mills. Their arrival affected the contours of Tucumán's rural society profoundly.[43]

Workers in the Field, Workers in the Factory

Between 1869 and 1895 Tucumán's population doubled. During this period, the province experienced the country's fourth largest increase, after Buenos Aires, Santa Fe, and Entre Ríos.[44] However, unlike other areas in Argentina, Tucumán's demographic growth did not result from European immigration but from the arrival of thousands of men, women, and children from other provinces, in particular Santiago del Estero and Catamarca. Describing Tucumán's rural inhabitants in the late 1910s, Pierre Denis observed, "The population of immigrant workers has settled down and taken root. Besides creoles it includes a small number of Italians and Spaniards; but while the creoles have been definitely incorporated in the sugar industry, the European immigrants use their savings to buy a bit of land and take to farming."[45] Tucumán did not receive as many Europeans as other areas in the country, although their numbers increased over time. In some cases, French immigrants who had arrived in the province during the first half of the nineteenth century became ingenio owners. This was the case of the Nougués and Rougés families.[46] In 1895 foreigners represented only 4.9 percent of the province's population, while natives from other provinces accounted for 20 percent. By 1914 the share of foreigners had increased to 9.8 percent, although they were still outnumbered by migrants from the provinces. As in other parts of Argentina, immigrants settled in urban areas. In 1895, 53 percent of foreigners lived in San Miguel de Tucumán.[47] The largest majority were of French, Spanish, and Italian origin. According to the 1895 census, foreigners participated significantly in commerce and accounted for 37.5 percent of Tucumán's total population engaged in that sector.[48]

Few immigrants chose to reside in rural areas and their participation in sugar production was more the exception than the rule. For example, a random sample of notarial records reveals that out of thirty-two partnerships established to cultivate sugarcane only one included foreign nationals. Attracted by the possibility of high profits, two Italians invested some savings in the purchase of lands in the department of Chicligasta and established a five-year partnership with the purpose of planting sugarcane. The short duration of the agreement indicates the tentative nature of the partnership. Both partners acted equally as capitalist investors and were not involved in any manual labor or fieldwork.[49] A few years later the situation had not changed and only a small number of foreigners still chose to become sugarcane planters. For example, in his 1889 report, Rodríguez Marquina listed six families from Seville hired as colonos by Ingenio La Reducción as the only group of foreigners involved in sugarcane planting in the province.[50] According to the census manuscript schedules, in 1895, 9.6 percent of those who claimed to be agricultores were of foreign origin, in contrast to the 4.5 percent of foreigners who declared themselves to be jornaleros.[51] The large majority of foreigners engaged in the sugar industry performed skilled jobs. When new machines were purchased by an ingenio, technicians were also sent, to train workers and to provide general assistance. An 1879 contract between the Méndez brothers and the British firm Fawcett, Preston, and Company stipulated that a British engineer spend one year in the ingenio supervising their machinery's installation and operation.[52] Increasingly, foreigners trained Argentine workers and by the turn of the century, during his visit to sugar areas, Juan Bialet Massé observed that foreign-trained personnel had been replaced by native workers.[53]

Therefore, native-born Argentines constituted the bulk of the working force in Tucumán's sugar industry. Attracted by the labor opportunities offered by the sugar economy, thousands of men, women, and children traveled to Tucumán every year during the harvest season. The arrival of workers from other provinces was not a new phenomenon in Tucumán. During the 1860s the province's prosperity had attracted migrants, in particular from neighboring provinces. In 1869 the first national census revealed that 9 percent of the provincial population came from other areas in Argentina, mainly Santiago del Estero and Catamarca. By 1895 the share of migrants in the total population had significantly increased, to 20 percent. The industry's impressive expansion offered additional labor possibilities for people from other provinces, in particular those with less dynamic economies, thus reinforcing preexisting migration patterns. Mark Jefferson observed, "The peon class in Santiago found a poor but easy sustenance in the fruit of the algarrobo [carob] tree . . . but by autumn the algarrobo had become scarce, and the three months of irksome toil in the sugar factories were an escape from starvation."[54] According to Jorge Balán, migration to Tucumán was one component in a pattern of "multiple seasonal migrations" in the area, in which migrants moved from the sugar harvest to the logging industry to the cotton harvest.[55] The two largest groups of migrants originated in Santiago del Estero and Catamarca. In 1895 their numbers totaled twenty-nine thousand and accounted for 70 percent of nonlocal Argentines residing in Tucumán. The department of Cruz Alta had the largest number of migrants in the province. Santiagueños and Catamarqueños constituted 27 percent of the population.[56] The 1895 census reveals that of this group 75 percent were over fourteen years old and most were single men. The median age was twenty-five and most individuals were illiterate; less than 15 percent of the surveyed adults could read and write. Literacy rates were slightly higher among workers from Catamarca, which may explain why a majority of natives from that province worked in sugar factories performing semiskilled jobs.[57]

The numbers of married individuals and children recorded in the 1895 census manuscript schedules suggest that at least one-fourth of the men who made the trip to sugar areas brought their families with them. There was a clear sexual division of labor. The most popular occupation declared by males in the sample was that of jornalero, while most women for whom an occupation was listed were employed in service activities, mostly as laundresses and cooks.[58] Only a few women declared themselves jornaleras, even though contemporary visitors remarked the importance of female contribution to fieldwork. By 1914 the number of Santiagueños and Catamarqueños

Figure 4.3. A family of seasonal workers arriving at Ingenio Bella Vista. Contemporary sources agree that the number of seasonal workers that migrated to Tucumán reached tens of thousands. *(Courtesy of Photographic Department, Archivo General de la Nación, Buenos Aires.)*

in the province had increased to almost forty thousand. That increase, however, did not mirror the significant expansion experienced by the labor force in the sugar industry, a clear indication that during the 1910s the industry was drawing a larger proportion of workers from the local workforce, old locals, and first-generation Tucumanos born in the ingenios, since, as observed by Juan Alsina in 1905, "more and more families from neighboring provinces who came [to the harvest] in prior seasons, have adapted to Tucumán well, to the point that they are settling permanently."[59]

As in other sugar economies in Latin America, work in the fields was extremely harsh. During the three or four months of the harvest, workers labored seven days a week.[60] The workday began early in the morning and lasted for about twelve to fourteen hours. Workers had half an hour for breakfast and one hour for lunch, although sometimes they could barely take a break during the entire workday. Harvest work consisted of cutting, peeling, and hauling cane. Although payment systems varied over time and from one plantation to the other, fieldworkers were usually expected to fulfill a daily quota, or *tarea,* for which they received one *jornal* (wage earned for one full day of labor). The quota was determined on the basis of the area to be harvested or a specific amount of sugarcane harvested.[61] The quota system reduced the need for worker supervision, thus enabling ingenios and planters to save significant resources that otherwise would have been used to control large numbers of workers dispersed throughout the vast sugarcane fields. However, it did require more careful inspection of the finished work, in particular for planters whose contracts with ingenios contained very specific delivery stipulations. Even though the establishment of a daily quota might have been intended as an incentive to increase productivity, in most cases it was difficult for the average worker to fulfill it in one day. In 1905, Juan Alsina pointed out that when the task was based on the area to be harvested rather than the weight of the harvested cane, workers still needed more than a day to complete their quota, clearly undermining their earnings, which the author estimated never exceeded a total of twenty jornales per month despite their seven-day workweek.[62] It is in this setting that the assistance of family members acquires significance and explains the migration patterns of those involved in Tucumán's harvest. Bialet Massé observed in 1904 that the productivity of a male worker increased twice when helped by his family.[63]

Whereas fieldwork was mostly the same for everybody, tasks and conditions in the factories varied depending on the job and the ingenio. In the mill, workers performed skilled and unskilled tasks such as feeding the rollers, monitoring sugar making, or repairing the machinery. During harvest season, ingenios milled twenty-four hours a day; work was done in two twelve-hour shifts.[64] Mill workers seem to have enjoyed a higher status than fieldworkers, more job security, and higher wages. So, despite harsh working conditions, factory work was a coveted position. Ingenio owners and overseers used it as a reward for workers' loyalty. By the same token, acts of insubordination were punished through demotion from mill to fieldwork. According to the trial records of a robbery case, an overseer transferred a worker from the mill to the cane fields—not only to separate him from the machinery and prevent further robberies but also to reprimand him for his alleged actions.[65] The need to keep the machines working constantly dictated that control be exercised more closely in the mill than in the fields. In certain cases, ingenios issued written regulations. The Reglamento del Ingenio Bella Vista, for example, was an attempt to establish a modern work ethic by laying down workers' duties and rights and punishing negligence and indiscipline with severity.[66] According to the code, the workday was clearly demarcated by the clock; the beginning and end of work periods were indicated by a loud steam whistle. The code rewarded performance and attendance with bonuses, and permanence and loyalty with pensions and education for workers' children.

Despite their constant presence in the ingenio, owners did not monitor workers directly but relied on the assistance of overseers and administrators.[67] Overseers (*mayordomos* or *capataces*) became the link between worker and administration and bore responsibility for keeping order as well as guaranteeing the completion of daily tasks. These individuals secured the synchronization of the tasks involved in sugar making and were thus essential to the successful operation of the ingenio. Supervision in the mill was indispensable to avoid delays in milling caused by unexpected events, work slowdowns, or sabotage. In some instances overseers were given bonuses or salary increases based on their workers' productivity.[68] In turn, overseers responded to, and were under the supervision of, the ingenio's administrator.

Administrators were in charge of keeping the ingenio running through the implementation of the owner's decisions. In charge of coordinating all operations in the ingenio and the fields, administrators oversaw investments in machinery and infrastructure, supervised contracts with conchabadores, and made day-to-day operational decisions. As payment for their work, after deducting workers' debts or any additional expense incurred, administrators received monthly or annual stipends as well as a share in the ingenio's profits. For example, the six-year contract between Ingenio Concepción and Samuel Vickess stipulated the responsibilities of the administrator, established that the ingenio owner was to be consulted on important decisions dealing with production, and guaranteed the administrator 10 percent of the revenue obtained from the sugar, in addition to a monthly sum that covered living expenses.[69] Tucumán's ingenio owners were not an absentee group but they did rely on subordinate personnel to assist them with day-to-day operations. While maintaining control over major productive decisions, ingenio owners delegated duties and responsibilities to administrators and relied on material incentives to increase productivity. Administrators and overseers carried out the owners' decisions, often resorting to strategies that ranged from the implementation of a strictly regimented work schedule to physical force.

Field and factory labor was not only extremely harsh but dangerous. In the fields, workers could be cut either by machetes or by the sharp edges of sugarcane leaves. They were also exposed to heat exhaustion, venomous snakes, rodents, and mosquito-borne diseases. In the mills, labor conditions were no better, although they varied significantly from one ingenio to the other. For example, Bialet Massé contrasted the cleanliness of Ingenio Esperanza and Ingenio Mercedes with the problems he saw at Ingenio San Felipe and the ingenios that belonged to the Compañía Azucarera Tucumana.[70] Despite those differences, excessive heat and the dangers associated with toxic fumes were a constant problem for workers' health. Work in the mills was repetitive and monotonous but demanded skill and constant attention. At times workers were crushed by rollers, fell into boilers, inhaled toxic fumes, or were burned by hot liquids.[71] Thus, workers' safety was a frequent concern among sugar producers. Over time ingenios implemented a number of safety measures, such as a prohibition against wearing ponchos while operating machinery, as well as the installation of handrails near the boilers and special guards for the sharp edges of the rollers. In 1910, Federico Figueroa observed that such improvements accounted for the absence of accidents in the province's ingenios for 1909.[72]

Payment systems and amounts varied depending on the ingenio. Generally, workers received an advance, or *socorro* (lit., help), for cigarettes or other small needs and, until 1904, collected the remaining wages at the end of the month in scrip, redeemable only at the ingenio's *proveeduría* (company store). The notes had either a cash value or were exchangeable for a specific commodity such as meat or yerba mate. Some ingenios gave workers bonuses for good performance, which at Ingenio Bella Vista and Ingenio Mercedes included saving fuel or having perfect attendance for the month. Besides their wages, workers received a daily ration that consisted on average of one and a quarter kilogram of meat, one kilogram of maize, and half a kilogram of bread, some sugar and salt, and firewood. Food quantities and quality varied from ingenio to ingenio. For example, Ingenio Concepción, Ingenio Mercedes, and Ingenio Esperanza added milk and sometimes coffee to workers' rations. Workers in other ingenios were not as lucky. Juan Alsina noted that rations among sugar workers were deficient in quality and quantity and resulted in malnutrition and a number of other physical ailments. Ingenio Bella Vista established differential rations for workers depending on their shifts; for example, those on the night shift received 25 percent more meat than day workers did. One way for workers and their families to supplement their nutritional needs was by sucking on sugarcane. In 1904 a visitor to the province observed that "it is estimated that workers consume 2 percent of the harvest, enough to make two thousand tons of sugar."[73] In his report, Bialet Massé observed that the caloric contribution of sugarcane to the average worker's diet was indispensable for the nutrition of those who brought their families to the ingenio.[74] Workers' "unalienable right to the two finest canes they cut," as Harry Franck put it, became one way for ingenios to compensate for a scanty food ration.[75]

Work in sugar production was frequently a family affair. Women and children were an essential part of the workforce. In the fields, girls and boys were usually in charge of peeling and hauling the sugarcane to the carts or portable railroads. Using smaller machetes, they worked side by side with their parents. In 1889 children under fourteen years old accounted for 11 percent of the workers in Tucumán's sugar industry. By 1919 that ratio had decreased to 6 percent, although photographs and newspaper reports clearly reveal that children still worked in the cane fields as late as the 1930s. Children performed a number of other tasks for the ingenios. At Ingenio Esperanza, for example, twelve-year-old boys were admitted as apprentices and remained in the mill until they became adults. Other ingenios employed children as young as six to perform unskilled jobs, such as feeding the rollers or carrying wood. Usually children received half the wages and rations of adult workers, but their labor conditions were just as harsh. In his 1910 report Figueroa insisted on the need to regulate child labor in order to prevent abuses and accidents.[76]

Women's contribution to sugar production was significant as well. According to official statistics, in 1889 they represented 9 percent of the workforce. Three decades later their participation had decreased to only 7 percent of all laborers. Their occupations varied. For example, at Ingenio Providencia they milked cows; at Ingenio San Felipe and Ingenio Esperanza they made burlap bags for sugar. Many women took care of the single males of the ingenios. Groups of men would often pay a woman to cook for them and wash their clothes. In the late 1880s, Jefferson observed that when performing these tasks women received credit from the company store. At the end of the month, the ingenio settled each worker's account, charging the credit advanced against his wage.[77] Planters' wives also used homemade trapiches to mill small amounts of sugarcane to make such confections as hard candies. Bialet Massé observed that many women set up small posts near the sugar towns, where they marketed their products as well as homegrown fruits and legumes.[78]

Women in sugar areas also found employment as laundresses and ironers. Some washed clothes in their houses and were paid by the unit. According to the census manuscript schedules, a significant number of laundresses came from neighboring provinces (in particular Santiago del Estero), were married, and had the lowest literacy rates among women.[79] Since entire families moved to sugar areas, many wives took in laundry, as it allowed them to remain at home. In 1898, Rodríguez Marquina observed that the poorest women were the ones engaged in this occupation.[80] Bialet Massé described them as "unhappy, emaciated, and most miserably poor."[81] Tucumana ironers were more likely to be married than laundresses and enjoyed a higher literacy rate.[82] Bialet Massé commented that Tucumanas were expert ironers, although not many women chose this occupation as it required basic equipment and Tucumán's hot weather made the work difficult. Nevertheless, ironing and washing enabled women to supplement the family income without leaving the home or breaking the family routine. Furthermore, both activities allowed wives to help their husbands in the fields when needed to fulfill the quota.

Between 1876 and 1916 the labor demands of the sugar industry resulted in the incorporation of thousands of men, women, and children into sugar production. The modern sugar industry imposed a regimented, routinized, and closely supervised work discipline on all those involved in sugar production. Sugar workers were subjected to a double system of control that relied on both legal mechanisms and the more informal, unwritten, and customary—albeit stricter—rules of the ingenio. In his 1904 assessment of labor in sugar areas, Bialet Massé observed, "The improvement of the working class in Tucumán has been fast, although not complete . . . there is still the brutally long workday, labor without rest, and many accidents not yet prevented."[83] The pace of modern factory work and the hierarchies of sugar production invaded Tucumán's countryside and significantly altered the province's rural society. The arrival of thousands of workers profoundly affected the physiognomy of Tucumán's countryside and contributed to the emergence of a new social complex, the sugar community.

The Sugar Community

The society that emerged in sugar areas responded to the needs of the sugar industry and was rigidly organized around its hierarchies and unique rhythms of production. Workers from neighboring provinces joined Tucumanos and became indispensable in the impressive expansion experienced by the industry. The seasonal arrival of thousands of workers during the harvest season altered Tucumán's rural patterns of settlement and precipitated changes that gradually became permanent features. The establishment of sugar towns surrounding ingenios not only transformed the countryside but also resulted in the development of a complex rural society. During his visit to sugar areas in the 1920s, Franck observed, "Every important factory has a village clustered about it, a community complete from bakers to priest."[84]

As in most sugar economies, sugar towns replicated the hierarchies of the ingenio. In every town the ingenio owner's chalet occupied a central location.[85] During his 1904 trip to the Argentine northwest, Manuel Bernárdez praised the quality of these often two- and three-story *palacetes* as well as the beauty of their environs. These large buildings, with their many rooms, European furniture of the finest materials, and modern features, rivaled urban dwellings in luxury and comfort.[86] Housing for workers revealed significant variation, depending on the ingenio and the worker's position there.[87] Administrators and technicians lived in houses that usually consisted of two or three rooms and were located near the mill. Since the early 1880s ingenios invested heavily in housing, especially for their permanent staff. For example, in 1886, Ingenio La Providencia built fifty rooms for those workers and their families who stayed after the harvest was over.[88] Workers' housing

Figure 4.4 *(above)* Permanent workers' houses and owner's chalet, Ingenio San Pablo, 1910. *(Courtesy of Photographic Department, Archivo General de la Nación, Buenos Aires.)*

Figure 4.5 *(below)* Ingenio owner's chalet, Ingenio San Pablo, 1910. Residence of the Nougués family, owners of the ingenio. *(Courtesy of Photographic Department, Archivo General de la Nación, Buenos Aires.)*

conditions changed over time. When visiting Ingenio Esperanza, Bialet Massé found two different types of dwellings. Older houses consisted of only a single three-by-four-meter room and shared a communal kitchen with neighboring houses; newer houses had bigger rooms, a porch, and a kitchen for each family.[89] Seasonal workers' houses were of lower quality. During his visit to the sugar areas in the early 1900s, Georges Clemenceau described the housing for seasonal workers as temporary encampments whose huts were made of sugarcane trash (the dry leaves left after the harvest). The rooms followed a primitive design that left thirty-centimeter openings at the base of the wall for air circulation.[90] Material possessions among the working class were modest and basic, in particular for those who only stayed in the area for a few months every year. Furniture consisted of planks laid across flimsy frames, a stove adapted for open-air cooking, tree trunks for seats, and a few kitchen utensils, such as spoons, knives, a kettle, a pot, and a mate (gourd for drinking tea), with its corresponding *bombilla* (filter straw).

Figure 4.6. Housing for permanent workers, Ingenio San Pablo. *(Courtesy of Photographic Department, Archivo General de la Nación, Buenos Aires.)*

Sugar towns included schools that were, in most cases, financed by the provincial government.[91] Ingenios contributed the buildings and school materials, as with Ingenio Santa Ana's school, whose building was donated by Clodomiro Hileret in 1894.[92] By 1899 several ingenios, such as La Reducción, Nueva Trinidad, San Pablo, Paraíso, Los Ralos, and San Miguel, provided educational facilities for those children living and working in the area.[93] Most of the schools offered instruction up to the third grade and were attended by both girls and boys. Some offered night courses for adults. However, school attendance was low, especially during harvest season. As Alsina observed, children's labor was indispensable to fulfill the tarea; therefore parents were forced to put their children to work.[94] Indeed, census data reveal lower school attendance in sugar areas than in nonsugar areas.[95] The number of schools and education programs in ingenios increased over time. By 1915 there were fifty-three schools located in sugar towns, with a total of 6,700 registered students, although rates of attendance were still significantly low since less than 50 percent of all children in sugar areas attended school.[96]

In most cases, sugar towns provided first aid for workers, and physicians visited them periodically. However, these basic medical facilities could not assist patients suffering from serious problems; therefore workers were usually treated in San Miguel's public hospitals. *El Orden* denounced ingenios' common practice of sending their workers to public hospitals and demanded from them more than their usual "token contribution"—a small monthly stipend or a bag of sugar.[97] Harsh working conditions, overcrowding, inadequate diet, and bad hygiene (including unsanitary water supplies) resulted in the spread of such ailments among the working population as smallpox, malaria, tuberculosis, syphilis, pneumonia, and intestinal disorders. In 1902, *El Orden* urged the authorities to intercede for workers by demanding from ingenios better living conditions and, above all, a supply of clean water.[98] To improve health conditions in sugar areas, the provincial authorities required that sugarcane be planted farther apart (to facilitate the passage of air), expanded vaccination programs to reach rural areas, and passed legislation regulating the disposal of sugar waste (*vinaza*).[99] Over time ingenios improved their health facilities. In the late 1910s Ingenio Bella Vista opened a hospital with a capacity of twenty patients; Ingenio San Pablo built public baths for both permanent and seasonal workers.[100]

Since rations received by workers did not provide enough provisions for an entire family, workers obtained additional supplies from proveedurías or

Figure 4.7. Public baths in a sugar town. Public baths and hospitals occupied a central location in sugar towns, although in most cases they could not satisfy the needs of the entire working population of the ingenio. *(Courtesy of Photographic Department, Archivo General de la Nación, Buenos Aires.)*

cantinas located in sugar towns. These stores, which were run by friends or relatives of ingenio owners or commissioned to entrepreneurs, sold all the necessary living supplies for the worker and his family. Proveedurías kept careful records of workers' purchases and required them to settle their debts on payday. According to contemporaries, purchases from the proveeduría took up more than half of workers' earnings.[101] In 1903, *El Orden* conducted a campaign against proveedurías and called on authorities to intervene and end "the tyranny that subjects workers to the absolute will of the ingenio owner."[102] Workers were not only unable to travel the long distances required to search for better prices but were threatened with dismissal if they did not make their purchases at the ingenio's store, thus transforming these stores into extremely lucrative enterprises. In 1904, Bialet Massé estimated that proveedurías realized a 300 or 400 percent annual return, and even more when workers were paid in scrip rather than cash. Besides their monopoly over the sales of staples, these stores obtained much of their profit from alcohol sales.

The availability of alcohol and gambling opportunities, despite the authorities' attempts to restrict them, transformed company stores into popular gathering places for workers, in particular on Sunday afternoons and holidays. References to the abuse of alcohol and its consequences among Tucumán's working population abounded throughout this period.[103] In 1882 almost 45 percent of the arrests in San Miguel resulted from disturbances caused by drinking.[104] The authorities saw gambling as another serious hindrance to worker productivity. The most popular games among workers were cockfights, roulette (known in Tucumán as the Japanese game), and horse races. Ingenio owners complained regularly that vices such as alcoholism and gambling encouraged disorderly behavior and absenteeism, and they pleaded for stricter legislation to eliminate them.

The ruling classes perceived indolence as a character trait of Tucumanos; alcohol abuse and gambling were seen as its direct consequence. Legislation to control workers' excesses was conceived as a necessary step toward the consolidation of a modern workforce. The government passed several laws to prevent workers from visiting cantinas and gambling places, and ingenios disciplined drunken workers severely with corporal punishment, detention, and, in case of frequent offenders, dismissal. As another way of keeping workers from alcohol and gambling, ingenios promoted sports and supported a number of other entertainment activities. By the late 1910s several ingenios had built gymnasiums for workers and their families and had organized their own soccer teams. Ingenio Santa Ana offered weekly film screenings and hired a small orchestra to play on special occasions.[105] In this ingenio, administrative employees enjoyed additional privileges as they had access to tennis courts and polo games, which were beyond the reach of regular workers. Control over leisure time and recreational activities became an additional mechanism of social control imposed on the working population by ingenio owners.

Between 1876 and 1916 important sugar towns emerged in sugar areas and evolved as independent living communities. Sugar towns not only provided workers with a place to live but also facilitated the submission of the working population to the needs and rhythms of sugar production. Ingenio owners created a microcosm in which their authority and that of their overseers was almost absolute. Since workers depended on employers for their jobs, sustenance, housing, and entertainment, sugar towns offered the possibility of exercising complete control over the lives of the working population. By keeping the workforce within a discrete living area and under direct surveillance, ingenio owners secured the availability of a disciplined and obedient workforce that was at the same time isolated from outside influences. In 1892, Julio Avila noted that since workers' dwellings in sugar towns were located "in the most convenient areas for the interests of the employer, work can become systematized, peons' excesses, always a result of lack of police vigilance, can be prevented, and they can be subjected, since they are all together, to the most detailed control."[106]

Control, however, was never absolute; workers managed to challenge managerial abuses regularly. Workers' actions responded to and were limited by the patterns of social relations and formal and informal mechanisms of control created by the distinctive nature of sugar making. Small and episodic, these cases of resistance reflected popular notions of justice and presented an alternative way to channel grievances and to express defiance. Furthermore, they contributed to the climate of social effervescence that created anxiety among the ruling groups in Tucumán, as clearly articulated by Governor Próspero García in 1892 when he made an appeal to the legislators to increase police control in sugar areas to end the "alarming increase of disorderly behavior among sugar workers."[107]

One such behavior was flight, which was endemic in sugar areas.[108] Despite capataces' constant supervision, sugar workers enjoyed freedom of movement and managed to run away, in particular on Sundays and holidays, when control was more relaxed. The popularity of this strategy can be verified by private reports. In his account of 1860s Tucumán, British consul Thomas Hutchinson recalled a conversation with an ingenio owner who "complained of the losses and annoyances to which they are subject by the desertion of peons after a portion of their wages has been advanced."[109] Flight was the second most common cause of jail sentences during the late 1870s and early 1880s.[110] Adjustments in labor legislation clearly illustrate the incidence of flight among sugar workers. The 1888 Servants' Law incorporated more precise mechanisms to register workers, as well as harsher sentences for those who failed to show up for work. While in 1877 the law had held workers responsible for covering any losses incurred by their employer as a result of their absence, the Servants' Law established prison terms and fines for those who committed similar crimes. Flight not only produced a sense of broken discipline but also had a significant financial impact on employers. Besides the direct effect that the loss of a worker had on the workforce, workers left substantial debts, clearly undermining the effectiveness of debt as a mechanism to guarantee a stable workforce. In some cases, workers who showed loyalty by not running away received material benefits; peons hired by Ingenio Nueva Baviera received higher cash advances for such loyalty.

Theft was another common occurrence in sugar areas. Stealing not only inflicted material losses but also challenged property rights while providing immediate, albeit small, material gains to those directly involved. Workers stole machine parts, money, animals, and sugarcane. Individuals working in the mill had free access to machinery and tool sheds, often only a few meters away from the mill, these rooms lacked close supervision, in particular during the peak season, when most workers were desperately required in the factory. In 1899, Victoriano Herrera was caught stealing metal bars from Ingenio Esperanza. During the trial it became clear that the worker was using the stolen pieces to supply a small shop he owned. Herrera accepted the blame but claimed it was his first offense and that he had been drunk.[111] In other instances theft was not the result of deliberate planning. Hermenegildo Angulo and Vicente Vega were caught stealing alcohol in Ingenio Bella Vista, but the accused workers claimed to have been drunk and to have no recollection of the episode.[112]

Even though the workers in both cases were convicted, the authorities considered alcohol abuse an attenuating circumstance and sentenced Herrera, Angulo, and Vega to only a few months of jail time. Workers knew that premeditated acts were punished more severely than those that resulted from ignorance or alcohol abuse and, as several court cases reveal, they used those excuses regularly. The complicit assistance of the community made reaching a guilty verdict very difficult, which must have served not only to validate workers' actions but also to create a sense of solidarity among the members of the sugar community. In 1891, Felix Molina, an indebted worker from Ingenio San Andrés, was assisted by a friend to run away with a mule and the ingenio's safe. The police caught Molina's accomplice but, despite the clear evidence against him, charges were never filed because his alibi was corroborated by many of his neighbors.[113]

Besides animals, money, and tools, workers stole sugar and sugarcane. Storage and shipping problems plagued the industry's early years, in particular during the 1880s, when railroads' cargo capacity could not fulfill ingenios' increasing demands. Shipments of sugar, left unattended in railroad stations, waited for days until shipped to their final destinations. Industrialists complained that significant quantities of sugar disappeared regularly from the stations and demanded improved security at terminal stations. Sugarcane also disappeared from the fields. It was customary for workers to chew sugarcane while performing their jobs. Bialet Massé noted that if mills failed to supply sugarcane to the workers, they found ways to obtain it.[114] However, it is difficult to determine whether the theft of sugarcane constituted an act of social protest or simply a survival strategy, as workers were arguably supplementing their own and their families' caloric needs.

Sabotage, on the other hand, was clearly an act of defiance. The nature of sugar making made sabotage common and easy to perform since workers operating machinery went unsupervised for extended periods of time, in particular during night shifts. Furthermore, workers' knowledge of the delicate process of sugar making allowed them to strike effectively by either bringing the machinery to a halt or directly disrupting the sugar-making process. The most common cases took place inside the mills, where metal objects and rocks were thrown into the rollers, halting the mill for hours or days until the machine was repaired. Sabotage was common because it could be accomplished within the daily work routine and could easily be denied by blaming others or claiming ignorance. In order to convict a suspect, authorities had to prove intent. In 1889, Santos Rojas was accused of throwing a metal bar into the mill. In his defense, the suspect declared he had been completely drunk and had no recollection of the crime. The judge denied his claim, however; before the incident witnesses had seen Rojas knocking down a pile of sugarcane, an indication that he was "not drunk enough" and had a "clear intention" of committing the crime.[115]

Determining whether an act was accidental or premeditated was not always easy. In 1892, Ingenio Esperanza's overseer caught Eduardo Frabuchet on his way to the boiler room with enough explosives to blow it up. The worker claimed he just wanted to "show the dynamite to the administrator" but had no intention to do any harm to the mill. Even though witnesses at the trial testified he had made explicit threats against the administrator and the mill, the authorities acquitted Frabuchet on the grounds that his criminal intent had never been proven.[116] Cases of arson were even more difficult to prove.[117] Planters and ingenio owners regularly started controlled fires to destroy weeds and facilitate the cutting and peeling of the sugarcane. An accident could easily occur during the process. Thus only few cases of arson were taken to court and no suspect was ever convicted.

Fellow-workers' complicity played an important role in the success of these acts of defiance. Their assistance not only legitimated their coworkers' actions but also made reaching a guilty verdict very difficult. In 1885, Juan Gómez was found throwing a piece of metal into the mill in Ingenio Luján. Caught in the act, Gómez admitted he had committed the crime and also confessed his involvement in a previous incident. Gómez declared that he had been persuaded by the overseer of Ingenio Esperanza to disrupt the milling operations at Ingenio Luján. Witnesses insisted that Gómez was indeed convinced by a stranger to commit the crime, although nobody ever saw the stranger. Since the authorities were given only the first name and a vague description of the mysterious instigator, they were unable to locate him. It is not known whether or not Gómez was formally charged, although the cause was finally dropped years later without a verdict having been reached.[118] What became clear throughout the trial were witnesses' attempts to diffuse the worker's culpability by depicting him as involved in a larger problem between competing firms, over which he had no control. Initially, sabotage and other acts of resistance were not considered serious enough to lead to long jail sentences. However, over time the authorities adopted a tougher attitude, which is clearly indicated by changes in the language used during trials. While in 1885 sabotage was described as a regular crime that ought to carry a "mild punishment," during the 1890s mill owners and prosecutors sought "to punish harshly" those who committed these acts.

Cases involving violence against individuals were the most severely punished. In most cases, violent acts in sugar areas were spontaneous and not destructive enough to pose significant material losses to the industry. Such disturbances sought the amelioration of specific grievances and took place within a limited geographic area. For example, in September 1884, after the harvest was over, *El Orden* reported with extreme alarm a series of incidents that took place in the department of Cruz Alta. According to the newspaper report, on September 1 the authorities jailed twenty-four workers who had participated in a riot against the administrator of an ingenio.[119] A day later, even though police records clearly show that the incident had taken place, the ingenio owner altered the reports.[120] In a clear attempt to purge any defiant element from the incident and downplay the events, he depicted the episode as a minor crime and claimed the problem was just the result of a group of alcoholics who got out of control.[121] A similar episode took place only a week after the first riot. In this case, according to the newspaper, the revolt involved workers from several ingenios in the same region.[122] Once again, a few days later, a representative from one ingenio rectified this initial report without providing too many details.[123]

Violent acts against the overseer or administrator were the most common occurrences. In charge of the discipline in fields and factories, these managers were both hated and feared by workers. In 1889 a group of workers at Ingenio San Felipe attacked the administrative office but were jailed almost immediately by the authorities.[124] The overseer at Ingenio Concepción met a different fate in 1901 when he was stabbed by a worker. When the police came to take the worker into custody, a group of fifty individuals attacked the authorities. The uprising had to be controlled with the help of police brigades from other towns and left several casualties.[125] Because open, organized, and collective acts of defiance were not viable during the first decades of sugar expansion, workers resorted to spontaneous resistance through individual tactics that required little planning and avoided direct confrontation, such as flight, theft, sabotage, and sudden outbreaks of violence.

Initial spontaneity also characterized the first organized act of resistance that took place in sugar areas. In June 1904, several weeks after the beginning of the harvest, laborers from Ingenio San Miguel went on strike. After a couple of days, peons and factory workers from other mills halted their activities and joined the protest. Lack of organization put the movement at risk, so local leaders in Tucumán called for support from the Unión General de Trabajadores (UGT) in Buenos Aires. The national union sent Adrián Patroni, who assumed leadership of the movement immediately.[126] A first meeting at Ingenio San Miguel brought together six hundred workers, and a week later thirty-five hundred workers attended a second convocation. Workers' demands included a monthly wage of fifty pesos without ration, in cash, and paid every other week. The final arrangement was a success for the strikers as it established a wage of forty-three pesos, payable biweekly, in cash, and eliminated the ration. The new minimum wage represented an important increase in wages since the average wage before the strike was thirty pesos. Furthermore, the requirement that payments be given in cash eliminated company vouchers, thus allowing workers to purchase goods outside the abhorred proveeduría.

The 1904 strike revealed a shift in sugar workers' forms of protest in response to changes in institutional, economic, and social circumstances that reduced impediments to collective action. The abrogation of the Servants' Law in 1896, in conjunction with the authorities' growing concern for "*la cuestión social*," contributed to the creation of an environment more conducive to organized resistance.[127] Living and working conditions in sugar areas were systematically criticized by the press thus providing a favorable atmosphere for workers' demands. The provincial government of Lucas Córdoba, more receptive to workers' grievances than previous governments in the province, made a commitment to not intervene or repress. Furthermore, the strike took place during Juan Bialet Massé's visit to the province and achieved national significance when the UGT in Buenos Aires got involved.

Other circumstances also helped workers achieve success. In 1904 labor shortages were affecting the province. According to *El Orden*, the number of workers from Santiago del Estero and Catamarca had decreased as more workers chose to work in railroad construction, where they obtained higher wages and better working conditions.[128] Furthermore, the twentieth century brought a new period in sugar production characterized by profound fluctuations and instability, thus increasing the risk of financial losses in case of work stoppages and, consequently, improving workers' bargaining power. The combination of favorable political, institutional, and economic circumstances bolstered workers' possibilities to reach a positive outcome in their struggle. Despite its successful outcome, the 1904 strike did not result in the consolidation of an organized labor movement and proved a wasted opportunity for sugar workers' organization, as the initial coordination and strength were lost in the following months.

Workers' individual and collective strategies of resistance were a clear manifestation of deeper social grievances in sugar areas. During this period, their actions set limits on abuses and challenged the ruling group's monopoly on violence but failed to consolidate a strong labor movement. The absence of organized confrontation during the early period of sugar production reflects workers' acute appreciation of the reality in Tucumán. The migrant and seasonal nature of sugar workers as well as their patterns of residence in enclosed and isolated communities acted against the consolidation of a cohesive labor organization that could have included all rural workers. Because open, organized, and collective acts of defiance were not viable during the first decades of sugar industry expansion, workers resorted to "everyday forms of resistance."[129] Flight, theft, sabotage, and violence aimed at immediate improvements and obtained short-term material benefits. During the early 1900s workers' strategies gradually took on a collective and more organized form, although it was not until decades later that sugar workers could actually claim an organized labor movement.[130] Collective forms of protest emerged only in the twentieth century, when a combination of political, economic, and institutional circumstances resulted in an environment more suitable for open resistance. As union leader Luis Lotito observed in 1907, "Workers' actions revealed a constant rebellion, individual, passive . . . a movement without theoretical premises, spontaneous and instinctive . . . which not only elevated the material conditions of workers but also showed the path of their future defense: organization and strike."[131]

IN 1904 Manuel Bernárdez praised the "civilizing effect" and material benefits that the sugar industry had had on the Argentine-born worker and observed, "What would be the situation of all those workers without these five months when they can secure an earning that will improve their humble lives for the rest of the year?"[132] Since the late 1870s thousands of men, women, and children made the journey to Tucumán and toiled side by side with the locals until the harvest was over. In the fields, they cut, peeled, and hauled millions of tons of sugarcane. In the mill, they fed the rollers, supervised the process of sugar making, and repaired machinery and ingenio facilities. A body of legislation systematized mechanisms of control and provided the legal framework needed to sustain the diverse strategies developed by sugar producers to fulfill their labor needs. Organized recruitment mechanisms ensured the availability of workers, whereas material incentives combined with coercion guaranteed their discipline and stability in sugar areas. The arrival of thousands of men, women, and children to work in the sugar industry not only contributed to the sector's growth but also altered Tucumán's rural society significantly. Self-sufficient communities emerged around factories and fields and evolved as independent living communities in rural Tucumán. These enclosed settlements facilitated the surveillance of the working population and their subjection to the unique needs of the sugar economy. The rhythms of sugar production moved beyond the field and the factory and regimented the lives of workers in Tucumán. The industry changed work routines and imposed a new time discipline. In rural Tucumán, sugar production became the principle around which human life was organized. The industry created and dispersed families and resulted in new complex sets of relationships characterized by consensus and conflict. As the most dynamic sector in Tucumán's economy, the sugar industry not only affected Tucumán's economy and rural society but also had a significant impact on the province's public sources of revenue and spending patterns.

Chapter 5

Sugar and the Province

DURING THE LAST quarter of the nineteenth century, the sugar industry became the most dynamic sector in Tucumán's economy. The changes experienced by Tucumán's productive structure had a significant impact on the province's public finances. Between 1876 and 1916 the composition of Tucumán's sources of revenue underwent dramatic changes as the province reduced its dependence on the financial assistance provided by the national authorities and increased its reliance on local sources of income. In response to the changes brought about by the sugar economy, Tucumán's authorities carried out periodic tax revisions, which in turn increased provincial revenues and the ability to finance public expenditures. In 1893 a report made by Tucumán's budget committee observed, "In the absence of public revenues it is necessary to create them, and the committee has the obligation to carry on this idea by imposing on our main industry [sugar] a minor contribution.... We must save the province's honor by settling our financial obligations."[1]

Four Decades of Tax Policies: The Old and the New

Between 1876 and 1916, Tucumán relied on both national and provincial funds to meet its financial obligations. The participation of both sources of funds varied over time. Initially, the province depended largely on national resources that consisted of general subsidies allocated periodically to cover for budget deficits and specific subventions for public education. The concession of general subsidies from the nation to the provinces was not new in Argentina. The practice was informally used by Juan Manuel de Rosas and Justo José de Urquiza as a means to assist provinces in need and maintain internal peace. During the 1860s subsidies became political tools that secured provincial support and loyalty to the nascent national state.[2] Even though they provided an invaluable source of funding, subsidies had serious limitations, since they depended both on political alliances and on the health of the national economy. For example, the 1875 crisis affected subsidy disbursements to the provinces. For Tucumán, funds during this period were not distributed regularly and more often than not fell short of government's expectations, although they still represented an important contribution to provincial finances. This was true especially during the late 1860s and early 1870s, when general subsidies made up more than 15 percent of the total provincial public income.[3] The importance of securing more stable sources of income did not escape the attention of the local authorities. In his 1877 annual message to the legislature, Tucumán's governor, Tiburcio Padilla, highlighted the negative effect of budget cuts on the government's ability to function properly and called for the establishment of new sources of public revenues to reduce the province's dependence on the national authorities.[4]

Aside from general subsidies, the national authorities also contributed to provincial finances through a separate fund for public education. National subventions for education were established for the first time in 1857, as provided for by article 67 of the national constitution.[5] Initially, the absence of clear disbursement mechanisms made the distribution of funds more dependent on political than educational concerns.[6] During President Domingo Faustino Sarmiento's administration (1868–74), Argentina became deeply committed to public education. Distribution mechanisms were improved and the national subvention for education quadrupled.[7] Most important, in 1871 the national congress passed a law that established clear mechanisms for the distribution of funds to the provinces thus institutionalizing a method that facilitated and supervised their allocation. The law tied the subsidy to local spending; each province received from the nation an amount that ranged from one-fourth to three-fourths of the resources assigned by provincial budgets to education for each given year.[8] To prevent fraud and guarantee responsible use of the allocations, the law established complex mechanisms to regulate the disbursement of funds. Each province was required to send budget reports detailing their expenses and planned investments. Moreover, provincial governments were requested to supply evidence that local funds had already been deposited in a bank at the time of each disbursement, which was made four times a year. In spite of its efforts, the national government failed to deliver the funds with the expected regularity, leaving local authorities to make up the difference. In 1877, Governor Padilla complained that the national authorities had failed to supply the resources to many provinces and noted that in the previous year Tucumán was the only province that did not suspend services or financial support for education.[9]

Tucumán's authorities understood the dangers that excessive reliance on national subsidies could pose for the financial health of the province. Between 1876 and 1916 the government became committed to the creation of alternative and more stable sources of income through periodic revisions of provincial taxes that targeted in particular the sugar industry. Tucumán's government increased demands on the industry through periodic revisions in the tax system since the early 1870s, especially adjustments to the patentes. Distilleries and sugarcane plantations had paid these taxes on economic activities since the 1860s. In 1872 the provincial government instituted a new patente applied directly to ingenios.[10] The law classified ingenios according to their technological level and the amounts they were to pay were determined based on the area of each ingenio cultivated in sugarcane. The first of the three categories specified by the law included those ingenios that possessed iron mills. The second group consisted of ingenios with wooden mills. The third encompassed those planters without milling technology. The law reflected the initial years of the industry, when both stages of production, agricultural and industrial, were integrated. However, it failed to recognize that some ingenios had already adopted additional technology, such as alternative sources of power or modern machinery, thus increasing their plant capacity and sugar output. The resulting tax system was thus unfair. For example, Justiniano Frías, who owned fifty hectares of sugarcane and an iron mill that used animal power was taxed as much as the Méndez brothers, who planted a similar area in sugarcane but relied on more modern technology, including an iron mill and a hydraulic centrifuge that likely yielded much more sugar.

In 1878 the government passed a new law that created six categories, based on a more accurate assessment of technological improvements, taking into consideration both the machinery and the source of energy. The tax burden on ingenios was thus made more equitable.[11] Ingenios in the top categories were taxed at a higher rate than before and ingenios using wooden mills, a technology that had already become outdated among Tucumán sugar producers, paid less. The law also introduced a seventh category, which specified an even lower levy for those cultivators who did not own mills. The latter category signaled an official recognition of the distinction between agricultural and industrial sectors as well as of the increasing participation of outside sugarcane growers in the industry. Finally, the 1878 law established a new criterion to determine the productive unit based on a standard unit (the *cuadra,* just over two hectares), rather than on the nominal one that had been in use until 1878 (the *surco,* or furrow), to end the discrepancies and abuses that plagued the provincial tax system.[12] This law was the first important modification in provincial tax policies affecting the sugar sector. It clearly shows increasing government interest in exercising tighter control over an industry that was already perceived as an important source of provincial revenues.

In 1880, Tucumán's acting governor, José Mariano Astigueta, denounced irregularities in collection mechanisms and placed special emphasis on the problems that resulted from tax evasion. He also remarked the unfairness of Tucumán's tax system—a cattle rancher with a capital investment of 75,000 pesos, for example, was taxed almost as much as a sugar industrialist with a capital investment of 600,000 pesos. Crude and outdated tax brackets that failed to reflect the increasingly complex sugar industry, he argued, were to be blamed for this inconsistency. Astigueta demanded revisions to provincial taxes to reflect the changes experienced by the economy and proposed heavier and more "responsible" taxes on the sugar industry, since it was the productive sector that received the most benefits from local and national authorities.[13] Soon after, sugar patentes experienced another change.[14] In this case, the new law modified the taxable unit from the cuadra to the hectare to be in accord with the national adoption of the metric system, in 1877.[15] The significance of this law resides, however, in other modifications that were described as urgent by the authorities. The new law revised ingenio classifications and incorporated a higher tax bracket, reflecting once again the industry's fast technological modernization. Even more important, the adjustments resulted in substantial tax increases that affected the top four brackets and sugarcane planters. Once again, the bracket comprising wooden mills was the only one to experience a decrease, confirming the declining significance of wooden mills within the industrial sector. Sugarcane planters with no milling technology still remained within the lowest tax bracket, although their taxes were increased as well.

The 1880s witnessed not only an increase in ingenios' plant capacity but also significant changes in the organization of production. Outside sugarcane suppliers, who had existed in small numbers before the adoption of modern technology, became an indispensable component in the sugar industry. In 1880 an official report stressed the importance of that group for the industry as a whole, which resulted in changes in tax policies the following year.[16] In 1881 a new law imposed on ingenios within the top two brackets an additional tax on the sugarcane purchased from independent planters.[17] Even though industrialists were expected to cover this additional levy, it is likely that they managed to transfer the cost to the planter, through additional provisions in their contracts. This modification reveals the authorities' understanding of the industry's evolution as well as their interest in sharing in its prosperity. However, in September 1887, Tucumán's governor, Lídoro Quinteros, pointed out that despite economic prosperity, an imperfect tax system was still affecting the financial health of the province. The governor called for improved mechanisms of collection and for taxes that reflected with more accuracy the progress made by Tucumán's economy.[18]

A few months later the legislature passed two laws in direct response to Quinteros's request. One created a new agency in charge of tax policies, while the other reformed, one more time, the patentes on sugar.[19] To simplify tax collection, the law reduced the number of ingenio categories to five and established a new mechanism to tax the sugarcane purchased from outside suppliers. The new legislation standardized the output of one hectare at fifty thousand kilograms of sugarcane, thus facilitating official monitoring over purchases from outside suppliers. Furthermore, for the first time, this law included detailed provisions to both prevent and prosecute tax evasion. The changes incorporated by the 1887 patente legislation were not radical but clearly revealed Tucumán authorities' interest in increasing control over the industry.

Throughout the 1880s the provincial government incorporated provisions to modernize the tax system as well as to increase public vigilance over the sugar industry. However, sugar taxes still contained a number of loopholes that limited Tucumán's authorities' efforts to increase the revenues obtained from the industry. For example, besides purchasing sugarcane from independent planters, ingenios placed plots under the direct management of colonos, who, as part of their arrangements, were responsible for the taxes on the land under their care. Patentes were determined based on total cultivated area, but tax brackets varied depending on an ingenio's technological level. The lowest rate included planters with no milling technology. Since colonos did not own milling machinery, they were taxed in the lowest bracket, even though the land belonged to the ingenio; the potential income from such properties was thus reduced. In 1889 the authorities modified sugar patentes to account for this oversight.[20] An ingenio's tax bracket remained determined by its machinery, although rates were changed to a fixed amount based on the ingenio's production capacity rather than on cultivated hectares. Therefore, all the lands that belonged to one ingenio were classified and taxed depending on the ingenio's technology, regardless of who worked the land. The 1889 law established three categories for ingenios, but in doing so it benefited the largest ones, which were producing more than twice as much sugar as those in the second category. This problem was addressed in 1893 with a more realistic classification for ingenios.[21] The new law's classification system considered the industry's impressive expansion in plant capacity and potential sugar output. Moreover, the new tax rates were raised substantially. Now, for example, an ingenio producing around 240,000 arrobas of sugar paid more than twice as much as it had before.[22] The increases also affected the agricultural sector, since the tax on cultivated land was more than doubled. The new tax established a fixed rate of three pesos per hectare cultivated in sugarcane.

During the 1880s periodic revisions to the tax laws indicated the Tucumán authorities' efforts to create a fiscal system that kept pace with the modernization and expansion of the sugar industry. The government did so without imposing an unbearable toll, which could have inhibited the industry's growth by discouraging additional investment. In any case, tax modifications reveal the provincial government's appreciation of the important changes affecting the industry as well as recognition of its potential as an important source of income.[23] As a result of government's direct intervention, patentes increased their contribution to provincial revenues during the 1880s. But the seasonal nature of patente collection posed a significant challenge to the stability of public finances. In 1892 an official report recognized this deficiency and observed that for half the year the province "does not have more income than the one provided from other taxes, which are too insignificant to fulfill

Tucumán's monthly financial obligations."[24] A year later, in an attempt to address this problem and to find a larger and more stable source of public income, the legislature shifted its tax policies and altered the balance between the sugar industry and public revenues in profound and permanent ways.

A significant watershed in the Tucumán government's attitude toward sugar taxes occurred in 1893. Unable to meet its financial obligations in the early months of that year, and as an emergency measure, the government imposed provisional levies on tobacco, rice, alfalfa, and sugar. The additional tax on sugar was half a cent per kilogram.[25] The toll fell only on ingenio owners, since the levy was applied to the final product. The legislature justified the increase as a modest contribution that the industry, thus far deeply protected by the national authorities, could make to provincial finances. Furthermore, during the debates, legislators claimed that most of the tax would be returned to the sugar industry in the form of public works such as irrigation canals and road construction. Since the main purpose of these taxes was to balance the provincial budget, they were considered a temporary measure. Indeed, that was the case for alfalfa, tobacco, and rice.[26] The fate of sugar was completely different. In 1894 the government maintained the tax and managed to avoid debates in the provincial legislature that could have challenged its legitimacy. By then, the taxes on the industry amounted to one-fourth of the total provincial income, and their elimination would have inflicted a profound blow to Tucumán's public finances. Industrialists joined forces and, assisted by the media, initiated a strong campaign against a levy that, according to its detractors, was imposed on the industry only to "compensate for administrative squandering."[27] Sugar producers' opposition to the levy put the government, very much dependent on their political support, in a very difficult position.

In March 1895, in an attempt to reach an agreement with producers, Tucumán's legislators presented a project that included five potential alternative revisions to the existing tax.[28]

1. Raise three and a half times the patente on ingenios, double the land tax, and eliminate the half-cent tax on sugar.

2. Eliminate the patente on ingenios, maintain the land tax, and increase the tax on sugar to three-quarters of a cent.

3. Eliminate the patente on ingenios, double the land tax to six pesos, and maintain the half-cent tax on sugar.

4. Maintain the patente on ingenios with small changes in their classification, increase the land tax to ten pesos, and eliminate the half-cent tax on sugar.

5. Increase the land tax to four pesos, maintain the half-cent tax on sugar, and eliminate the patente on ingenios.

The final law, passed in 1895, eliminated the patente on ingenios and maintained both the land tax and the half-cent tax on sugar in what Donna Guy has called a compromise between the sugar sector and the government.[29] Besides being a compromise, the law clearly embodied the most rational economic and political choice available to the provincial authorities. In revisions 1 and 4 the elimination of the sugar tax would have resulted in a significant reduction in Tucumán's public income. On the other hand, revisions 2 and 3 would have led to substantial increases in provincial revenues but would have encountered opposition from sugar producers, as it raised their taxes significantly. The last option would have placed an unfair burden on landowners. Provincial finances depended on the income supplied by the industry, but at the same time the government could not afford to alienate the sugar sector, which provided important political support. The 1895 tax law maintained a delicate balance between the financial and political needs of the province and those of the industry. On the one hand, with the 1895 law, both groups involved in sugar production (industrial and agricultural) were equally required to pay taxes. The elimination of the land tax would have placed the tax burden exclusively on the industrial sector. Moreover, since sugarcane cultivation was still expanding, its elimination would have had an important impact on future governments' income. Conversely, an increase in the land tax would have had an unbearable impact on planters already hit by decreasing sugarcane prices. Instead, the law eliminated patentes on ingenios, which gave a bit of relief to the industrialists without resulting in a significant loss of provincial revenues. Since taxes on a particular input discourage investments on that input, the elimination on machinery tax also must have acted as an incentive for ingenios to keep adopting modern technology and increasing their output.[30] The tax on sugar was maintained, since its elimination would have resulted in an important loss for public revenues that could have been compensated only by significant increases in the other taxes paid by the sector, a high political price to pay. Finally, and most important, taxes on output were not only more efficient but also easier to transfer to the consumer, in particular if the commodity enjoyed protection from cheap international competition, as was the case for Tucumán's sugar.

Therefore, the 1895 law enabled the government to consolidate its tax policy and secure a steady and increasing source of revenue without alienating the support of the groups involved in sugar production or compromising the growth of the industry. The incorporation of additional taxes constituted an important innovation in tax policies and inaugurated a new period in the history of sugar taxation. Announced as a temporary measure to deal with public debt and acute budget deficits, increases in the taxes paid by sugar producers became a permanent feature in the province and consolidated the industry's role as the largest contributor to the provincial treasury. At the same time, Tucumán's tax policies increased the local authorities' stake in the enactment of protective legislation for the sugar industry at the national level. It was clear to the provincial authorities that sugar producers would accept higher taxes only if they could transfer to the final consumer the brunt of the tax increase by means of a protected domestic market. Local tax policies had the effect of tying the financial health of the province to national politics even more. During the following four years sugar taxes did not experience further revisions, as increases in cultivated area and sugar output kept public revenues from the sector high.

This situation changed during the first decade of the twentieth century, when sugar taxes were again significantly revised. In 1900 a new law revised patentes paid by the agricultural sector.[31] Rates were changed from 3.00 pesos per hectare to one-fifth of a cent per kilogram of sugar, assuming a 6 percent average sugar yield.[32] The revision resulted in a significant increase in the taxes paid by planters—from 3.00 pesos to approximately 4.80 pesos per hectare.[33] The government justified the change on the grounds that it improved collection but also benefited planters since new taxes were due at the end of the harvest, thus relieving them from cash disbursements at the beginning of the year, when patentes were due. In 1903 the government imposed a special levy to indemnify the industrialists who had been affected by the provincial law of 1902, or machete law, that established limits to sugar production and also changed the sugar tax from one-fifth of a cent per kilogram of sugar to fifteen cents per ton of sugarcane.[34] The change meant a substantial increase in the land tax, since, considering the average output of sugarcane per hectare, a planter would now be paying 6.00 pesos per hectare. Once again, changes in tax policies hit the agricultural sector the hardest. This situation reversed in 1906 when a new law created a special quarter-cent tax per kilogram of sugar imposed on ingenios and exempted sugarcane plantations from the fifteen-cent tax if the cane was to be used to make sugar nectar or as seed for future plantations.[35] The governor argued that "the industry's prosperity and the precariousness of public finances" justified an additional imposition on the industry that was to be devoted to investments in public works.[36] Additional taxes on sugar and increasing government reliance on the sector to bail out the province in times of financial distress continued throughout the late 1900s and 1910s. In 1907, after the imposition of two additional special taxes of a quarter cent per kilogram of sugar, sugar producers were paying, including regular and special levies, one cent per kilogram of sugar and fifteen cents per ton of sugarcane.[37] To make past increases permanent, in 1908 the patente for sugar was doubled to one cent per kilogram of sugar.[38] From 1908 to 1916 the legislature approved, as part of its annual budget, additional half-cent increases on sugar taxes every year. In 1916 sugar producers were paying one and a half cents per kilogram of sugar and fifteen cents per ton of sugarcane. During the two decades following 1895, provincial revenues expanded dramatically and sugar taxes accounted for much of that increase. In 1894 revenues from sugar taxes represented 24.5 percent of the total provincial income. Two decades later, Tucumán obtained 58 percent of its income from the sugar industry.[39]

Besides revisions, increases, and additional taxes, the provincial government made important changes in the mechanisms of tax collection. Provincial taxes were collected through two different systems. In some cases, rights over tax collection were auctioned annually to individuals while in other cases, the majority, taxes were collected directly by the government or by specific commissioners appointed for that purpose, who received a percentage of the amount collected in partial compensation for their job.[40] During this period, in order to centralize and improve the system of tax collection, the provincial government created several agencies, such as the Oficina de Estadística Provincial (Office of Provincial Statistics) (1881), the Receptoría General de Rentas (General Office of Revenue) (1887), the Dirección General de Rentas (General Bureau of Revenue) (1892), and the Oficina Central de Recaudación (Central Office of Tax Collection) (1898). During the 1890s and early 1900s the authorities also paid special attention to collection and approved several regulations to control and punish tax evasion, a rampant problem in the province.[41] Improved mechanisms of collection combined with increasing demands on the sugar industry led to a dramatic growth in public revenues. For example, in 1895, patente and contribución directa collections amounted to 65.9 and 49.7 percent of the projected collection estimated by the authorities, respectively. By 1912 the province was collecting 95.4 and 72.5 percent of the projected collection estimated for both levies.[42]

Until 1893 tax revisions constituted part of a program of modernization of the provincial tax system intended to reflect the changes experienced by Tucumán's economy and the sugar industry. After 1893 revisions illustrate the government's attitude toward the industry that was perceived as an "unlimited fountain of wealth and public revenue."[43] The sugar industry became the most important source of provincial revenue as well as a convenient and easy mechanism to cover budget deficits. The new taxes targeted the commodity rather than wealth or personal income. Therefore, the potential negative effects that new levies could have had on local producers were avoided by transferring the costs to the consumer in Buenos Aires and the littoral areas, where the largest markets were located. The national government's commitment to protect Tucumán's sugar through high tariffs enabled the provincial authorities' policies to increase fiscal pressures on the industry. However, a significant drawback of this tax policy was that it tied the future of Tucumán's public finances to the preservation of protective policies at the national level, thus reducing provincial financial autonomy. In any case, modifications to tax policies increased provincial revenues and the government's ability to finance public expenditures. This period witnessed not only increased public income but also a significant change in the government's spending priorities.

Public Investment: Education and Health

Rising revenues from taxes came together with changes in spending priorities, revealing that Tucumán's authorities conceived the sugar industry not only as a long-lasting fountain of wealth but also as an instrument to further provincial modernization. Taxes from sugar allowed the provincial government to embark on programs that extended the benefits of the industry to a larger sector of society. Throughout this period, the composition of public expenditures underwent important quantitative and qualitative changes. Funds allocated to areas that can be classified as social expenditures, such as health and education, experienced a more dramatic and steady increase than expenditures in other areas, such as security and government. The two areas that experienced the most significant changes were police and education. Whereas in the last quarter of the nineteenth century police had absorbed a significant share of provincial resources, over time the situation reversed and investments in education experienced a gradual but steady expansion. In 1876 police spending made up 37 percent of the total provincial budget, whereas by 1916 its participation had declined to 18 percent. Conversely, during the same period funds invested in education increased from 16 to 28 percent of total public spending.[44] Public health revealed a similar pattern, although its relative share of the provincial budget throughout the period never exceeded 3 percent of the total provincial budget.[45]

Interest in popular education had always been a part of the Argentine authorities' agenda. The national authorities conceived education as a tool to convey symbols and values that would assist in the creation of a common identity, an important component in the process of social construction and consolidation of the national state.[46] Therefore, besides creating a legal institutional framework to sustain the new state, the 1853 constitution included provisions on public instruction and required that each province take the necessary steps to guarantee free and obligatory education within its boundaries. Since the late 1850s, Tucumán's authorities had joined in the national trend and made efforts to advance the province's public educational system as a "unique base and foundation of our system of government, whose development, improvement, and maintenance the people are required to care for" through the creation of a body of regulations and institutions such as the Junta Central in 1857 and the position of chief inspector of public instruction a few years later.[47] The provincial authorities blamed low literacy levels on absenteeism and took an aggressive stance on attendance problems. A law passed in 1861 established mandatory education for children under the age of twelve and exempted those families with one child only if they could prove that the child's work was indispensable for the material sustenance of the family.[48] In 1873 the legislature passed another law that allowed for no exceptions to mandatory education and imposed fines on those parents who failed to send their children to school.[49] The police were put in charge of registering all children and prosecuting offenders.[50] As was the case with labor, the use of the police to enforce regulations on public instruction indicates that the authorities not only considered education an instrument to create consensus and support for the ruling classes but also attributed to it a moralizing and disciplining role in society. Furthermore, the public school system could "initiate children in manual labor and other experimental branches, providing notions on agriculture or cattle ranching that could be applied immediately, to form men of action and productive labor," an indication that for the authorities education was equally important in the consolidation of a modern labor force in the province.[51]

Tucumán's ability to invest in public education was hindered by insufficient funds, which in turn resulted in late payments to teachers and the impossibility to invest in infrastructure. Provincial funds allocated to education came from the national subsidy as well as local resources and were determined every year by the legislature in the provincial budget. However, the exact amount available was difficult to predict since it depended ultimately on tax collections and the timely arrival of the subsidy. In 1877, Governor Padilla observed that Tucumán's instructional system was suffering from the absence of a specific law that, among other provisions, would create stable funding for education. Confronting that problem, the governor argued, would eliminate the "absurdity that Tucumán, despite so many improvements, is still so behind in education."[52] Securing a stable source of funds for public instruction became one of the main goals that guided the provincial government's efforts in education during the late nineteenth century.[53] After several failed attempts, in 1883 the legislature approved a comprehensive law that provided the basis for the creation of a modern educational system in the province. The Education Law of 1883 reiterated that education was free and mandatory and maintained the fines and penalties for those who failed to comply. Most important, the law included specific provisions to create permanent funds for education and to guarantee responsible use of those funds.[54] Public instruction was to be financed through a combination of sources that included national subsidies, a provincial subsidy, provincial taxes, municipal funds, and other minor sources, such as inheritance taxes and donations. The Education Law of 1883 represented an important step toward the consolidation of permanent funding for education, although it failed to clearly stipulate the sources that would constitute the provincial subsidy. A revision addressed this problem more than a decade later and determined that 15 percent of the provincial patentes and 15 percent of the contribución directa were to be allocated to education. The consolidation of a permanent fund for education, in conjunction with the rising tide in the collection of sugar taxes during the 1890s and 1900s, had a significant effect on Tucumán's public education system. Between 1892 and 1912 the total resources allocated to public instruction increased sixfold and the relative contribution of national and provincial sources reversed. While in 1892 the province was contributing 24 percent of the funds allocated for education, by 1912 its share was 72 percent.[55] Therefore, it was local funds that accounted for most of the increase experienced by Tucumán's investments in public education.

The dramatic expansion of funds for public education allowed Tucumán's authorities to carry out a number of measures that modernized the provincial school system. In 1883, Governor Benjamín Paz observed that Tucumán was suffering from a severe teacher shortage.[56] To confront this problem, the legislature increased budget allocations to pay for teachers' salaries, especially after 1895. From 1896 to 1912 provincial expenditures for teacher salaries more than doubled.[57] The need to improve teachers' qualifications was also another concern for Tucumán's policymakers. In 1896 only one-fourth of those working in public elementary schools had a degree in education. In 1875 the first Escuela Normal (School for Teachers), an institution devoted to training teachers, opened its doors. Teachers were required to take specific courses in several disciplines unless they could pass qualifying exams in those fields. The provincial government allocated special funds for fellowships and grants for those willing to pursue a career in education. The success of the Escuela Normal encouraged the opening of other institutions of higher learning, such as a second Escuela Normal, the Escuela de Ayudantes (later renamed the Escuela Pedagógica Sarmiento), and the National University of Tucumán (UNT). During the first decade of the twentieth century, the number of teachers working in public schools more than doubled, thus improving the ratios of students to both schools and teachers. For example, in 1876 the average number of students per school was 106, while in 1914 the number had dropped to 83, despite significant increases in attendance. Similarly, while in 1882 the teacher-student ratio was 1:55, by 1914 it had dropped to 1:31.

Infrastructure problems, in particular an acute shortage of buildings, also affected the public school system in Tucumán. Private houses and small rooms were still serving as substandard classrooms as late as 1889. Furthermore, their location did not respond to the specific needs of the student population but rather depended on availability. Since the early 1890s the authorities devoted increasingly larger shares of educational expenses to

Figure 5.1. School of Agriculture, UNT. *(Courtesy of Photographic Department, Archivo General de la Nación, Buenos Aires.)*

build, rent, and repair school facilities. An 1895 decree set basic construction standards for schools, appointed a supervisory commission, and allocated special funds for new school buildings. Between 1896 and 1912 investments in infrastructure increased almost threefold and the number of schools grew from 162 to 208.[58] However, the composition of investments in infrastructure reveals significant shares devoted to rent and furniture purchases rather than building construction and repair, a clear indication that despite the construction of new facilities, a significant number of schools still relied on available buildings, either through leases or donations.[59]

Increasing investments in education had a significant impact on the education levels of Tucumán's population. Between 1869 and 1914 enrollment in public schools rose steadily. In 1869, according to national figures, only 12.1 percent of Tucumán's school-age population attended school.[60] By 1914 that number had grown to 46 percent. Not surprisingly, provincial literacy levels increased dramatically over the same period, from 11.7 percent to 45.9 percent. Tucumán's literacy rates, as well as the province's position relative to other provinces, improved over time. Between 1869 and 1914,

Tucumán climbed from thirteenth to eleventh place in literacy among Argentina's twenty-five provinces and territories. This modest improvement is explained by the fact that in 1914, 17 percent of Tucumán's population had recently migrated from other provinces (especially Santiago del Estero and Catamarca) that had extremely high illiteracy rates. Other indicators suggest that Tucumán made more significant improvements in education than other provinces during this period. Among school-age population literacy rose from fourteenth to ninth place, the highest in the Argentine northwest. The most dramatic improvement occurred in school attendance. During the same period, the province moved from fourteenth place to eighth, with more than half the province's school population attending, a rate extremely close to the national average.

Health care was also affected by changes in the allocation of public resources, although not as dramatically as education. Throughout this period the share of health care in the composition of public expenditures increased, even though investments in that sector were still small, not exceeding 3 percent of all provincial spending. In 1876 health care investments amounted to only 0.4 percent of public expenses. By 1916 spending on health care

Figure 5.2. Geography class, Escuela Pedagógica Sarmiento. *(Courtesy of Photographic Department, Archivo General de la Nación, Buenos Aires.)*

accounted for 2.5 percent.[61] Tucumán's sanitary conditions were a source of concern among provincial policymakers. In the early 1880s a national report described the province as a "vast cemetery, with significantly higher death rates than in the rest of the country."[62] To address health care issues, the authorities acted on two fronts. On the one hand, the government allocated larger funds to programs on prevention and care. On the other hand, the provincial authorities created agencies in charge of regulating sanitary matters, such as the Consejo de Higiene (Department of Hygiene), the Oficina Química (Chemical Office), and the Laboratorio de Bacteriología (Laboratory of Bacteriology).[63]

Infant mortality was the most acute health problem affecting Tucumán and was the top priority in the government's health care agenda. In 1897 infant deaths in Buenos Aires accounted for 11 percent of all deaths, while in Tucumán they represented 24 percent. In his 1898 report Paulino Rodríguez Marquina cited as leading causes of infant mortality the absence of prenatal care, unqualified professionals, substandard treatment facilities, and bad living conditions.[64] One obvious area of concern was childbirth. The government took important steps to improve childbirth conditions and in 1885 the Hospital Mixto opened a maternity ward.[65] Other institutions such as the Instituto de Puericultura (Prenatal Care Institute), Hospital de Niños (Children's Hospital), Casa Cuna (Infant Care Institute), and Asilo Maternal (Maternity Hospital) opened their doors during the first decade of the twentieth century and represented important steps toward improving infant care in the province. New facilities, however, could not compensate for the lack of qualified professionals. In 1885 there was only one registered midwife in the province.[66] Ten years later, the 1895 census recorded a total of thirty-seven midwives, a significant increase, although still insufficient to fulfill the needs of Tucumán's population. In many cases, pregnant women still resorted to *hábiles* (lay midwives), women who assisted birth procedures without following basic hygiene or medical guidelines.[67] More than a decade later, the government inaugurated the first Escuela de Parteras (School for Midwives). But the demand for qualified professionals remained high, and in 1914 the authorities created the Escuela de Idóneas (School for Assistant Midwives). The institution offered workshops and basic training to assist women in childbirth. In spite of the government's efforts, as late as 1916 a survey revealed that 75 percent of childbirths in the province were still being assisted by hábiles.[68]

Besides childbirth, Tucumán's authorities made significant efforts to reduce the effects of malnutrition among Tucumán's infant population. In 1908 the provincial authorities commissioned Dr. Cayetano Sobrecasas to visit maternity facilities in Paris. In his report, Sobrecasas encouraged investments in milk dispensaries, as they represented inexpensive ways to improve the health of mothers and infants. Their goal was to decrease health risks for newborns through the distribution of sterilized milk and sanitary educational campaigns.[69] In 1909 two milk dispensaries (*gotas de leche*) opened in San Miguel and provided low-income mothers with free medical assistance and food for their children. Mothers received daily rations and were required to bring the child once a week for checkups and vaccination. The institution also offered assistance to midwives through training courses and the distribution of boxes of sterilized medical supplies. The success of San Miguel's dispensaries encouraged the opening of similar facilities in Lules, Bella Vista, Monteros, and Medinas, as well as regular care facilities in Leales and Cruz Alta during the 1910s. In 1916 a report presented to the authorities commended the positive effects of dispensaries in improving newborns' health.[70] Data for the period corroborate this assertion; between 1900 and 1914 infant mortality in Tucumán declined dramatically.[71]

However, since children were also exposed to maladies in the adult population, any effort that tended to improve children's health had to be accompanied by changes in adult care. Endemic diseases such as malaria and tuberculosis, as well as recurrent epidemics of cholera and chickenpox, affected the population very often. Tucumán's government invested resources in both preventive and outpatient care programs. The Consejo de Higiene conducted periodic vaccination campaigns, in particular during epidemics, as well as preventive campaigns intended to educate the population on sanitary issues. For example, in the early 1880s, during a chicken pox epidemic, the authorities initiated an aggressive campaign to prevent the spread of the disease. Doctors, nurses, and teachers traveled throughout the affected areas administering vaccines. As a result of subsequent campaigns, the number of vaccinated individuals increased from less than five hundred in 1895 to more than thirty thousand in 1910.[72] To protect the entire population, in 1911 the legislature passed the first mandatory vaccination law. Tucumán's population was also affected by endemic diseases such as malaria. In 1897, 21 percent of deaths were attributed to malaria. In 1901 the disease was still a source for concern, a tourist guidebook even gave advice to prospective visitors in case they experienced intermittent fevers.[73] Assisted by the Oficina Química, the provincial authorities created a program of free distribution of quinine in affected areas that by 1908 was helping almost four thousand individuals. Despite these efforts, malaria remained endemic among Tucumanos, in particular in rural areas, where running water, trash collection, and drainage and sewage systems did not exist.

The authorities paid special attention to improving medical and sanitary facilities. In 1871, Tucumán had only one hospital, in the city of San Miguel. A new facility, the Hospital Mixto opened its doors in 1883, also in the provincial capital. By 1916 it had expanded to four wards with the capacity to treat three hundred patients, as well as surgery rooms, a pharmacy, an autopsy room, a morgue, and rooms for outpatient care. Both men and women were assisted until 1898, when the Hospital San Miguel opened to care for women exclusively. In 1916 that hospital also had four general wards, a maternity and nursery room, six doctors, two midwives, and two assistants. In 1900 a quarantine hospital opened in San Miguel to treat those suffering from tuberculosis, leprosy, and other infectious diseases.

Increases in health expenditures resulted in a gradual improvement of provincial health patterns. Between 1900 and 1910 mortality rates declined from 36 to 25 per thousand, although they still remained higher than the national average of 17.5 per thousand.[74] Throughout the same period, the number of deaths among people with no access to medical assistance also declined, from 78 percent to 65 percent.[75] On the other hand, the province kept experiencing bouts of epidemics and extreme fluctuations in the mortality rate for at least two more decades, especially in sugar areas.[76]

Between 1876 and 1916, Tucumán's authorities increased their tax pressure on the sugar sector, which became the most important source of provincial revenue. At the same time, the government revealed a change in spending priorities and embarked on programs that benefited a larger sector of society, in particular through increases in public expenditures in education and health. However, the effects of new spending policies did not affect the province evenly. Nowhere were the modernizing effects of the sugar industry more apparent than in Capital Department. John Foster Fraser observed of San Miguel in the 1910s, "There is no difficulty in imagining that this is a bit of Madrid instead of being a little-visited town tucked away in the north of Argentina."[77]

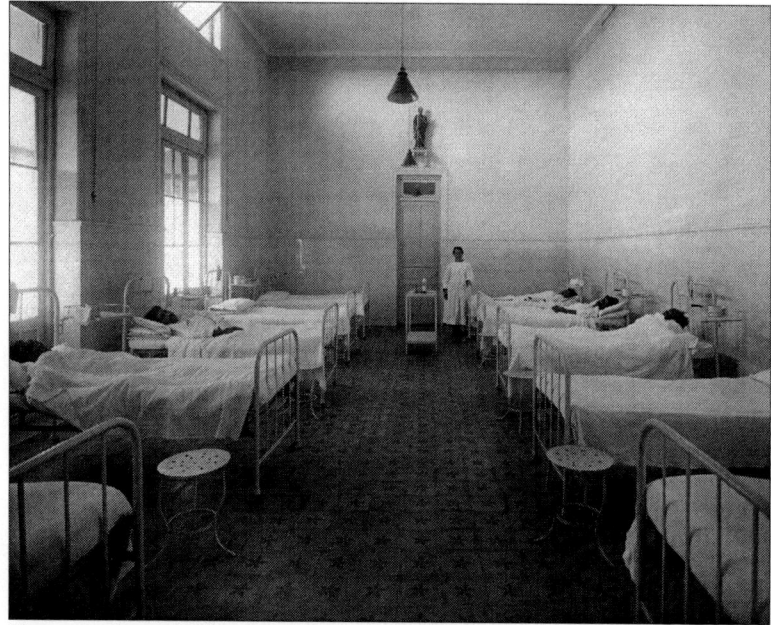

Figure 5.3. Hospital Mixto, 1920. During the early twentieth century, sanitary facilities in Tucumán improved significantly as a result of investments made by the provincial authorities. *(Courtesy of Photographic Department, Archivo General de la Nación, Buenos Aires.)*

San Miguel de Tucumán: The City within the Province

During the last decades of the nineteenth century, San Miguel de Tucumán experienced an impressive transformation and became the most important urban center not only in the province but the Argentine northwest. By providing commercial and administrative services to the expanding sugar industry, the city reinforced its role as Tucumán's political, bureaucratic, financial, and even cultural center. With three railroad lines meeting within city limits, San Miguel consolidated its role as the distribution center and commercial hub of the province, reinforcing patterns that had begun before the 1870s. By 1914, 59,333 inhabitants, more than half the department's population and almost 20 percent of the total provincial population, resided in the 252 square blocks delimited by San Miguel's four boulevards.

Paralleling developments taking place in other cities in Argentina, San Miguel de Tucumán experienced a dramatic urban transformation in the last decades of the nineteenth and early twentieth centuries. The creation of the municipality of San Miguel de Tucumán, in 1868, and the passage of the Ley Orgánica de la Municipalidad, in 1883, provided an institutional framework that facilitated the city's modernization. During the early 1870s the municipal authorities, assisted by the provincial government, undertook the construction and renovation of many buildings, such as the municipal jail, a casino, the government palace, churches, a cemetery, and a new public market. Street and sidewalk conservation occupied an important place in the authorities' agenda as poorly maintained streets and potholes posed a constant danger for pedestrians and carriages alike. Likewise, improved street lighting and night security concerned the municipal authorities, who made investments to upgrade services in the city.[78] Improvements in urban transportation occupied a significant place in the municipal authorities' agenda. By the end of the century, five tram lines served passengers within the city limits and telegraph and telephone lines facilitated communication.[79]

Along with improvements in infrastructure, the city government carried out a number of measures intended to increase its control over public and private hygiene. San Miguel's authorities paid close attention to improving the living conditions of the city's inhabitants by regulating garbage disposal, setting periodic housing inspections, establishing pest control measures, and imposing strict regulations on latrine construction. A municipal report in the early 1880s observed that the accumulation of trash in the streets and the absence of regular collection posed significant health hazards to the population. In 1881 the municipal authorities contracted with a private company for sweeping services in the downtown area. A decade later the city council took direct control of public sanitation and allocated significant funding for the purchase of cleaning equipment.[80] Attention to urban sanitation came together with attempts to protect San Miguel's inhabitants from the Río Salí's periodic floods and their devastating effects on lives and property. Efforts to build defenses to protect the city increased during the 1880s and gradually improved the lives of those most affected, those who resided in the low-lying areas of downtown San Miguel. Besides material destruction, contamination of drinking water was a serious consequence of the periodic flooding.[81] San Miguel's inhabitants drank rainwater collected in cisterns, subterranean water from wells, and water from the Manantial de Marlopa spring, collected and sold by water carts. The 1890s witnessed significant efforts to improve the quality of the city's water supply systems. In January 1899, San Miguel's running-water system opened for public service. The most modern water system in the Argentine northwest, it served twenty thousand people living in 3,141 houses in a ninety-square-block area.[82]

Throughout this period the government devoted important resources to improve the health of San Miguel's population. During the first decade of the twentieth century, municipal spending in health increased much more quickly than it did at the provincial level.[83] In 1913, *El Orden* published an extensive piece highlighting the progress of sanitation in the city of San Miguel. According to the report, government efforts had also affected other areas in the province, although, as a result of the inaction of "rural personnel, not always active or efficient," there was still much to be done for the countryside.[84] For example, the report noted that medical facilities in the rest of the province lacked the modernity attained in San Miguel, giving the rural population no other choice but to travel to the city or resort to unqualified professionals and thus transforming the capital city into the most modern center for health care in the province.[85]

Stone- or wood-paved streets, brick sidewalks, electric lighting, and regular cleaning and night patrolling of streets made visiting San Miguel a pleasant and safe experience. Foreign travelers noted the city's cosmopolitan and modern flair with amenities "with which most of us are acquainted in European cities."[86] As with other former Spanish cities, San Miguel's focal point was the central plaza. Early in the evening Tucumanos could promenade among the orange trees, sit on marble benches to listen to the local orchestra, or just sip a cup of coffee and smoke a cigar in any of the surrounding cafes. Periodic balls and kermises organized by the Sociedad Española or Sociedad Italiana guaranteed the foreign visitor a taste of Europe.[87] Visitors could also enjoy themselves in the parties at the Club Social, El Círculo, or at the *tertulias* held in the luxurious residences of the sugar barons. As the capital of the province, San Miguel also hosted annual religious and patriotic celebrations in which all the city's inhabitants participated, without social distinctions.

A natural consequence of the city's modernization during this period was its emergence as an incredibly active cultural center. Theaters, libraries, and museums transformed San Miguel into a major hub of intellectual activity. Half a dozen theaters offered a variety of performances for a wide range of prices and audiences. Important national and local figures gave frequent lectures in the city's public libraries, which also offered many local and international

Figure 5.4. Government palace. Built during the first decade of the twentieth century, the palace became a symbol of Tucumán's progress. *(Courtesy of Photographic Department, Archivo General de la Nación, Buenos Aires.)*

publications and an amazing collection of almost thirty thousand volumes from all over the world.[88] San Miguel had the largest number of schools and teachers and boasted higher literacy rates than the rest of the province (in 1895, 46 percent versus 27 percent). School attendance was much higher than in the rest of the province, with gradual and progressive increases from 17.9 percent in 1869 to 65 percent in 1914, always exceeding provincial rates and exacerbating the disparities between Capital Department and the rest of the province.

IN 1900, in an article entitled "Tucumán's Evolution: Progress or Deterioration?" the owner of Ingenio La Invernada observed, "From an economic and commercial point of view, the situation is not bad. It would be even better if we were not overwhelmed by national and provincial levies with their extortionist nature, the former truly unconstitutional and the latter extremely abusive."[89] Since the late 1870s, recognizing the potential of the sugar industry as a source of public revenue the government adjusted tax rates periodically. Initially, revisions reflected the rapid changes experienced by the industry. In an attempt to cover budget deficits and raise additional funds, Tucumán's authorities increased demands on the sugar sector through additional ad hoc taxes that became permanent. The year 1893 marks a significant shift in the provincial government's perception of the role of the industry. By the late 1890s the sugar industry had become the most important source of provincial income and Tucumán's financial health was extremely dependent on its growth. Modifications in tax policies increased provincial revenues and the ability to finance public expenditures. Larger allocations of provincial resources in areas such as education and health represented an important innovation in provincial policies. Changes in spending priorities resulted from carefully considered decisions that had the effect of partially redistributing the benefits of the sugar boom among the broader provincial population. Therefore, the effects of Tucumán's sugar industry trickled down to local society by reason of specific governmental policies. However, the sugar boom did not affect the province evenly. Between 1876 and 1916 San Miguel consolidated its role as the province's political, bureaucratic, financial, and cultural center, and while the city shared the same comforts as its counterparts in the littoral, the rest of the province lagged behind. In any case, revenues from sugar allowed Tucumán to partake in Argentina's nineteenth-century transformation, albeit in its own terms—that is, by encouraging the development of a high-return commercial crop that supplied almost exclusively the demands of the domestic market and grew due to the implementation of protective policies at the national level.

Conclusion

The World That Sugar Created

IN 1916, San Miguel de Tucumán hosted the centennial celebration of Argentina's independence. Thousands of visitors attended the nearly month long festivities and were surprised to find in the capital city of Argentina's tiniest province the same amenities found in many other major cities in the world. Within San Miguel's city limits, and for a modest ten-cent fare, steam or electric tramways provided transportation to any point in the city. For those used to more luxurious vehicles, a phone call guaranteed a private five-peso tour of San Miguel or a guided visit to the province's first sugar mill. But the province had more to offer its guests than modern amenities. A three-hour motor car trip took one to sugar areas where, as Harry Franck commented, "some sixty immense *engenios* [*sic*] grind incessantly during the rather short but exceedingly busy season. . . . Tucumán province is a hive of activity."[1] The centennial gave the City of Sugar an opportunity to celebrate its accomplishments. For the provincial authorities, the sugar industry had become both instrument and symbol of progress. In four decades Argentina had consolidated its position in the international market as a producer of foodstuffs, while Tucumán emerged as the country's main sugar producer. As the most dynamic sector in Tucumán's economy, the sugar industry unleashed an intense process that produced profound and long-lasting consequences in Tucumán's economy and society.

Sixty years earlier, few Argentines could have imagined such developments. During the 1850s Buenos Aires and the Argentine Confederation coexisted as two competing political forces. While President Urquiza struggled to foster the confederation's economic growth, the coastal city maintained control over customs revenues and enjoyed a more prosperous economy than the rest of the country. In any case, in those days Tucumán enjoyed a diversified and dynamic economy. The province's population made for a strong local market that was complemented by active exchange with neighboring provinces and foreign countries. Patterns of trade during this period revealed the survival of colonial networks but also the intensification of a shift toward the Atlantic that, having started many decades earlier, achieved supremacy as a result of the country's unification under one national authority. The battle of Pavón, in 1861, put an end to the fight between Buenos Aires and the confederation, thus creating favorable conditions for the consolidation of the national state and a capitalist economy. From Buenos Aires, the authorities combined coercion and compromise to consolidate their position at the national level. Bartolomé Mitre and Domingo Faustino Sarmiento quelled rebellious foci in the northwestern and western regions of Argentina, while Nicolás Avellaneda established contacts with provincial elites through a national alliance that brought him to the presidency in 1874.[2] The Liga de Gobernadores enabled Avellaneda, and later Julio Roca, to consolidate an interprovincial coalition that strengthened the nascent state. Through patronage, the authorities in Buenos Aires built links with provincial governors and increased the power of the national state at the expense of local political autonomy. The federalization of Buenos Aires, in 1880, sealed the alliance by creating a new balance in the country in which provincial political networks acquired previously unknown preeminence on the national scene.

After asserting effective political control over the country, Argentina's national authorities became strongly committed to economic growth. In the 1860s sheep farming forced cattle ranching into peripheral areas. As the first export boom of the country, wool not only generated significant revenue but also strengthened Argentina's position in the international economy as a producer of raw materials. In a few decades, exports of beef and grain replaced wool and transformed Argentina into the breadbasket of the world. The pampas's comparative advantage in these products placed the area at the forefront of these economic changes. Tens of thousands of hectares of virgin lands were placed into production, immigrants settled in urban and rural areas, British companies built railroads that connected the port with the pampas, and foreign investment expanded dramatically. It soon became clear to the national government that failure to integrate other regions into Argentina's economic bonanza jeopardized the future of the national political coalition. Sugar, a cash crop that was gradually increasing its participation in Tucumán's economy, offered a possible point of convergence between national and provincial projects that did not entail excessive political risks or an unbearable financial burden. As Donna Guy has pointed out, "The encouragement of certain regional industries was seen as the most successful way to maintain peace, facilitate the economic integration of the nation and bolster the interior provinces against undue economic domination by Buenos Aires."[3]

The promotion of the sugar industry neither interfered with nor threatened the export model and took place at a time when the Argentine economy was strong enough to tolerate it. It hastened the industry's development and offered important political dividends by guaranteeing Tucumán's elites' continuing support of and participation in the national coalition. However, the growth of the industry did not respond exclusively to coincidental political interests between provincial and national elites.[4] Sugar demand rose as a result of changes in consumption patterns stimulated by demographic growth and higher incomes in Buenos Aires and the littoral. The sugar boom in Tucumán was part and consequence of a larger process of expansion of a national capitalist economy and the consolidation of the national market.

The national authorities embarked on a program of active promotion and protection of the sugar industry. The arrival of the Central Norte railroad in 1876 marked a significant turning point in active state intervention. A state-funded project, the line unleashed an intense process that altered Tucumán's economy profoundly. Improved, faster, and cheaper transportation with coastal areas facilitated communications between sugar producers and consumer markets, thus stimulating the demand for sugar. Railroad expansion made for a continuous reduction in the cost of shipment, thus accelerating the incorporation of modern sugar-processing technology.[5] The first line paved the way for the development of a railroad network that catered exclusively to the interests of the industry; as a result the development of alternative economic activities was discouraged. Since the lines radiated outward from San Miguel and served mostly the sugar-producing departments of Tucumán, they consolidated the role of the capital city as commercial hub and administrative center and reinforced a pattern of economic growth that privileged sugar areas over the rest of the province. The railroad revolution facilitated the technological revolution that confronted industrialists with an increasing need for sources of capital. The national state took the lead in the creation of modern banking institutions in response to the financial demands of the nascent industry, although as José Antonio Sánchez Román has demonstrated, the capital market remained fragmented and sugar industrialists still relied for several decades on informal credit mechanisms to finance the expenses involved in technological modernization. Even though Tucumán's sugar supplied the domestic market, its expansion took place at the time of an intensively protected and fluctuating international market. Therefore, sugar industrialists required additional assistance from the authorities to shield the infant industry from foreign competition, and that came in the form of high tariffs and bounties.[6]

In 1895, after decades of relying on imports from Cuba and Brazil, Argentina achieved self-sufficiency in sugar and Tucumán became the country's main producer. The province accounted for 93 percent of Argentina's area cultivated in sugarcane and produced more than 80 percent of all the sugar consumed in the country. That year also witnessed the first crisis of overproduction and inaugurated a new era in Tucumán's sugar economy, characterized by price instability and an imbalance between supply and demand. Confronted with serious problems that threatened the industry's future, Tucumán's industrialists lobbied actively for solutions at the national and provincial levels. In response to those demands, the national authorities shifted from promotion to active protection at the same time that the provincial authorities implemented more drastic measures intended to correct overproduction. Both strategies provided only short relief to the industry since they failed to realize that the main problem lay in a distorted model of growth that had encouraged specialization within a context of uncertain international and domestic markets.

As this study shows, sugar expansion provoked profound changes in Tucumán's economy and society. The impressive growth experienced by the industry produced long-lasting consequences for the provincial economy as sugar specialization replaced Tucumán's diversified productive structure. Sugarcane took over thousands of hectares of land previously planted in cereals and tobacco. Changes in methods of sugar manufacturing took place in conjunction with the division between the industrial and agricultural sectors of production. In order to realize fuller use of the newly acquired modern technology, rather than opting for vertical integration, Tucumán's ingenios took advantage of preexisting patterns of landownership and relied on outside growers who owned small and medium-size plantations for a large share of their raw material. Tucumano farmers, who had previously produced for self-consumption and the local market, adapted successfully to the requirements of the nascent industry and supplied a large share of the raw materials processed by Tucumán's ingenios.

The incorporation of outside sugarcane suppliers had its counterparts in other sugar-producing regions such as Brazil and Cuba. Since colonial times the Bahian sugar economy had depended on outside suppliers, or *lavradores da cana,* for much of the sugarcane processed by Bahian *engenhos.*[7] Lavradores remained an essential part of the Bahian sugar economy throughout the nineteenth century, although the group's composition changed.[8] In Pernambuco, another sugar producing area in Brazil, the situation was somewhat different. During the 1870s and 1880s attempts to create central mills failed as a result of speculation and lack of control over sugarcane supply and prices. Therefore, Pernambuco's sugar producers found it difficult to guarantee a stable supply of raw materials for their *centrales.*[9] The last decade of the century witnessed Pernambuco's return to vertically integrated enterprises, with the new *usina,* "a modern reincarnation of the traditional engenho on a more complicated and far larger scale."[10] Initially, *usineiros* relied on *fornecedores* (outside suppliers) for the provision of the sugarcane, but gradually mill owners purchased plantations and cultivated the lands with wage laborers or tenants under direct management of the mill owner, a pattern of production that had long-lasting consequences for the region.[11]

In Cuba, colonato arrangements emerged in response to the labor needs created by the abolition of slavery. The system, which was devised to attach freedmen to sugar areas, drew instead a majority of Cuban white farmers, as well as Spanish immigrants.[12] In the twentieth century, when vertically integrated ingenios were replaced with large central mills, colonato arrangements acquired a different nature, as the group adopted a more managerial role. Since Cuba's sugar economy had important regional differences, this shift was more apparent in those centrales located in the east and was a result of the adoption of continuous-processing technology and economies of scale.[13] In the island's western areas, centrales relied for the supply of much of their sugarcane on independent colonos.[14] That group consisted of planters who owned the land and, unable to modernize their ingenios, ceased milling their own cane and became suppliers of those ingenios that had successfully made the conversion to centrales.[15] In any case, even though the incorporation of outside suppliers had its counterparts in other sugar-producing regions, what makes Tucumán's case unique is that ingenios resorted to a large and heterogeneous number of outside growers and never depended on a single source of supply to obtain the sugarcane for their mills.

To operate efficiently, Tucumán's sugar industrialists adjusted to the local reality, thus reinforcing rather than altering provincial land tenure patterns. By avoiding vertical integration, ingenios were able to disperse the costs and risks of investment among a larger group. At the same time, this arrangement offered farmers an alternative to move beyond subsistence agriculture by enabling smallholders to gain a foothold in the most modern sector of the provincial economy. During the last decades of the nineteenth century, a large number of farmers responded to new market conditions and adapted land use to the pull of the expanding sugar economy. Rather than being a homogenous group, sugarcane farmers in Tucumán revealed significant disparities in socioeconomic background, size of their holdings, and patterns of land tenure and use. While small farmers maintained their adherence to food staples, revealing a more diversified pattern of cultivation that combined subsistence farming with sugarcane planting, large planters became more specialized and devoted most of their lands to sugarcane. Therefore, in Tucumán, sugar expansion resulted in the consolidation of a socially differentiated planter group and a complex rural society.

In the same way, in other sugar economies the group of sugarcane planters was socially heterogeneous. During colonial times, Bahian sugarcane farmers represented a farmer elite, or "proto-planters," an adjunct to the engenho owners' group "united by interest and dependence on the international market," who aspired to become engenho owners.[16] In the early nineteenth century the social status of lavradores changed from that of protoplanters, as the group "came to form one of the most thoroughly mixed social groups in Northeastern Brazil," and included small farmers, tenants-at-will, and lavradores da cana.[17] Similarly, in Cuba and Puerto Rico the term *colonos* implied "a multiplicity of social layers. . . . A large farmer operating thousands of acres of land with wage labor and a small farmer working his cane lands only with family labor."[18] The arrival of American investments in the early twentieth century contributed to the increasing internal differentiation of the group. As in Tucumán, the heterogeneous nature of Cuban colonos precluded the consolidation of a group's identity or a rural middle class in Cuba.[19]

Small, medium, and large landholders became essential components in the development of Tucumán's sugar economy. Therefore, in Tucumán the penetration of capitalist relations of production did not result in massive land dispossession, as in other sugar economies, such as the vertically integrated sugar enterprises of Peru and Mexico. Northern Peru is a prototypical example of land concentration by mills, as capital-intensive plantations expanded their landholdings at the expense of smallholders, thus giving rise to the modern corporate sugar plantation.[20] Control over water supplies appears to be one main reason for the consolidation of large properties as well as a main source of conflict between hacendados and small and middle landholders. Similarly, sugar haciendas in the Mexican state of Morelos expanded the area under cultivation during the second half of the nineteenth century at the expense of smallholders and tenants.[21] By the end of the century, half the territory in Morelos belonged to seventeen estate owners.[22] In this state, land concentration not only gave sugar producers full control over water and land resources but also became a mechanism to meet the intensive labor demands of the sugar industry.[23]

In stark contrast, Tucumán's farmers' access to land limited the pool of local workers available to fulfill the labor demands of the sugar industry, especially during the harvest season. Since few foreigners chose to settle in the province, planters and industrialists resorted to workers from neighboring provinces to meet the industry's increasing labor demands. A body of legislation systematized mechanisms of control and provided the legal framework needed to sustain the diverse strategies developed by sugar producers to fulfill their labor needs. Organized recruitment mechanisms ensured the availability of workers, whereas material incentives combined with coercion guaranteed their discipline and stability in sugar areas. The need to guarantee a stable and disciplined labor force was not exclusive to Tucumán. In Peru sugar producers resorted to a wide array of strategies ranging from the quasi slavery of Chinese coolies to the labor contracting of highland natives to guarantee laborers for the expanding sugar economy. After the coolie traffic ended, in 1874, sugar producers were forced to seek new sources of labor. As in Tucumán, Peruvian sugar hacendados resorted to the local population to fulfill the needs of the sugar industry through a form of contract labor known as *enganche*. Attracted by professional contractors (*enganchadores*), workers from the highlands came seasonally to work on coastal sugar plantations. Gradually these workers took up residence on the plantations, thus leading to the emergence of a permanent workforce.[24] A different mechanism was used in Morelos, where sugar hacendados relied on the labor available in the area and combined wage labor with share tenancy or renting arrangements. Tenants obtained access to small plots of land and compensated the landowners with shares of their crops and by working a few days a week for the sugar plantation. During the peak season, sugar haciendas relied on additional seasonal workers, who received wages and housing.[25] A rather different situation was the one found in Pernambuco. There plantation workers were a disparate lot that ranged from wage and salary earners to nonpropertied farmers, such as sharecroppers. Sharecroppers received a plot of land and were required to grow sugarcane and sell it to the mill. Payment for the plot consisted usually of half the cane produced or the sugar obtained from it. Larger sharecroppers paid lower percentages and enjoyed slightly better conditions.[26]

Throughout Latin America the expansion of sugar production had a profound impact on society. In Tucumán the rhythms of modern factory work invaded the countryside and a modern workforce took shape. The arrival of thousands of men, women, and children changed rural society dramatically as entire self-sufficient communities emerged around the factories and sugarcane fields and evolved as independent living cells. Their internal organization replicated the hierarchies of the ingenio, creating a new social milieu that still persists. At the same time, the peculiar structure of sugar production in Tucumán acted against the consolidation of an organized labor movement, thus limiting the resistance strategies available to sugar workers. As the most dynamic sector in Tucumán's economy, the sugar industry affected more than those groups involved directly in sugar production; its effects trickled down to local society by reason of specific governmental policies. Between 1876 and 1916 the composition of Tucumán's sources of revenue underwent dramatic changes and sugar became the most important source of public income. Periodic revisions in tax policies increased provincial revenues and therefore the government's ability to finance public expenditures. Increased literacy levels and improvements in health indicators revealed that new expenditure patterns had partially redistributed the benefits of sugar among a larger sector of Tucumán society, in particular the capital city, San Miguel de Tucumán. New spending priorities resulted from carefully considered decisions that enabled the provincial state to appropriate resources that were transferred to larger sectors, thus legitimizing its position and reinforcing its presence in society.

Revenues from sugar enabled Tucumán's government to participate in the modernizing movement that was sweeping turn-of-the-century Argentina. The sugar boom altered Tucumán's productive structure, shaped its society in profound new ways, and allowed the province to participate in Argentina's nineteenth-century modernization, although in its own terms—that is, through encouraging the development of a high-return commercial crop that supplied the demands of the domestic market. The sugar industry became an alternative path of growth that, as some scholars have affirmed, did not compete but rather complemented the export model.[27] Nevertheless, this reality had its own inherent limitations, which in turn produced profound and long-lasting effects on Tucumán's economy and society. The sugar industry did not provide sufficient economic multiplier effects to lead to self-sustaining growth, and the government's reliance on sugar revenues did little to foster diversification. Therefore, provincial growth required policies that could ensure a delicate balance between fiscal needs and those of the industry. The creation of taxes that could be transferred to the consumer through increases in domestic sugar prices was the mechanism chosen by the government to achieve that balance. However, high domestic prices in an international market flooded with cheap subsidized sugar were possible only with the implementation of national protection through high tariffs or bounties. The financial health of the province became inextricably linked to the export economy and ultimately to the preservation of favorable policies from the national authorities. In 1916 the inauguration of Hipólito Yrigoyen resulted in a major shift in national politics and ushered in a new era in relations between national and provincial authorities that revealed the inherent limitations of a pattern of growth dependent on protective policies at the national level.

Fifty years after the centennial celebrations, Tucumán's sugar industry faced the most dramatic crisis of its history. On August 22, 1966, federal troops occupied seven ingenios in the province and gave their owners three days to stop milling. A year later, more ingenios closed their doors, the area under cultivation with sugarcane decreased drastically, more than seven thousand independent planters abandoned sugarcane planting, and more than forty thousand workers lost their jobs. The effects on the province were terrifying. Unemployment skyrocketed, bankruptcies and foreclosures filled the courts, and the government faced a significant reduction in its sources of income, clearly revealing the risks involved in excessive specialization and dependency on limited sources of public revenues. Since those days the province has slowly and painfully diversified its agrarian sector. Even though sugarcane remains one of the most important crops in Tucumán, it is likely that those visiting the province during the bicentennial celebrations will find not only ingenios but also soybean fields and lemon groves. Nevertheless, the effects of the industry have left a profound imprint that will likely never disappear from the "City of Sugar."

Appendix

Census Manuscript Schedules, 1869 and 1895

DURING THE PERIOD covered in this book, the national authorities conducted three censuses: 1869, 1895, and 1914. This study has relied extensively on the information of these published censuses. However, published censuses offer only aggregate data, thus limiting the scope of analysis. To overcome these limitations, I have also relied on the census manuscript schedules for 1869 and 1895, as those for 1914 have been lost. The manuscript schedules corresponding to population provide extensive comparative and quantitative data such as age, gender, profession, marital status, ownership, and literacy levels, thus enabling a more thorough analysis of Tucumán Province's socio-occupational structure during the transition from a diversified economy to one specialized in sugar production. From the schedules corresponding to population I have compiled a sample of 20 percent of the population drawn from three of the province's departments: Capital, Cruz Alta, and Trancas. (Cruz Alta was created in 1888 and roughly covered the area classified as rural Capital in the 1869 census.) I used a random sample, the first twenty individuals recorded in each census booklet (libreta), selected to be representative of each department as a whole. For 1869 the sample consists of 8,376 cases for both Capital and Trancas, whereas for 1895 it totals 17,021 individuals including Capital, Cruz Alta, and Trancas.

In order to offer a complete understanding of Tucumán's agrarian structure, I have also relied on the unpublished census manuscript schedules of the Censo económico y social, Sección agricultura, corresponding to the 1895 census. The schedules contain disaggregated data on the total extension of the property, the area under cultivation, tenure arrangement, crops cultivated, and tools owned by each agricultural unit. I have examined the manuscript schedules for the entire province. The number of units surveyed is 10,470.

Notes

Abbreviations

AGN Archivo General de la Nación, Buenos Aires
AHT Archivo Histórico de la Provincia de Tucumán

Introduction: Setting the Stage

1. Harry Franck, *Working North from Patagonia* (New York: Century, 1921), 4.
2. Located east of the Andes, the Cuyo region encompasses the provinces of Mendoza, San Juan, and San Luis.
3. Between 1869 and 1914 Argentina's population increased fourfold.
4. David Rock, "Argentina in 1914: The Pampas, the Interior, Buenos Aires," in *Argentina since Independence,* ed. Leslie Bethell (Cambridge: Cambridge University Press, 1993), 125.
5. Franck, *Working North,* 57.
6. See, for example, Jorge Balán, "Migraciones, mano de obra y formación de un proletariado rural en Tucumán, Argentina, 1870–1914," *Demografía y economía* 10, no. 2 (1976): 201–34; Balán, "Una cuestión regional en la Argentina: Burguesías provinciales y el mercado nacional en el desarrollo agroexportador," *Desarrollo económico* 18, no. 69 (1978): 49–87; María Celia Bravo, "Sector cañero y política en Tucumán, 1895–1930" (PhD diss., Universidad Nacional de Tucumán, 2000); Daniel Campi, "Azúcar y trabajo: Coacción y mercado laboral, 1856–1896" (PhD diss., Universidad Complutense de Madrid, 2002); Marcos Giménez Zapiola, "El interior argentino y el 'desarrollo hacia fuera': El caso de Tucumán," in *El régimen oligárquico: Materiales para el estudio de la realidad argentina hasta 1930,* comp. Giménez (Buenos Aires: Amorrortu Editores, 1975), 72–115; Noemí Girbal de Blacha, "Estado, modernización azucarera y comportamiento empresario en la Argentina (1876–1914)" in *Estudios sobre la historia de la industria azucarera argentina,* ed. Daniel Campi, 2 vols. (Jujuy: Ediciones del Gabinete, 1992), 1:17–59; Daniel Greenberg, "The Dictatorship of the Chimneys: Sugar, Politics and Agrarian Unrest in Tucumán, Argentina 1914–1930" (PhD diss., University of Washington, 1985); Donna Guy, *Argentine Sugar Politics: Tucumán and the Generation of Eighty* (Tempe: Center for Latin American Studies, Arizona State University, 1980); Carlos León, "El desarrollo agrario de Tucumán en el período de transición de la economía de capitalismo

incipiente a la expansión azucarera," *Desarrollo económico* 33, no.

130 (1993): 217–36; Roberto Pucci, *La élite azucarera y la formación del sector cañero en Tucumán (1880–1920)* (Buenos Aires: Publicaciones del Centro Editor de América Latina, 1984); Gustavo Rubinstein, *Los sindicatos azucareros en los orígenes del peronismo tucumano* (Tucumán: Universidad Nacional del Tucumán, 2006); José Antonio Sánchez Román, *La dulce crisis: Estado, empresarios e industria azucarera en Tucumán, Argentina (1853–1914)* (Seville: Diputación de Sevilla, Universidad de Sevilla; Madrid: Consejo Superior de Investigaciones Científicas, Escuela de Estudios Hispano-Americanos, 2005); Daniel Santamaría, *Azúcar y sociedad en el noroeste argentino* (Buenos Aires: Ediciones del Instituto de Desarrollo Económico y Social, 1986).

7. The census manuscript schedules for 1914 have been lost.

8. Guy, *Argentine Sugar.*

9. Luis Alberto Romero, *A History of Argentina in the Twentieth Century,* trans. James Brennan (University Park, Pennsylvania: Pennsylvania State University Press, 2003), 2.

10. Bravo, "Sector cañero"; Greenberg, "Dictatorship of the Chimneys."

11. For the specific case of Tucumán's sugar industry, Donna Guy's *Argentine Sugar* is the only English monograph dealing with the topic. Other landmark studies focusing on the Argentine "interior" are James Brennan, *Labor Wars in Córdoba, 1955–1976: Ideology, Work, and Labor Politics in an Argentine Industrial City* (Cambridge, MA: Harvard University Press, 1994); James Brennan and Ofelia Pianetto, eds., *Region and Nation: Politics, Economy, and Society in Twentieth-Century Argentina* (New York: St. Martin's, 2000); Miron Burgin, *The Economic Aspects of Argentine Federalism, 1820–1852* (Cambridge, MA: Harvard University Press, 1946); Ariel de la Fuente, *Children of Facundo: Caudillo and Gaucho Insurgency during the Argentine State-Formation Process (La Rioja, 1853–1870)* (Durham: Duke University Press, 2000); James Scobie, *Secondary Cities of Argentina: The Social History of Corrientes, Salta, and Mendoza, 1850–1910,* completed and ed. Samuel Baily (Stanford: Stanford University Press, 1988); Mark Szuchman, *Mobility and Integration in Urban Argentina. Córdoba in the Liberal Era* (Austin: University of Texas Press, 1988).

12. This trend is also seen among English-speaking scholars, as indicated by a number of doctoral dissertations dealing with Argentina's provinces that have emerged from American universities in the last decade. See, for example, Oscar Chamosa, "Archetypes of Nationhood: Folk Culture, Sugar Industry, and the Birth of Cultural Nationalism in Argentina, 1895–1945" (PhD diss., University of North Carolina, Chapel Hill, 2003); Alistair Hattingh, "Cuyo and Goliath: The Province of San Juan and the Argentine Federal Government, 1930–1943" (PhD diss., University of California, Santa Barbara, 2003); Mark Healey, "The

Ruins of the New Argentina: Peronism, Architecture, and the Remaking of San Juan after the 1944 Earthquake" (PhD diss., Duke University, 2000); Sofía Martos, "The Balancing Act: Ethnicity, Commerce, and Politics among Syrian and Lebanese Immigrants in Argentina, 1890–1955" (PhD diss., University of California, Los Angeles, 2007); Gustavo Paz, "Province and Nation in Northern Argentina: Peasants, Elite, and the State, Jujuy, 1790–1880" (PhD diss., Emory University, 1999).

Chapter 1: Foundations for Growth

1. Hermann Burmeister, *Descripción de Tucumán* (1858; repr., Buenos Aires: Imprenta y Casa Editora de Coni Hermanos, 1916), 39.

2. Enrique Tandeter, *Coercion and Market: Silver Mining in Colonial Potosí, 1692–1826,* trans. Richard Warren (Albuquerque: University of New Mexico Press, 1993).

3. Upper Peru, modern territory of Bolivia, received a significant influx of population during this period. Besides *mitayos* (indigenous people forced to perform rotational work in the mines), the area attracted permanent workers, such as Basques, who settled near the mining areas or on the outskirts of the city. Spanish officials lived in the downtown areas of Potosí. Jonathan C. Brown, *A Socioeconomic History of Argentina, 1776–1860* (Cambridge: Cambridge University Press, 1979), 10–11.

4. According to Carlos Sempat Assadourián the "Peruvian space," an economic area characterized by complex links that connected centers of population from Lima to Buenos Aires, emerged as a result of the mining industry's increasing demands for goods. This vast area extended as far as Ecuador, Paraguay, Argentina, and Chile; each subregion specialized in the production of specific goods to supply the demand of the two growth poles, in Lima and Potosí. Recent studies have demonstrated the survival of this vast network of interregional trade throughout the nineteenth century. Erick D. Langer and Viviana Conti have identified two phases in the development of economic trading relationships in the central Andean region. The first lasted until 1890 and was characterized by the circulation of Bolivian silver throughout the region and the participation of indigenous peasants in the annual fairs reproducing patterns of colonial trade, although on a smaller scale. The second phase, during which railroads connected regions with both the Atlantic and the Pacific, eroded colonial patterns of trade and resulted in the final consolidation of national economies. Assadourián, *El sistema de la economía colonial: Mercado interno, regiones y espacio económico* (Lima: Instituto de Estudios Peruanos, 1982), 1–25; Langer and Conti, "Circuitos comerciales y cambio económico en los Andes centromeridionales (1830–1930),"

Desarrollo económico 31, no. 121 (1991): 91–111; Conti, "Articulación económica de los Andes centromeridionales, siglo XIX," *Anuario de estudios americanos,* no. 46 (1989): 423–53.

5. These towns supplied provisions and equipment to the mining areas and also contributed to consolidate Lima's political control over the region through the establishment of a line of permanent settlements. Armando Raúl Bazán, *Historia del noroeste argentino* (Buenos Aires: Editorial Plus Ultra, 1986), 18–26.

6. The jurisdiction of San Miguel de Tucumán became the province of Tucumán after independence.

7. In order to take advantage of new trading opportunities, many vecinos had established themselves in small and precarious huts in La Toma even before the authorities approved the relocation of the city.

8. Concolorcorvo, *El Lazarillo: A Guide for Inexperienced Travelers between Buenos Aires and Lima, 1773,* trans. Walter D. Kline (Bloomington: Indiana University Press, 1965), 108.

9. Horacio William Bliss, *Del virreinato a Rosas: Ensayo de historia económica argentina: 1776–1829* (Tucumán: Editorial Richardet, 1958).

10. In 1622 the Spanish authorities established the Aduana Seca in Córdoba, which consisted of a tariff line intended to increase the crown's control and revenues over its dominions by preventing contraband between Potosí and Buenos Aires. The measure persisted for more than a century, although the line was moved to Jujuy in 1696. David Rock, *Argentina, 1516–1987: From Spanish Colonization to Alfonsín* (Berkeley: University of California Press, 1987), 28.

11. Gabriela Tío Vallejo, *Antiguo régimen y liberalismo: Tucumán, 1770–1830* (San Miguel de Tucumán: Facultad de Filosofía y Letras, Universidad Nacional de Tucumán, 2001), 40.

12. Klaus Müller-Bergh, "Comercio interno y economía regional en Hispanoamérica colonial: Aproximación cuantitativa a la historia económica de San Miguel de Tucumán, 1784–1809," *Jahrbuch für Geschichte von Staat, Wirtschaft und Gesellschaft Lateinamerikas,* no. 24 (1987): 265–334.

13. Tulio Halperín-Donghi, *Politics, Economics, and Society in Argentina in the Revolutionary Period* (Cambridge: Cambridge University Press, 1975), 38.

14. After the wars of independence were over, the Argentine northwest gradually reestablished colonial trading relations with Bolivia, although on a much smaller scale. Erick Langer, "Espacios coloniales y economías nacionales: Bolivia y el norte argentino (1810–1930)," *Siglo XIX* 2, no. 4 (1987): 135–60.

15. The province of Tucumán replicated patterns that were taking place at the national level as part of the consolidation of the national state. After the promulgation of the 1853 national constitution and the reincorporation of Buenos Aires into the Argentine Confederation, the national authorities became committed to

institutional modernization as a means to raise the effectiveness of the state apparatus as well as to promote rapid economic growth. There is a vast literature on state formation in Argentina; for some studies on the topic, see Jeremy Adelman, *Republic of Capital: Buenos Aires and the Legal Transformation of the Atlantic World* (Stanford: Stanford University Press, 1999); Natalio Botana, *El orden conservador: La política argentina entre 1880 y 1916* (Buenos Aires: Editorial Sudamericana, 1977); Oscar Cornblit, Ezequiel Gallo, and Alfredo O'Connell, "La generación del 80 y su proyecto: Antecedentes y consecuencias," *Desarrollo económico* 1, no. 4 (1962): 5–45; Ezequiel Gallo and Roberto Cortés Conde, *Argentina: La república conservadora* (Buenos Aires: Editorial Paidós, 1972); Tulio Halperín-Donghi, *Una nación para el desierto argentino* (Buenos Aires: Centro Editor de América Latina, 1982); Colin Lewis, "The Political Economy of State-Making: The Argentine, 1852–1955," in *Studies in the Formation of the Nation-State in Latin America,* ed. James Dunkerley (London: Institute of Latin American Studies, 2002), 169–81; Oscar Oszlak, *La formación del estado argentino* (Buenos Aires: Editorial de Belgrano, 1982); David Rock, *State Building and Political Movements in Argentina, 1860–1916* (Stanford: Stanford University Press, 2002); Hilda Sábato, *The Many and the Few: Political Participation in Republican Buenos Aires* (Stanford: Stanford University Press, 2001); James Scobie, *Argentina: A City and a Nation,* 2nd ed. (New York: Oxford University Press, 1971).

16. During their formative period, states create new mechanisms to impose their authority, increase revenues, and regulate social relations. In this sense the establishment of systems of collection not only guarantees the economic survival of the state but also legitimates its power and consolidates conditions for economic expansion. Oszlak, *Formación,* 30–32.

17. In his 1878 study, Alfredo Bousquet identified two periods in the history of the province's tax system. During the first, between 1820 and 1853, Tucumán obtained most of its revenues from tithes, customs duties, and forced loans from local citizens. The second period, from 1853 to 1878, was characterized by significant financial reforms that mirrored changes at the national level. The most important changes were the abolition of domestic customs and the tithe, the creation of new taxes, and the improvement of collection mechanisms. Besides the patente and the contribución directa, the province during this period also collected taxes on postage stamps, meat, hides, cattle exports, branding, in addition to sales and municipal taxes. Bousquet, *Estudio sobre el sistema rentístico de la Provincia de Tucumán de 1820 a 1876* (Tucumán: Imprenta La Razón, 1878).

18. Manuel Lizondo Borda, *Historia de Tucumán (siglo XIX)* (Tucumán: Universidad Nacional de Tucumán, 1948), 174.

19. Central to tax payers' cooperation and compliance is the creation of institutions for assessment and collection that rely on the participation of the taxpayers

themselves. Martin Daunton, *Trusting Leviathan: The Politics of Taxation in Britain, 1799–1914* (Cambridge: Cambridge University Press, 2001), 11–13.

20. Paul Groussac complained in 1881 that taxes did not reflect the increase in property values that had taken place as a result of railroad construction and sugar expansion. According to the authors, 1880 levies were based on six-year-old estimates. Groussac, Alfredo Bousquet, Inocencio Liberani, Juan M. Terán, and Javier Frías, *Memoria histórica y descriptiva de la provincia de Tucumán* (Buenos Aires: Imprenta de M. Biedma, 1882), 501.

21. Police Code 1856, sec. 6, arts. 48, 50, 51, 53, 56, 65, 66, 67; Ana María Ostengo de Ahumada, *La legislación laboral en Tucumán: Recopilación ordenada de leyes, decretos y resoluciones sobre derecho del trabajo y seguridad social, 1839–1969*, 3 vols. (Tucumán: Facultad de Derecho y Ciencias Sociales, Instituto de Derecho del Trabajo Juan Bautista Alberdi, Universidad Nacional de Tucumán, 1969), 1:12–16.

22. The use of *papeletas* (certificates of employment) and passports dates back to the colonial period and was not limited to Tucumán. In 1804, Viceroy Rafael de Sobremonte ordered workers to carry a license signed by their employers attesting that they were employed. The document was to be renewed every two months. After independence, both provincial and national governments reinstated the system. In 1815 the Bando Oliden required job certificates and punished those found without an occupation. During the 1820s and 1830s provinces passed legislation authorizing governments to draft into the military those without jobs and required passports for transient workers. In Buenos Aires, Bernardino Rivadavia enacted several vagrancy laws to control the unemployed population. Juan Manuel de Rosas did not implement any significant changes to the legislation, but his regime was characterized by a very effective application of the regulations. Six months after Rosas's defeat, Justo José de Urquiza reinstated passport requirements and police jurisdiction in labor matters. In Buenos Aires the legislature passed thorough labor legislation in 1865. The Rural Code regulated labor relations, rights of property, police duties, and rights and duties of employers and employees.

23. Ostengo de Ahumada, *Legislación laboral*, 1:13.

24. Ignacio Rickart, *Mineral and Other Resources in the Argentine Republic in 1869* (London: Longmans, Green, 1870), 238.

25. Ibid., 234–37.

26. For the purposes of this study, the northwest region encompasses the modern provinces of Jujuy, Salta, Tucumán, Santiago del Estero, La Rioja, and Catamarca.

27. Argentina, Comisión Directiva del Censo, *Primer censo de la República Argentina, verificado en los días 15, 16, y 17 de septiembre de 1869* (Buenos Aires: El Porvenir, 1872), 698.

28. Thomas Hutchinson, *Buenos Ayres and Argentine Gleanings: With Extracts from a Diary of Salado Exploration in 1862 and 1863* (London: Edward Stanford, 1865), 179.

29. Tucumán presents a varied ecosystem with three phytogeographic divisions–*selva tucumana, selva del monte,* and *selva chaqueña*–and two main regions–mountains and plains. Following a north-south direction, the western mountains are irrigated with streams that, united in the lowlands, contribute to the Río Salí located in the east portion of the province. Fertile soils and good irrigation west of the Río Salí sustain a varied agriculture, while the left bank experiences less humidity and requires irrigation. The mountainous region consists of the grand Sierra del Aconquija that reaches an altitude of three thousand meters (ten thousand feet). Exuberant vegetation covers the large and fertile plains located in the central areas of the province. The climate of the province differs according to altitude, although in general the year is divided in two main seasons–a rainy summer between October and March and a dry winter between April and September.

30. At the time of their expulsion, the Jesuit order owned almost four hundred thousand hectares in the area. Ana María Bascary, *Familia y vida cotidiana: Tucumán a fines de la colonia* (Tucumán: Universidad Nacional de Tucumán, 1999), 57–75; Cristina López de Albornoz, *Los dueños de la tierra: Economía, sociedad y poder; Tucumán, 1770–1820* (Tucumán: Facultad de Filosofía y Letras, Universidad Nacional de Tucumán, 2003), 130.

31. Patricia Fernández Murga, "La tierra en Tucumán en la primera mitad del siglo XIX: Propiedad, formas de acceso y de tenencia: El derecho y la realidad: Compraventas y compradores" (master's thesis, Universidad Internacional de La Rábida, 1996).

32. Arsenio Granillo, *Provincia de Tucumán,* Serie de artículos descriptivos y noticiosos (Tucumán: Imprenta de la Razón, 1872).

33. Argentina, *Primer censo,* 506–12.

34. A sample of census manuscripts schedules corresponding to the second national census provides information on property and gives additional information that could be extrapolated to understand proprietary status in 1869. In 1895, only 8 percent of those listed as peones and jornaleros, 36 percent of those listed as labradores, and 54 percent of those listed as agricultores owned land.

35. Argentina, Departamento Nacional de Agricultura, *Informe del Departamento Nacional de Agricultura.* Presentado por Juan Terán (Buenos Aires: Imprenta del Departamento Nacional de Agricultura, 1875).

36. Groussac et al., *Memoria histórica,* 441.

37. Between 1824 and 1832, British traveler Woodbine Parish visited Argentina in a mission that combined public and business goals. In the 1850s, Justo Maeso

translated Parish's account and enriched it with additional information compiled during several years of thorough research. For the province of Tucumán, Maeso used an 1853 official report. Parish, *Buenos Aires y las provincias del Río de la Plata, desde su descubrimiento y conquista por los españoles,* trans. Justo Maeso (1853; repr., Buenos Aires: Librería Hachette, 1958), 637–38.

38. Groussac et al., *Memoria histórica,* 407.

39. In 1853, according to the commission's report, Tucumán's lands produced ten thousand cargas of wheat. By 1880 the total wheat produced amounted to thirty thousand cargas. One carga equals about 160 kilograms. Parish, *Buenos Aires,* 637; Groussac et al., *Memoria histórica,* 411.

40. Before the expansion of Tucumán's milling capacity, the province had to export its grain and import flour from neighboring provinces. Groussac et al., *Memoria histórica,* 548.

41. Tobacco was grown in small family-operated units in other parts of Latin America as well. However, as with coffee and sugar, the crop's patterns of production varied widely, offering a complex reality that deserves particular analysis. For example, in Ambalema, the most important tobacco-growing area in Colombia, the crop's cultivation was carried out by sharecroppers (*aparceros*) and their families in plots of land that were part of large landholdings owned by Bogotá merchants and hacendados. On the other hand, Bahía's productive units were owned by tobacco growers. In this specific case, the family's work was complemented by slave work, although the slave population on tobacco farms never reached that on sugarcane plantations and consisted mainly of Creole slaves rather than Africans. The situation in Cuba was different still, as tobacco plantations consisted of small family-operated units that did not employ slave labor. For more on this topic, see William Paul McGreevey, *An Economic History of Colombia, 1845–1930* (Cambridge: Cambridge University Press, 1971); B. J. Barickman, *A Bahian Counterpoint: Sugar, Tobacco, Cassava, and Slavery in the Recôncavo, 1780–1860* (Stanford: Stanford University Press, 1998); Fernando Ortiz, *Cuban Counterpoint: Tobacco and Sugar* (New York: Knopf, 1947).

42. Alfredo Marbais du Graty, *La confederación argentina,* trans. from the French Sara Elena Bruchez (1858; repr., Buenos Aires: Comisión Nacional de Monumentos y Museos Históricos, 1968), 56–57.

43. Granillo, *Provincia de Tucumán,* 110.

44. Ibid., 103.

45. Groussac et al., *Memoria histórica,* 507.

46. The financial crisis in the aftermath of the Franco-Prussian war provoked a decrease in export revenues and a significant contraction of British investments in Argentina, thus reducing the country's ability to service its foreign debt. To deal with the crisis, the national government cut expenditures, borrowed from

local banks, and withdrew funds from the Banco de la Provincia de Buenos Aires, among other measures. In Tucumán, the crisis affected cereal cultivation, commercial and manufacturing activities, and public and private construction. A significant reduction in demand hit the provincial tanning industry, which experienced a decline in the number of operating tanneries and a decline in the productive capacity of those still operating. Rock, *Argentina,* 147–48; Donna Guy, *Argentine Sugar Politics: Tucumán and the Generation of Eighty* (Tempe: Center for Latin American Studies, Arizona State University, 1980), 12.

47. Groussac et al., *Memoria histórica,* 544.

48. Burmeister, *Descripción de Tucumán,* 51–52.

49. Argentina, Departamento Nacional de Agricultura, *Informe del Departamento de Agricultura.*

50. Cart manufacturing did not disappear but rather increased, albeit in a modified form, after the Central Norte railroad arrived in the province. The late 1870s witnessed a shift to lighter and faster mule-driven barrows. As the Central Norte did not provide service throughout the province, carts were used to carry merchandise and equipment to and from population centers in the interior of the province. Furthermore, carts were also used to transport sugarcane from the fields to the ingenios and sugar from the ingenios to the station. Thus, initially railroad expansion provided a significant boost to the local cart industry.

51. Michael G. Mulhall and Edward T. Mulhall, *Handbook of the River Plate; comprising Buenos Ayres, the Upper Provinces, Banda Oriental, and Paraguay* (Buenos Aires: Standard Printing Office, 1875), 264.

52. Müller-Bergh, "Comercio interno," 265–334.

53. Until the arrival of the railroad, oxcarts provided the only means of transportation for regional trade. Before railroads arrived in the province, travel time varied immensely depending on whether passenger or cargo transportation was used. In 1859 it took Hermann Burmeister nine days to travel from Córdoba to Tucumán and a similar number of days to make it from Buenos Aires to Córdoba. By 1875, according to Edward Mulhall, the 1,300 kilometers separating Buenos Aires and Tucumán were covered in seven days. In the case of cargo, the trip from Tucumán to Buenos Aires could take up to six months, depending on the cargo transported and the size of the convoy. A caravan of fourteen carts needed three hundred oxen, between twenty and twenty-five horses, and around thirty people for the six-month trip. In most cases, weather and unsafe roads acted against the fluidity of communications. Moreover, since it was necessary to make a round trip in order for the transaction to be profitable, sometimes convoys remained idle for several weeks.

54. Studies on the Bolivian economy demonstrate that contacts between northern Argentina and Bolivia survived after independence and remained, although in a more debilitated state, until the 1860s. During the late 1870s, the

intensification of commercial links between northern Argentina and the Atlantic as a result of new railroad lines and changes in Bolivian monetary policies led to the disruption of this trading network. Antonio Mitre, *El monedero de los Andes; Región económica y moneda boliviana en el siglo XIX* (La Paz: Hisbol, 1986); Langer and Conti, "Circuitos comerciales."

55. Marbais du Graty, *Confederación argentina,* 56.

56. Vicente Quesada, *Memorias de un viejo: Escenas de costumbres de la República Argentina* (Buenos Aires: Jacobo Peuser, 1889), 192–93.

57. Marbais du Graty, *Confederación argentina,* 57.

58. Archivo Histórico de la Provincia de Tucumán (hereafter cited as AHT), Sección protocolos, series C, 1862, fols. 224–29.

59. José Antonio Sánchez Román has identified three different credit mechanisms between 1850 and 1879, *habilitaciones* (start-up loans), *letras* (letters of exchange), and credit secured on mortgages. These mechanisms were also present in Buenos Aires during the same period. For a thorough analysis of credit mechanisms in Tucumán, see Sánchez Román, *La dulce crisis: Estado, empresarions e industria azucarera en Tucumán, Argentina (1853–1914)* (Seville: Diputación de Sevilla, Universidad de Sevilla; Madrid: Consejo Superior de Investigaciones Científicas, Escuela de Estudios Hispano-Americanos, 2005), 55–80.

60. Miguel Alfredo Nougués, *Los fundadores, los propulsores, los realizadores de San Pablo* (Buenos Aires: Club de Lectores, 1976). Even though technically the term ingenio encompasses the factory and the lands surrounding it, in Tucumán it was mostly used to refer to the sugar mill.

61. Michael G. Mulhall and Edward T. Mulhall, *The River Plate Hand-book, Guide, Directory and Almanac for 1863, comprising the City and Province of Buenos Ayres, the other Argentina provinces, and Montevideo* (Buenos Aires: Editors of the *Standard,* 1863), 195.

62. Argentina, *Primer censo,* 509–12.

63. Archivo General de la Nación, Buenos Aires (hereafter cited as AGN), Comisión Directiva del Censo, Primer censo de la República Argentina, unpublished census manuscripts, Boletines de población, vols. 441–49, 465.

64. The analysis of census manuscript schedules for the department of Trancas presents a similar high employment rate as 84 percent of the surveyed population over fourteen declared an occupation. However, this department reveals a significantly unbalanced occupational pattern, as 57 percent of the population was employed in the agropastoral sector.

65. Aggregate census results do not include the occupational breakdown by sex. Certain professions are listed using the feminine form of the noun, which clearly indicates women's predominant participation in those activities. Seamstresses, saddle blanket makers, cigar makers, weavers, and wool spinners belong in this group.

However, since the figures may also include some male workers, the aggregate data preclude accurate assessments of female labor before sugar expansion.

66. The department of Trancas revealed a similar pattern, with 78 percent of the women over fourteen declaring an occupation. Of those with an occupation, only 15 percent were employed in the agropastoral sector.

67. Tucumán was not the only province that benefited from female domestic manufacturing. Other provinces in the northwest and Cuyo depended on cottage industries for their livelihood. Donna Guy, "Women, Peonage, and Industrialization: Argentina, 1810–1914," *Latin American Research Review* 16, no. 3 (1981): 65–89.

68. In the specific case of Tucumán, women's participation in the cottage industries was not limited to Capital Department, and this is confirmed by census data. The 1869 national census officers reported that textile manufacturing in Chicligasta Department was an activity exclusively "reserved" for women. The census officers also predicted that the decrease in importance of textile manufacturing would affect female employment in the following decades.

69. Eduardo Quintero, *Ocho días en Tucumán: Apuntes de viaje* (Buenos Aires: Imprenta de M. Biedma, 1877), 10–11.

70. The department of Trancas also revealed a significant number of non-Tucumanos as 18 percent of the population over fourteen years old came from neighboring provinces. In the case of this department, almost 70 percent of the nonlocals were from the province of Salta.

71. Salta and Jujuy followed closely, with 8 percent of their population from other provinces. Argentina, *Primer censo,* 314–15, 464–65, 544–45, 580–81.

72. Quesada, *Memorias,* 209.

73. James Scobie, *Secondary Cities of Argentina: The Social History of Corrientes, Salta, and Mendoza, 1850–1910,* completed and ed. Samuel L. Baily (Stanford: Stanford University Press, 1988), 6–7. Even though Scobie's study focuses on Corrientes, Mendoza, and Salta, San Miguel de Tucumán fits his conceptualization of Argentina's secondary cities.

74. Teodoro Ricci, *Evolución de la ciudad de San Miguel de Tucumán* (Tucumán: Universidad Nacional de Tucumán, 1967).

75. Burmeister, *Descripción de Tucumán,* 42.

76. Granillo, *Provincia de Tucumán,* 60.

77. Alice Houston Luiggi, *65 Valiants* (Gainesville: University of Florida Press, 1965), 89–91.

78. Hutchinson, *Buenos Ayres,* 181.

79. Granillo, *Provincia de Tucumán,* 52.

80. Pompeyo Moneta, *Informe sobre la practicabilidad de la prolongación del Ferrocarril Central Argentino desde Córdoba hasta Jujuy* (Buenos Aires: Tipografía "La Tribuna," 1867), 4.

81. Moneta reported for Tucumán an output value of $1,429,572, for Salta $1,033,620, and for Catamarca $1,158,505. The population figures reported for the provinces were ninety thousand, one hundred thousand, and ninety nine thousand, respectively, which clearly places Tucumán's per capita output above the other two. Moneta's figures on population do not concur with other authors' estimations and it is possible that they are not completely accurate. However, they are used in the three cases in order to maintain a certain uniformity. Ibid., 57–62.

82. When Pompeyo Moneta turned in his final report, the line from Rosario to Córdoba was still under construction. One of the peculiarities of this line was that it was built on an area with strong economic potential but still to be developed, a big difference from the situation of the Ferrocarril del Sud. The system of guarantees offered by the government facilitated this process by attracting investment in the railroad lines.

83. Rickart, *Mineral and Other Resources*, 237.

84. The construction of the Ferrocarril Central Argentino was a difficult task. By the time the line reached Córdoba, in 1870, shareholders were not willing to make additional investments until securing some returns on their initial invested capital. Furthermore, the region extending from Córdoba to Tucumán lacked the same economic potential as the areas served by the Central Argentino or the Ferrocarril del Sud. Colin Lewis, *British Railways in Argentina, 1857–1914: A Case Study of Foreign Investment* (Atlantic Highlands, NJ: Humanities Press, 1983), 30–32.

85. Heraclio Mabragaña, ed., *Los mensajes: Historia del desenvolvimiento de la nación argentina, redactada cronológicamente por sus gobernantes, 1810–1910*, 6 vols. (Buenos Aires: Talleres Gráficos de la Compañía General de Fósforos, 1910), 3:213.

86. The Central Argentino ran between Rosario and Córdoba and the Ferrocarril del Sud extended south of Buenos Aires to the city of Chascomús. In both cases, the authorities awarded the concessions to British investors and guaranteed an annual dividend of 7 percent on their investment as well as plots of land on both sides of the tracks. For traditional studies on the development of the Argentine railroad system, see Horacio Juan Cuccorese, *Historia de los ferrocarriles en la Argentina* (Buenos Aires: Ediciones Macchi, 1984); H. S. Ferns, *Britain and Argentina in the Nineteenth Century* (Oxford: Clarendon Press, 1960); Lewis, *British Railways;* Mario Justo López, *Ferrocarriles, deuda y crisis. Historia de los ferrocarriles en la Argentina de 1887 a 1896* (Buenos Aires: Editorial de Belgrano, 2000); Raúl Scalabrini Ortiz, *Historia de los ferrocarriles argentinos* (Buenos Aires: Editorial Devenir, 1958); Winthrop Wright, *British-Owned Railways in Argentina: Their Effect on Economic Nationalism,*

1854-1948 (Austin: Institute of Latin American Studies, University of Texas Press, 1974).

87. Guy, *Argentine Sugar*, 4.

88. As a result, certain towns achieved new importance as points of convergence where cargo from the littoral was transferred to animal-driven carts for transportation to its final destination. Such was the case of the town of Medinas, about eighty kilometers south of San Miguel; Medinas developed into a commercial focal point in the area. Its importance increased even more with the emergence of big ingenios, such as La Trinidad in 1877, San Felipe los Vegas and Azucarera Argentina in 1882, Providencia in 1883, and Santa Bárbara in 1884. Around 1871, Arsenio Granillo described Medinas as small but "pretty." Fourteen years later, the Mulhalls' handbook depicted it as a "thriving" place with twelve hundred inhabitants, its own church, school, and brisk trade. The importance of Medinas was directly related to the fact that the Central Norte's rails covered only the eastern part of the province, leaving the western areas completely unattended. Granillo, *Provincia de Tucumán*, 64, Michael G. Mulhall and Edward T. Mulhall, *Handbook of the River Plate, comprising the Argentine Republic, Uruguay and Paraguay, with six maps*, 5th ed. (London: Trübner, 1885), 198. Tulio Santiago Otonello, "El ferrocarril y su influencia en el desarrollo y posterior decaimiento de la Villa de Medinas," in *Ensayos sobre la ciudad*, ed. Alba Omil (Tucumán: Ediciones del Rectorado, Universidad Nacional de Tucumán, 1995), 40-67.

89. The Argentine railroad network had three different gauges. The narrow (one meter) gauge was used for the Central Norte in Tucumán and for the Andino in Mendoza. Railroads in the Región Mesopotámica (the Argentine littoral) chose the middle gauge (1.435 meters). Finally, the Ferrocarril del Oeste de Buenos Aires, the Central Argentino, and the Ferrocarril del Sud used the broad gauge (1.676 meters). The estimated cost of construction for the narrow gauge was around £2,500 per kilometer (£4,000 per mile), against the £4,000 per kilometer (£6,400 per mile) for the broad gauge. Winthrop Wright has pointed out that during those years the narrow gauge was considered the "railroad of the future" and that several countries adopted it for their railroad systems. Wright, *British-Owned Railroads*, 2-45.

90. Tucumán's railroads did not escape the privatizing euphoria of the late 1880s. In October 1887, the national congress passed a law authorizing the Central Norte's privatization. In 1889 the line was sold to the Central Córdoba Railroad Co., a British firm created in 1887. Ten years later, the same company purchased the Noroeste Argentino, thus monopolizing transportation on sugar areas located in western Tucumán, south of San Miguel. The government maintained control over the section of the Central Norte between Tucumán and Salta. López, *Ferrocarriles, deuda*, 187.

91. *La Nación* (Buenos Aires), October 18, 1892, 2.

92. According to national statistics, Tucumán ranked sixth in the country in kilometers of track. Argentina, Comisión Directiva del Censo, *Segundo censo de la República Argentina, levantado el 10 de mayo de 1895, 3* vols. (Buenos Aires: Taller Tipográfico de la Penitenciaría Nacional, 1898), 2:469.

93. Studies on this topic emphasize the role that railroads played in the expansion of the sugar industry in Tucumán. In a recent and well-documented study, José Antonio Sánchez Román challenges this traditional interpretation and argues that modern banking institutions and protective tariffs played a more important role in Tucumán's sugar expansion. See Sánchez Román, *Dulce crisis*.

94. Argentina, Congreso Nacional, Cámara de Diputados, Comisión de Agricultura y Colonización, *Investigación parlamentaria sobre agricultura, ganadería, industrias derivadas y colonización: Ordenada por la Honorable Cámara de Diputados en resolución de 19 de junio de 1896.* Anexo G. Tucumán y Santiago del Estero por Antonio M. Correa. Rev. and expanded Emilio Lahitte (Buenos Aires: Tipografía de la Penitenciaría Nacional, 1898), 41.

95. Transportation improvements resulted in significant expansion in the area under cultivation in other sugar-producing regions in Latin America as well. However, the development of a railroad system in each region followed different paths. For example, in Morelos railroad construction was undertaken by a group of estate owners through a society that in 1881 inaugurated its first line. In Pernambuco railroads were financed by the state government as a means to help out the sugar industry, which was undergoing a profound crisis. Scholars agree that in Cuba the construction of railroads on the east side of the island resulted in the unprecedented growth experienced by the industry at the turn of the century. However, there is disagreement on the consequences of railroad lines for the Cuban economy and society. In his traditional study on Cuban sugar, Ramiro Guerra y Sánchez argues that railroads encouraged the formation of latifundia and the disappearance of the independent colono. Alan Dye's analysis of the Cuban sugar industry contends that track construction should be understood in the context of the adoption of continuous processing technologies, which created additional demands for sugarcane. Roberto Melville, *Crecimiento y rebelión: El desarrollo económico de las haciendas azucareras en Morelos, 1880–1910* (Mexico City: Centro de Investigaciones del Desarrollo Rural, 1979); Peter Eisenberg, *The Sugar Industry in Pernambuco: Modernization without Change, 1840–1910* (Berkeley: University of California Press, 1974); Ramiro Guerra y Sánchez, *Sugar and Society in the Caribbean: An Economic History of Cuban Agriculture* (New Haven: Yale University Press, 1964); Alan Dye, *Cuban Sugar in the Age of Mass Production: Technology and the Economics*

of the Sugar Central, 1899–1929 (Stanford: Stanford University Press, 1998); Oscar Zanetti Lecuona and Alejandro García, *Sugar and Railroads: A Cuban History, 1837–1959* (Chapel Hill: University of North Carolina Press, 1998).

96. Jules Huret, *De Buenos Aires al Gran Chaco*, 2 vols. (1900; repr., Buenos Aires: Hyspamérica, 1988), 1:203–4.

97. Besides assisting the nascent industry, Argentina's first "crisis of development" brought to the forefront debates on the importance of protectionism and economic diversification for the national economy. Vicente Fidel López and Carlos Pellegrini, among others, favored different degrees of protection to foster infant industries, promote regional development, and eliminate the country's excessive dependence on a limited number of exports. The crisis opened a breach in the strong orthodox free-trade policies of many Argentine leaders and sanctioned a protectionist discourse that would be used by sugar interests during the following decades. José Carlos Chiaramonte, *Nacionalismo y liberalismo económicos en Argentina, 1860–1880* (Buenos Aires: Solar/Hachette, 1971), 121–45.

98. In Argentina duties were expressed in either ad valorem or specific terms. While in the latter case the duty was a fixed sum paid by the importer, in the former duties consisted of a percentage applied to an estimated unit value (*aforo*) established by the government on each imported good. In 1877 imported sugars paid 25 percent ad valorem duty. In 1883 sugar duty was changed to a specific duty: five cents per kilogram. This change was part of an overall tariff revision that affected other goods as well. The revised duty amounted to the equivalent of 25 percent and 36 percent ad valorem duties for refined and unrefined sugar, respectively. Since Tucumán produced only unrefined sugar, the revision increased protection for the province's sugar and encouraged local sugar manufacturing; by maintaining lower duties for imported refined sugars, it also maximized tariff revenue. In 1885 a new tariff revision increased duties one more time. The new duty for refined and unrefined sugars was raised to seven cents, which, based on the 1885 aforo established by the government for refined and unrefined sugars, represented equivalent ad valorem rates of 39 percent and 52 percent, respectively. Revisions maintained a higher level of protection for unrefined over refined sugars, thus preserving the dual goal of protection and fiscal revenue. Three years later another tariff revision redressed disparate rates between both types of sugar and raised the duties for refined sugars to nine cents per kilo while maintaining the duties for unrefined sugars to seven cents. The revision reduced the gap between both types of sugar in an attempt to protect the interests of the first Argentine refinery, which opened in Rosario in 1889. Over the last years of the 1880s, protection of the industry was clearly taking precedence over fiscal needs.

99. From 1875 to 1891 the valuation of paper money to gold went from 1:1 to 3.75:1.

100. For example, in 1891 a consumer in Argentina paid 1.48 pesos for ten kilograms of sugar, while the same amount cost a British consumer 0.656 pesos. Argentina, *Investigación parlamentaria,* 187.

101. During the last quarter of the nineteenth century, tens of thousands of immigrants, mainly from Spain and Italy, traveled to Argentina. Between 1869 and 1895 the country's population increased from 1.8 to 3.9 million. While in 1869, 12 percent were foreign born, in 1895 almost one-quarter of Argentina's population was of foreign origin. The littoral region concentrated almost two-thirds of the country's population. In Buenos Aires, three out of four adults were foreigners. Immigrants did not provide plantation labor for the nascent sugar industry, but they constituted an important consumption market for sugar, in particular for the refined type, a staple in the diet of Italians and Spaniards.

102. In 1897, after intense sugar lobbying in the congress, a new law established a six-cent production tax per kilo of sugar, along with a twelve-cent bounty for the export of 35 percent of the total national production. Other provisions established special taxes and bounties for stocks from previous crops. Finally, to prevent further price increases, the law granted the national government the power to suspend bounties if the price of sugar in the domestic market exceeded four pesos per ten kilos. The law experienced two adjustments. In 1898, a change provided for a four-cent increase in bounties but reduced the bountied amount to be exported to 25 percent. The second modification, in 1901, exempted from production taxes all sugar exported without bounties.

103. During the late 1870s a new law replaced the old method of sugar classification by color, known as the Dutch standard, with measurement by the polariscope, which measured the purity of sugar. According to international standards, pure refined sugar had 98 degrees of sucrose strength. The new law established a lower standard, 96 degrees, for refined sugars, thus benefiting Rosario's refinery.

104. During the late 1890s most of South America consumed Peruvian and Brazilian sugars. The United States offered small commercial prospects, not only because American markets consumed Hawaiian and Cuban sugars but also because high import duties were imposed on sugar by the Dingley Tariff in 1897. Continental European markets were flooded with subsidized beet sugar from France and Germany. Therefore, only Great Britain, Paraguay, Bolivia, and Uruguay offered possibilities for the Argentine sugar industry, but exports to those markets never reached industrialists' expectations.

105. Since the early 1860s, Caribbean sugar producers had made efforts to limit the excessive protection enjoyed by European beet sugars. Sugar producers

reached several partial agreements in 1861, 1864, 1873, 1877, 1887, and 1898. In 1902, Germany, Austria, Belgium, Spain, France, Great Britain, Italy, the Netherlands, Sweden, and Norway met in Brussels and pledged to abolish all direct and indirect bounties on sugar production. The agreement also established fines for bountied sugar. Moreover, the participating countries agreed to grant special low duties to sugar imports from any of the signatory countries. This agreement affected Argentina's possibility to export bountied sugar, since one kilogram of sugar that had received a sixteen-cent bounty was to be charged an additional duty of twenty-three cents if sold on the British market. Ph. G. Chalmin, "The Important Trends in Sugar Diplomacy before 1914," in *Crisis and Change in the International Sugar Economy 1860–1914,* ed. Bill Albert and Adrian Graves (Norwich, UK: ISC Press, 1984), 9–21.

106. The new law established a fifteen-cent tax per kilogram on 25 percent of the sugar produced, unless it was exported. One important innovation of the bill was a clause authorizing the national authorities to intervene in the market, reducing import duties or increasing the fifteen-cent tax when the price of sugar in the domestic market exceeded three pesos. The authorities applied this clause in 1907, 1910, and 1911.

107. In 1907 the national congress appointed a commission to study tariffs on sugar once again. The report recommended a modification in the duties from nine and seven cents to 80 percent ad valorem, and from that point, progressive annual reductions until 30 percent ad valorem was reached during the sixth year. The law was not approved, but it did reveal a change in the national authorities' attitude toward the industry, a change that became reality in the following decade.

108. *El Orden* (San Miguel de Tucumán), February 5, 1912, 2.

109. Sánchez Román's analysis has uncovered the high levels of protection received by the sugar industry during the period under consideration. According to his estimates, between 1883 and 1913 the ad valorem protection received by the industry averaged 128.18 percent. Sánchez Román, *Dulce crisis,* 110. Capital accumulated during this period was later invested in the sugar business. Marcos Giménez Zapiola, "El interior argentino y el 'desarrollo hacia afuera': El caso de Tucumán," in *El régimen oligárquico. Materiales para el estudio de la realidad argentina hasta 1930,* comp. Giménez (Buenos Aires: Amorrortu Editores, 1975), 86.

Chapter 2: The Sugar Industry and Tucumán's Economy

1. Harry Franck, *Working North from Patagonia* (New York: Century, 1921), 58.

2. In 1895, according to provincial tax records, the area cultivated with cane amounted to 40,606 hectares. Tax evasion explains the discrepancy between

census data and tax records. Since the census had no taxing purposes, land-owners' declarations were more accurate than those provided for the tax rosters. Ramón Cordeiro, Carlos Dalmiro Viale, Horacio Sánchez Loria, and Ernesto del Moral, eds., *Compilación ordenada de leyes, decretos y mensajes del período constitucional de la Provincia de Tucumán que comienza en el año 1852*, 33 vols. (Tucumán: Prebisch y Violeto, 1915–19), 18:106.

3. Nicholas Cushner, *Jesuit Ranches and the Agrarian Development of Colonial Argentina, 1650–1767* (Albany: State University of New York Press, 1983).

4. Emilio Schleh, *La industria azucarera en su primer centenario, 1821–1921* (Buenos Aires: Ferrari Hermanos, 1921), 65.

5. According to Paulino Rodríguez Marquina, sugar production was already a profitable investment in 1845, although few planters were financially ready to make large investments in modern technology. Tucumán, *Anuario estadístico de la Provincia de Tucumán*, published under the direction of Paulino Rodríguez Marquina, 20 vols. (Tucumán: Tipografía y Encuadernación La Razón, 1895), 1:496–97.

6. Benefiting from the technological advances that had been made in the beet sugar industry, the sugarcane industry experienced important technological innovations in the nineteenth century. See Noël Deerr, *The History of Sugar*, 2 vols. (London: Chapman and Hall, 1949–50); J. H. Galloway, *The Sugar Cane Industry: An Historical Geography from Its Origins to 1914* (Cambridge: Cambridge University Press, 1989); Hedrick Prinsen-Geerligs, *The World's Cane Sugar Industry, Past and Present* (Manchester: Norman Rodger, 1912).

7. Paul Groussac, Alfredo Bousquet, Inocencio Liberani, Juan M. Terán, and Javier Frías, *Memoria histórica y descriptiva de la provincia de Tucumán* (Buenos Aires: Imprenta de M. Biedma, 1882), 524.

8. Ignacio Rickart, *Mineral and Other Resources in the Argentine Republic in 1869* (London: Longmans, Green, 1870), 231, 233.

9. Arsenio Granillo, *Provincia de Tucumán*, Serie de artículos descriptivos y noticiosos (Tucumán: Imprenta de la Razón, 1872), 97–101.

10. Schleh, *Industria azucarera*, 67.

11. Granillo, *Provincia de Tucumán*, 97–101. In those years, the median size for an ingenio was twelve cuadras. One cuadra equals 2.066 hectares.

12. Woodbine Parish, *Buenos Aires y las provincias del Río de la Plata, desde su descubrimiento y conquista por los españoles*, trans. Justo Maeso (1853; repr., Buenos Aires: Librería Hachette, 1958), 637–38.

13. José Antonio Sánchez Román, *La dulce crisis: Estado, empresarions e industria azucarera en Tucumán, Argentina (1853–1914)* (Seville: Diputación de Sevilla, Universidad de Sevilla; Madrid: Consejo Superior de Investigaciones Científicas, Escuela de Estudios Hispano-Americanos, 2005), 40.

14. AHT, Sección protocolos, series A, 1874, fols. 364–67.

15. Jorge Sábato has argued that the Argentine economic elite presented a diversified investment portfolio that favored commerce and finances over other economic activities. This investment behavior allowed them to respond with flexibility to changing economic opportunities. Despite high returns in the short term, in the long run this pattern precluded development as it discouraged large investments in key economic sectors. Recently, Roy Hora has refuted this idea by focusing on the pampas's landowners. The author's thorough analysis of probate records uncovered the importance of land in the group's investment portfolio, therefore showing that specialization in rural production, rather than diversification, characterized the investment strategies of this group, in particular until the 1920s. Jorge Sábato, *La clase dominante en la Argentina moderna: Formación y características* (Buenos Aires: Grupo Editor Latinoamericano, 1988); Roy Hora, *Los terratenientes de la pampa argentina: Una historia social y política, 1860–1945* (Argentina: Siglo Veintiuno de Argentina Editores, 2002).

16. Michael G. Mulhall and Edward T. Mulhall, *Handbook of the River Plate, comprising Buenos Ayres, the Upper Provinces, Banda Oriental, and Paraguay* (Buenos Aires: Standard Printing Office, 1875), 263.

17. Brazil produced and exported different types of sugar that varied greatly in quality. The most famous type was the clayed, or white, sugar called Brazil sugar. A lower-quality sugar, Brazilian *muscovado,* had higher molasses content that gave it a brown color. Even though consumers preferred the white variety, both types were exported to Argentina during the nineteenth century.

18. John Foster Fraser, *The Amazing Argentine. A New Land of Enterprise* (London: Cassell, 1914), 254–56.

19. Groussac et al., *Memoria histórica,* 521.

20. Michael G. Mulhall and Edward T. Mulhall, *Handbook of the River Plate, comprising the Argentine Republic, Uruguay, and Paraguay, with six maps,* 5th ed. (London: Trübner, 1885), 522–29.

21. Groussac et al., *Memoria histórica,* 520–21.

22. Eduardo Quintero, *Ocho días en Tucumán: Apuntes de viaje* (Buenos Aires: Imprenta. de M. Biedma, 1877), 28–29.

23. Argentina, Departamento Nacional de Agricultura, *Boletín del Departamento Nacional de Agricultura* (Buenos Aires: Imprenta del Departmento Nacional de Agricultura, 1884), 7:436.

24. Argentina, *Estadística gráfica: Progreso de la República Argentina en la exposición de Chicago* (Buenos Aires: Taller Tipográfico de la Penintenciaría Nacional, 1892), 557.

25. Cámara Azucarera Regional de Tucumán, *Cincuentenario del Centro Azucarero Argentino: Desarrollo de la industria en medio siglo: Trabajo preparado*

por el Gerente-Secretario del Centro Azucarero Argentino, Sr. Emilio Schleh (Buenos Aires: Imprenta Ferrari Hermanos, 1944).

26. AHT, Sección protocolos, series A, 1879, fols. 218–22.

27. Groussac et al., *Memoria histórica,* 532–33.

28. AHT, Sección protocolos, series A, 1881, fols. 395–98.

29. Tucumán's ingenios operated 69 roller mills, 44 diffusers, 177 clarifiers, 57 evaporators, 78 vacuum pans, 468 centrifuges, and 275 boilers powered by steam and hydraulic engines. Argentina, Comisión Directiva del Censo, *Segundo censo Nacional de la República Argentina, levantado el 10 de Mayo de 1895,* 3 vols. (Buenos Aires: Taller Tipográfico de la Penitenciaría Nacional, 1898), 3:342–43.

30. Ibid., 3:349.

31. Groussac et al., *Memoria histórica,* 522.

32. In August 1885, *El Orden* reported the creation of a partnership to construct a refinery in Tucumán. However, the Refinadora Argentina failed to raise the capital needed and never started operation. The same year Guillermo Hill presented another project to open a sugar refinery in Santa Fe. Investors requested fifteen years of tax exemptions and permission to construct a railroad branch to the refinery in exchange for a commitment to have the facilities built in three years. The national authorities failed to provide the guarantees required and the project failed as well. *El Orden* (San Miguel de Tucumán), August 31, 1885, 1; September 9, 1885, 2.

33. Sugar producers Clodomiro Hileret, David Metheven, and Pedro G. Méndez; local politicians Marco Avellaneda and Delfín Gallo; and investors Teodoro de Bary and Federico Portalis joined forces to make the project happen. Túbal C. García, *La industria azucarera y las consecuencias de su protección* (Buenos Aires: Imprenta Mercatali, 1920), 57.

34. Following policies similar to those implemented for British railroads, the congress granted the refinery a 7 percent guarantee for fifteen years. Even though the implementation of the guarantee system followed the pattern of railroad guarantees commonly used in Argentina, Donna Guy's analysis indicates that sugar interests had to exercise much pressure on the congress in order to obtain concessions for the refinery. With annual profits amounting to 10 percent, the refinery never used the government's guarantee. Guy, *Argentine Sugar Politics: Tucumán and the Generation of Eighty* (Tempe: Center for Latin American Studies, Arizona State University, 1980), 53.

35. García, *Industria azucarera,* 58.

36. Cordeiro et al., *Compilación ordenada,* 18:106.

37. The estimate for Capital Department includes Cruz Alta and Tafí departments. In 1888 the authorities divided Capital Department into three separate

departments. Tafí Department was located in the northwest portion of Capital Department, while the southeast portion became Cruz Alta, and the remainder of the original department retained the name Capital.

38. Schleh, *Industria azucarera*, 92–120.

39. *El Orden,* May 2, 1891, 1; May 4, 1892, 1.

40. During the 1920s and 1930s producers reached an agreement and established production quotas to guarantee minimum profits.

41. Marcelo Lagos, "The Organization of Jujuy's Sugar Ingenios in a Regional Context (1870–1940)," in *Region and Nation: Politics, Economy, and Society in Twentieth-Century Argentina,* ed. James Brennan and Ofelia Pianetto (New York: St. Martin's, 2000), 103–29.

42. Schleh, *Industria azucarera,* 112.

43. As a result of immigration, the country's population experienced impressive growth during the last quarter of the nineteenth century and the beginning of the twentieth. In 1869 the country's population totaled 1,737,076. By 1895 the second national census recorded 3,954,911 inhabitants. By 1914, Argentina's population had doubled once again.

44. During the early 1900s, when a large amount of unsold sugar led to another slump in sugar prices, Tucumán's governor, Lucas Córdoba, invited sugar industrialists to propose alternative projects to limit production. A law approved in 1902 stipulated that Tucumán's sugar production for that year should not exceed seventy-one thousand tons. It devised a quota system based on each ingenio's highest monthly output. Each kilogram of sugar produced within the authorized quota would pay the regular half-cent provincial tax, whereas each kilo over the limit would be taxed forty cents. The additional tax would be partially or fully reimbursed to the industrialist, depending on whether sugar was exported with or without the bounty. The law also determined that the amount collected from the additional tax was to be used to indemnify those planters with unsold sugarcane or those who chose not to plant at all. The following year, 1903, the provincial government passed a second law that increased sugar production to eighty-four thousand tons and maintained the same quota system and tax on sugar. The machete laws, as they were known by their detractors, indicate a turning point in government policies. The strategy, which required, for the first time, a sacrifice from sugar producers, was a success. Even though the government abrogated the laws, Tucumán's sugar production shrank and wholesale prices increased from 1.50 to 2.80 pesos by the end of the harvest. Two different interpretations have dominated the debate on the effects of the laws on the agricultural sector. Marcos Giménez Zapiola has emphasized their destructive effects on sugarcane planters. In stark contrast, María Celia Bravo and Roberto Pucci have argued that the laws prevented planters' ruin. Their

interpretations differed in the group of planters benefited since for Bravo the laws benefited only large and middle planters while Pucci does not make any distinction. Giménez Zapiola, "El interior argentino y el 'desarrollo hacia afuera': El caso de Tucumán," in *El régimen oligárquico: Materiales para el estudio de la realidad argentina hasta 1930,* comp. Giménez (Buenos Aires: Amorrortu Editores, 1975), 103; Roberto Pucci, *La élite azucarera y la formación del sector cañero en Tucumán (1880–1920)* (Buenos Aires: Centro Editor de América Latina, 1984); María Celia Bravo, "Las leyes 'machete' y la ruptura del frente azucarero tucumano," in *Estudios sobre la historia de la industria azucarera argentina,* ed. Daniel Campi, 2 vols. (Jujuy: Ediciones del Gabinete, 1992), 1:97–139.

45. Around the same time, Cuba produced almost two million tons of sugar, Morelos, fifty thousand tons, Peru, two hundred thousand tons, and Brazil, three hundred and fifty thousand tons.

46. Sugar firms in Jujuy underwent a similar process during the late nineteenth and early twentieth centuries, although foreign investors in the province acquired a much larger significance than in Tucumán. Lagos, "Jujuy's Sugar Ingenios," 107–8.

47. Changes in firm organization also affected the industrial sector in other parts of Argentina. During the first decade of the twentieth century, big business emerged in Buenos Aires, leading to the development of a dual industrial complex in which small workshops coexisted with big firms. For recent studies on industrialization in Argentina, see Fernando Rocchi, *Chimneys in the Desert: Industrialization in Argentina during the Export Boom Years, 1870–1930* (Stanford: Stanford University Press, 2006); Yovanna Pineda, "The Firm in Early Argentine Industrialization, 1890–1930: A Study of Fifty-five Joint-Stock Companies' Owners, Finance Sources, Productivity, and Profits" (PhD diss., University of California, Los Angeles, 2002).

48. Cámara Azucarera Regional, *Cincuentenario del Centro Azucarero.*

49. Noemí Girbal de Blacha, "Estado, modernización azucarera y comportamiento empresario en la Argentina (1876–1914)," in *Estudios sobre la historia de la industria azucarera argentina,* ed. Daniel Campi (Jujuy: Ediciones del Gabinete, 1992), 1:31.

50. For example, in 1898 the company signed a contract with the Padilla brothers, owners of Ingenio Mercedes. According to the agreement, the ingenio would not mill its sugarcane in order to become exclusive supplier of the CAT for three years. The company made similar arrangements with other ingenios, such as Cruz Alta and Lastenia. *Revista azucarera* (Buenos Aires), November 1898, 341–42; *El Orden,* October 18, 1898, 1.

51. Monthly statistics published by the *Revista azucarera* corroborate that the CAT's participation in the total provincial production oscillated between 20 and 25 percent.

52. Argentina, Comisión Nacional del Censo, *Tercer censo nacional, levantado el 1 de junio de 1914 ordenado por la Ley no. 9108 bajo la presidencia del dr. Roque Saenz Peña, ejecutado durante la presidencia del dr. Victorino de la Plaza*, 10 vols. (Buenos Aires: Talleres gráficos de L. J. Rosso, 1916–19), 5:929.

53. Whereas the *Criolla* sugarcane variety yielded 1,434 kilograms of sugar per hectare, the Java variety was capable of yielding up to 5,100 kilograms per hectare.

54. Ingenios and big plantations conducted it first. Small independent planters did not have the financial resources to undertake the investment. In 1920, about 85 percent of Tucumán's production was from Javanese sugarcane. However while 92 percent of ingenios' lands had already made the switch only 68 percent of independent planters had done so. Among planters, there were differences as well since while 81 percent of planters with plots larger than 10 hectares had switched to the Java variety, only 32 percent of planters with small plots had been able to make the conversion.

55. *El Orden*, November 22, 1884, 1.

56. Franck, *Working North*, 58.

57. Tucumán, *Album de la Provincia de Tucumán* (Buenos Aires: Establecimiento Gráfico Rodriguez Giles, 1917).

58. Groussac et al., *Memoria histórica*, 410.

59. Argentina, *Tercer censo*, 5:929.

60. Tucumán, *Memoria del Ministerio de Hacienda e Instrucción Pública correspondiente al año 1895, presentada a las Honorables Cámaras Legislativas en 1896* (Tucumán: Imprenta La Velocidad, 1897), V.

61. Argentina, *Tercer censo*, 5:929.

62. Approximately 1 percent of the surveyed units did not include tenure arrangement, so they have not been considered for the analysis. AGN, Comisión Directiva del Censo, Segundo censo de la República Argentina: Censo económico y social, unpublished census manuscripts, Sección agricultura, bulletin 27, vol. 3, fols. 46–133.

63. At the national level, 61 percent of the units were worked by their owners. Argentina, Comisión Directiva del Censo, *Segundo censo*, 3:37.

64. Argentina, *Agricultural and Pastoral Census of the Nation: Stock-Breeding and Agriculture in 1908* (Buenos Aires: Argentine Meteorological Office, 1909), 236–37.

65. Argentina, *Tercer censo*, 5:720.

66. The 1895 published census provides more information than the 1869 census on the provincial occupational structure since it lists occupations and workers segregated by sex and origin.

67. Also significant is the incorporation in the 1895 census of a new category, "no occupation." One-third of men and women over fourteen years old were listed in this category.

68. Argentina, Comisión Directiva del Censo, *Primer censo de la República Argentina, verificado en los días 15, 16, y 17 de septiembre* (Buenos Aires: El Porvenir, 1872), 509–12; Argentina, *Segundo censo*, 2:552–55.

69. Argentina, *Segundo censo*, 2:552–55.

70. Rocchi, *Chimneys in the Desert*, 31–32.

71. Census data may not accurately reflect the labor situation of women, due to census takers' biases and instructions. Furthermore, women's jobs tended to be in those areas in which underrepresentation was common. For example, in 1895 census takers received specific instructions to include housewives in the no-occupation category, as families with more than one income were required to report only the highest. Therefore, seamstresses or laundresses who claimed to be housewives or worked part-time were not recognized as workers, even though their activities must have supplemented the family income. Women's own perception of their contribution in the household economy must have also played a role in their responses to the surveyors. In a patriarchal society in which, as Juan Bialet Massé noted, a "woman's mission is to be a mother, to have, raise and educate her children," there is a likelihood that the first response was housewife, thus automatically including those women in the no-occupation category. Another problem was the categories used by the census. In an attempt to modernize and simplify census methodology, the 1895 census reduced the number of occupations from 491 in 1869 to 186. That reduction was based on previous censuses taken in areas with large numbers of male immigrants that did not account for female employment. Therefore, the new occupational categories did not correspond to Tucumán's job market, and that might have decreased census takers' ability to account for Tucumanas' participation in the workforce. A paradigmatic case is the elimination of the categories saddle-blanket maker and wool spinner from the 1895 census. For census categories and instructions, see Argentina, *Segundo censo*, 2:cxl–cxlv.

72. National figures for females in the same category revealed similar results. Ibid., 2:cxc–cxciii.

73. AGN, Comisión Directiva del Censo, Segundo censo de la República Argentina, unpublished census manuscripts, Boletines de población, vols. 1320–31, 1334–38, 1362. This pattern also repeated in other areas in Argentina. See Donna Guy, "Women, Peonage, and Industrialization: Argentina, 1810-1914," *Latin American Research Review* 16, no. 3 (1981): 65–89.

74. However, it is very important to recognize that women's activities in the home were centrally important for the survival of the family. Male workers

depended heavily on the unpaid or undeclared labor of family members who produced goods and services that under other circumstances would have to be purchased.

75. Fraser, *Amazing Argentine*, 255.

76. García, *Industria azucarera*, 111.

Chapter 3: Sugarcane Planters

Sections of this chapter were originally published as part of Patricia Juarez-Dappe, "*Cañeros* and *Colonos:* Cane Planters in Tucumán, 1876–1895," *Journal of Latin American Studies* 38, no. 1 (2006): 123–47.

1. Pierre Denis, *The Argentine Republic, Its Development and Progress*, trans. Joseph McCabe (New York: Scribner's, 1922), 74.

2. The sugar industry in Jujuy was centered in the "ingenio-plantation" complex. As in other areas in Latin America, the need to obtain full control over water resources and to guarantee a stable supply of raw materials resulted in ingenios' acquisition of large holdings. Jujuy's large ingenios not only cultivated and processed their sugarcane but also took over the commercialization of sugar, thus leading to a high degree of capital concentration not found in other sugar areas in Argentina. Marcelo Lagos, "The Organization of Jujuy's Sugar Ingenios in a Regional Context (1870–1940) in *Region and Nation: Politics, Economy, and Society in Twentienth-Century Argentina*, ed. James Brennan and Ofelia Pianetto (New York: St. Martin's, 2000), 103–29.

3. Argentina, Congreso Nacional, Cámara de Diputados, Comisión de Agricultura y Colonización, *Investigación parlamentaria sobre agricultura, ganadería, industrias derivadas y colonización: Ordenada por la Honorable Cámara de Diputados en resolución de 19 de junio de 1896.* Anexo G. Tucumán y Santiago del Estero por Antonio M. Correa. Rev. and expanded Emilio Lahitte (Buenos Aires: Tipografía de la Penitenciaría, 1898), 38.

4. Paul Groussac, Alfredo Bousquet, Inocencio Liberani, Juan M. Terán, and Javier Frías, *Memoria histórica y descriptiva de la provincia de Tucumán* (Buenos Aires: Imprenta de M. Biedma, 1882), 522.

5. The 1870s and 1880s witnessed significant attempts to modernize banking institutions in the province in order to assist the needs of the sugar industry by increasing the availability of funds, extending the duration of loans, and reducing interest rates. Furthermore, besides their role in the promotion of the sugar industry, these institutions facilitated the incorporation of Tucumán into the broader national economy and became important political tools in the hands of the national authorities. For a thorough analysis of credit and Tucumán's financial modernization, see José Antonio Sánchez Román, *La dulce crisis: Estado,*

empresarions e industria azucarera en Tucumán, Argentina (1853–1914) (Seville: Diputación de Sevilla, Universidad de Sevilla; Madrid, Consejo Superior de Investigaciones Científicas, Escuela de Estudios Hispano-Americanos, 2005).

6. Sugarcane experiences significant losses in sucrose content twenty-four hours after being cut, so a well-defined timeline was indispensable to guarantee its quality, as measured by the amount of juice that can be extracted. Despite the existence of specific contractual stipulations on sugarcane quality, industrialists complained periodically about the difficulties in controlling and guaranteeing a crop's quality.

7. Groussac et al., *Memoria histórica,* 400. For a modern study on the costs of sugarcane planting, see Daniel Santamaría, *Azúcar y sociedad en el noroeste argentino* (Buenos Aires: Ediciones del Instituto de Desarrollo Económico y Social, 1986), 43–65.

8. Michael G. Mulhall and Edward T. Mulhall, *Handbook of the River Plate, comprising the Argentine Republic, Uruguay, and Paraguay, with railway map* (London: Kegan Paul, Trench, 1892), 508.

9. Argentina, *Investigación parlamentaria,* 27.

10. The department of Cruz Alta had better soil quality and irrigation systems than in the rest of the province, so not only were planting costs lower but higher sucrose contents resulted in higher prices for its cane.

11. Arsenio Granillo, *Provincia de Tucumán,* Serie de artículos descriptivos y noticiosos (Tucumán: Imprenta de la Razón, 1872), 98–99.

12. Argentina, *Informe del Departamento Nacional de Agricultura.* Presentado por Juan Terán (Buenos Aires: Imprenta del Departamento Nacional de Agricultura, 1875).

13. Argentina, Departamento Nacional de Agricultura, *Boletín Nacional de Agricultura,* 10 vols. (Buenos Aires: Imprenta del Departamento Nacional de Agricultura, 1878–1896, 1883), 7:5.

14. AGN, Comisión Directiva del Censo, Segundo censo de la República Argentina, Censo económico y social, Sección agricultura, unpublished census manuscripts, bulletin 27, vol. 3, fols. 46–133.

15. Emilio Lahitte, *La industria azucarera: Apuntes de actualidad* (Buenos Aires: Imprenta Europea de M. A. Rosas, 1902).

16. Argentina, Comisión Nacional del Censo, *Tercer censo de la República Argentina: Levantado el 1 de junio de 1914* (Buenos Aires: G. Pisce, 1917–19), 5:77, 539, 549.

17. *El Orden* (San Miguel de Tucumán), August 31, 1903, 1.

18. *El Orden,* July 19, 1909, 2.

19. The author of the play, Alberto García Hamilton, was a member of Tucumán's elite. According to *El Orden,* the play was performed on at least two occasions, to raves from the audience. *El Orden,* April 16 1909, 2.

20. *El Orden*, January 14, 1890, 1.

21. *El Orden*, January 7, 1893, 1.

22. Groussac et al., *Memoria histórica*, 522.

23. Granillo, *Provincia de Tucumán*, 99.

24. Herrera was involved in real estate investments, contracts with the government, tax collection, and private lending, such as short-term loans, bails, and long-term loans.

25. AHT, Sección protocolos, series D, 1883, fols. 1406v–8.

26. Ibid., series C, 1893, fols. 346–49.

27. Ibid., series A, 1882, fols. 556–58.

28. Ibid., series A, 1890, fols. 1309–10.

29. Ibid., series A, 1890, fols. 3567–87.

30. Ramón Cordeiro, Carlos Dalmiro Viale, Horacio Sánchez Loria, and Ernesto del Moral, eds., *Compilación ordenada de leyes, decretos y mensajes del período constitucional de la Provincia de Tucumán que comienza en el año 1852*, 33 vols. (Tucumán: Prebisch y Violeto, 1915–19), 14:462.

31. As late as 1895, Tucumán's minister of finance commented on the desperate situation of small and medium planters due to credit shortages. According to the minister, planters had to face increasing interest rates and draconian payment conditions, to the extent that they had to forfeit their property to pay their debts. He recommended an increase in the funds the government provided to the Banco Provincial in order for the institution to assist planters with long-term and low-interest loans. Similar demands were made during the last decade of the nineteenth century by *El Orden*. Tucumán, *Memoria del Ministerio de Hacienda e Instrucción Pública correspondiente al año 1895, presentada a las Honorables Cámaras Legislativas en 1896* (Tucumán: Imprenta de la Razón, 1897), v–vi.

32. AHT, Sección protocolos, series D, 1885, fols. 362–67.

33. Ibid., series D, 1883, fols. 736–39.

34. Ibid., series D, 1882, fols. 368–71.

35. Ibid., series D, 1882, fols. 1173–76.

36. Ibid., series A, 1881, fols. 516–19.

37. Ibid., series A, 1882, fols. 77v–81.

38. Ibid., series A, 1883, fols. 525–28.

39. Ibid., series A, 1882, fols. 249–53.

40. Ibid., series D, 1884, fols. 561v–63.

41. Ibid., series D, 1888, fols. 2051–53.

42. AGN, Comisión Directiva, Segundo censo.

43. Pedro Alurralde, "La Crisis Azucarera," *Anales de la Facultad de Derecho y Ciencias Sociales* 1 (1902): 360–67.

44. AHT, Sección protocolos, series A, 1882, fols. 529–31.

45. Ibid., series A, 1881, fols. 145–50.

46. AGN, Comisión Directiva, Segundo censo.

47. Fifteen units extending over 343 hectares did not include tenure arrangement, so they have not been considered for the analysis. Ibid.

48. AHT, Sección protocolos, series D, 1888, fols. 2671–675.

49. Ibid., series D, 1880, fols. 220–22.

50. AHT, Sección judicial civil, series A, 1885, box 190, file 12.

51. AHT, Sección protocolos, series A, 1887, fols. 1268–70.

52. Ibid., series A, 1885, fols. 645–47.

53. Ibid., series D, 1890, fols. 2076–78.

54. Ibid., series A, 1881, fols. 664–67.

55. Ibid., series D, 1876, fols. 137–40.

56. Ibid., series D, 1885, fols. 805–7. One arroba equals about eleven and a half kilograms.

57. Ibid., series A, 1890, fols. 3088–91.

58. AGN, Comisión Directiva, Segundo censo.

59. Sugar colonias in Tucumán were not comparable to the ones established in Santa Fe, Entre Ríos, and Corrientes. In those areas, European immigrants and their families were granted plots to cultivate cereals, mostly wheat. However, more important, in many of these colonias, colonos eventually gained title to the land. Tucumán's colonias are comparable to those established in eastern Cuba during the process of centralization that took place after the war for independence. Ezequiel Gallo, *La pampa gringa: La colonización agrícola en Santa Fe (1870–1895)* (Buenos Aires: Editorial Sudamericana, 1984); James Scobie, *Revolution on the Pampas: A Social History of Argentine Wheat, 1860–1910* (Austin: University of Texas Press, 1968).

60. *El Orden,* October 9, 1891, 1.

61. Vicente Padilla, *El norte argentino: Tucumán, Salta, Jujuy, Santiago del Estero, Catamarca: Historia política, administrativa, social, comercial e industrial de las provincias: Crónica de la época prehispana hasta nuestros días* (Buenos Aires: Imprenta Ferrari Hermanos, 1922).

62. Argentina, *Investigación parlamentaria,* 38.

63. In 1889, Ingenio Los Ralos obtained only half its sugarcane from colonos. By 1904 all the cane processed in the mill came from its own colonias.

64. AGN, Comisión Directiva, Segundo censo.

65. AHT, Paulino Rodríguez Marquina, "Memoria descriptiva de Tucumán y de la industria azucarera: Su presente, su pasado y porvenir estadístico" (unpublished manuscript, 1889), 192.

66. AHT, Sección judicial civil, series A, 1885, box 212, file 6.

67. *El Orden,* November 1890–February 1891.

68. *El Orden,* February 4, 1893, 1.
69. *El Orden,* January 14, 1893, 1.
70. AHT, Sección protocolos, series A, 1883, fols. 455–59.
71. Ibid., series D, 1884, fols. 448–53.
72. Ibid., series A, 1888, fols. 1921–25.
73. Ibid., series D, 1886, fols. 341–45.
74. Ibid., series D, 1883, fols. 1277–79.
75. Ibid., series D, 1884, fols. 1729–35.
76. Ibid., series D, 1883, fols. 713–17.
77. Annual interest rates higher than 10 percent were quite common, not only in Tucumán but in other regions in Argentina and Latin America as well. For example, in Santa Fe, Gallo argues, rates fluctuated around 12 percent during the 1880s. In Buenos Aires, Jeremy Adelman's analysis confirms that borrowers were paying between 6 and 12 percent annual rates in 1895. In Pernambuco, Peter Eisenberg has found, rates oscillated between 8 and 11 percent during the 1880s. In Cuba, Laird Bergad observes, planters were paying interest rates as high as 1 percent monthly in the 1850s. Gallo, *Pampa gringa,* 240; Adelman, "Agricultural Credit in the Province of Buenos Aires, Argentina, 1890–1914," *Journal of Latin American Studies* 22, no. 1 (1990): 83; Eisenberg, *The Sugar Industry in Pernambuco: Modernization without Change, 1840–1910* (Berkeley: University of California Press, 1974), 64; Bergad, *Cuban Rural Society in the Nineteenth Century: The Social and Economic History of Monoculture in Matanzas* (Princeton: Princeton University Press, 1990), 174.
78. Argentina, *Investigación parlamentaria,* 47.
79. AHT, Sección protocolos, series A, 1883, fols. 456–59.
80. *El Orden,* January 7, 1893, 2.
81. AHT, Sección protocolos, series D, 1884, fols. 1729–34.
82. AHT, Rodríguez Marquina, "Memoria descriptiva de Tucumán," 168–77.
83. AGN, Comisión Directiva, Segundo censo.
84. Although the evidence is only fragmentary, it is still possible to reconstruct planters' lives by piecing together bits of information from census manuscript schedules, newspapers, contracts, testaments, and the valuable photographs at the Archivo General de la Nación in Buenos Aires and included in Manuel Bernárdez's 1904 report of his visit to the province. Bernárdez, *La nación en marcha* (Buenos Aires: Talleres Heliográficos de Ortega y Radaelli, 1904).
85. Argentina, *Investigación parlamentaria,* 49.
86. Bernárdez, *Nación en marcha,* 15.
87. AHT, Sección judicial civil, series A, 1888, box 228, file 23.
88. Ibid., series A, 1887, box 203, file 7.

89. AGN, Comisión Directiva, Segundo censo.

90. Ingenio Esperanza had over two hundred houses surrounding the plantation for its colonos and workers. At Ingenio San Pablo, six hundred houses accommodated six thousand people, including colonos and workers. Tucumán, Exposición Nacional, *Album argentino: Provincia de Tucumán: Su vida, su trabajo, su progreso* (Tucumán: Tip. Lit. la Velocidad, 1910).

91. In Ingenio La Providencia, colonos' houses were bigger and located in the middle of the housing complex; workers lived in smaller apartments surrounding the colonos' living area. Padilla, *Norte Argentino*.

92. Bernárdez, *Nación en marcha*, 34.

93. AHT, Sección judicial civil, series A, box 187, file 8. According to Groussac, a peon's monthly salary at the time of Avila's death was 12 pesos. One fanega equals approximately 1.6 U.S. bushels.

94. Denis, *Argentine Republic*, 76.

95. AHT, Sección protocolos, series C, 1893, fols. 409–11v.

96. *Revista azucarera* (Buenos Aires), September 1, 1894, 201–5.

97. *El Orden*, September 4, 1884, 1.

98. *El Orden*, August 7, 1895, 1.

99. *El Orden*, October 29, 1897, 1.

100. AHT, Sección protocolos, series A, 1890, fols. 3568–587.

101. Ibid., series C, 1893, fols. 409–11v.

102. Ibid., series D, 1890, fols. 1099–1106.

103. Contemporary observers noted that the scarcity of wagons to transport sugarcane was a source of conflict among sugarcane planters and mill owners, in particular during the 1880s.

104. AHT, Sección protocolos, series A, 1890, fols. 3556–60.

105. Ibid., series A, 1888, fols. 1520–22.

106. *El Orden*, August 7, 1895, 1.

107. AHT, Sección protocolos, series A, 1890, fols. 3244–49.

108. Ibid., series D, 1884, fols. 448–53.

109. Interest rates varied depending on whether they came from formal or informal sources as well as on the total amount loaned. Disparities in interest rates were also likely related to a contract's stipulations, such as length and type of arrangement and the situation of the industry at the time of the arrangement. According to Sánchez Román's analysis, between 1880 and 1890, Tucumán's banking rates oscillated between 7 and 9 percent annually. Rates paid in the informal sector showed larger fluctuations, from 10.7 to 16.3 percent. The author also points to the existence of "professional loaners" who charged up to 48 percent annual rates. Sánchez Román, *Dulce crisis*, 159.

110. AHT, Sección protocolos, series A, 1890, fols. 3568–87.

111. Ibid., series D, 1883, fols. 1535v–39v.

112. Alan Dye, *Cuban Sugar in the Age of Mass Production: Technology and the Economics of the Sugar Central, 1899–1929* (Stanford: Stanford University Press, 1998), 197–99.

113. The conflict has been reconstructed using *El Orden* and criminal and civil court records.

114. The real cause of the conflict is unclear, although changes in tax policies might have played a significant role. When the conflict started, the provincial legislature was discussing a bill that provided for additional sugar taxes that, although characterized as extraordinary, affected the final product and not the raw material. The contracts between Medina and his colonos had been signed before the bill's inception. The ten-year arrangement would have had an impact on the ingenio owner's profits. Therefore, by revoking the contracts, Medina could renegotiate new deals that took into account changes in sugar tax policies.

115. *El Orden* gave daily updates on the colonos' situation. Moreover, the paper included editorials discussing the miserable living and working conditions of the farmers and urged the provincial authorities to intervene. *La Opinión,* a paper politically aligned with Medina, reported the mill owner's side of the conflict.

116. Violent events in Santa Fe's agricultural colonies must have convinced the authorities to be receptive to colonos' pleas in order to prevent the spread of similar violence in Tucumán's countryside.

117. It is likely that the entire group settled their disputes along the same lines as San Martín, although lack of evidence prevents a case-by-case analysis.

118. María Celia Bravo has identified the use of roads and the demarcation of property limits as another important source of constant conflict between ingenio owners and planters. According to her analysis, the impressive expansion of the area planted in sugarcane altered the old network of roads in the countryside. Ingenios and planters closed traditional paths, making it extremely difficult to determine rights of way for those in the area. The police became the authority in charge of mediating in those conflicts, thus leading in many cases to favoritism and unfair decisions. Numerous complaints from all those affected by these problems resulted in the approval of the Rural Code in 1897 that reorganized the use rural space in the province. María Celia Bravo, "Sector cañero y política en Tucumán, 1895–1930" (PhD diss., Universidad Nacional de Tucumán, 2000).

119. *El Orden,* August 7, 1895, 1.

120. AHT, Sección judicial civil, series A, 1886, box 196, file 32. The ingenio paid the planter the owed amount right after the case was taken to court.

121. In 1875, in his annual message to the legislature, the governor observed the need to regulate water sources to avoid the intensification of conflicts. Cordeiro et al., *Compilación ordenada,* 6:357.

122. The province of Tucumán is crossed by the Río Salí, which divides the sugar area into two sections. The region located east of the river, where a large number of mills and sugarcane plantations were located, required artificial irrigation since rainfall did not compensate for lack of natural streams.

123. AHT, Sección judicial civil, series A, 1886, box 196, file 32.

124. In his 1883 report on the Río Salí, engineer Mariano Lana y Sarto observed that as a result of unplanned irrigation, the river was losing 10 percent of its volume through evaporation every year. Cordeiro et al., *Compilación ordenada,* 9:82.

125. AHT, Sección protocolos, series D, 1888, fols. 1377-78.

126. AHT, Sección judicial civil, series A, 1893, box 171, file 6.

127. Cordeiro et al., *Compilación ordenada,* 9:79, 119.

128. *El Orden,* May 4, 1896, 1.

129. María Celia Bravo has indicated that the measure intended to protect the small planter, the group most affected by the 1895 crisis. Bravo, "Sector cañero," 25.

130. Antonio Correa mentioned that it was common for one-thousand-kilogram loads of sugarcane to be underweighed, resulting in a final payment equivalent to only five or six hundred kilograms. Argentina, *Investigación parlamentaria,* 47.

131. *El Orden,* June 5, 1885, 1.

132. AHT, Sección judicial del crimen, 1894, box 168, file 6.

133. *El Orden,* October 14, 1897, 2.

134. Juan Bialet Massé, *Informe sobre el estado de las clases obreras argentinas a comienzos del siglo,* 2 vols. (1904; repr., Buenos Aires: Hyspamérica, 1986), 1:229.

135. AHT, Sección judicial del crimen, 1897, box 235, file 24.

136. Ibid., 1897, box 182, file 4.

137. AHT, Sección judicial civil, series A, 1888, box 99, file 12.

138. AHT, Sección judicial del crimen, 1894, box 136, file 3.

139. *El Orden,* July 30, 1895, 1; August 7, 1895, 2; August 12, 1895, 1; August 14, 1895, 1.

140. *El Orden,* May 15, 1885, 1; September 4, 1884, 2.

141. In some instances local politics must have played a role in the press's support for the planter group. This was apparent in *El Orden*'s treatment of the conflict between Abraham Medina and his colonos. Medina, who was referred as "el satanás cojo de los ingenios azucareros," (the limping demon of the sugar mills) and *El Orden* were at opposite ends of the political spectrum. This explains the paper's extensive and detailed coverage of colonos' pleas and grievances as well as its indictment of the abuses committed by the ingenio owner and his people. *El Orden,* July 12, 1894, 1.

142. *El Orden*, February 26, 1893, 1.

143. Argentina, *Investigación parlamentaria*, 231.

144. Tucumán, *Memoria del Ministerio de Hacienda e Instrucción Pública correspondiente al año 1895, presentada a las Honorables Cámaras Legislativas en 1896* (Tucumán: Imprenta La Velocidad, 1897), vi.

145. This situation changed during the twentieth century with the consolidation of a Centro Cañero and new patterns of government involvement clearly illustrated by the Laudo Alvear. In 1928, Argentine president Marcelo T. de Alvear intervened to put an end to the conflict between sugarcane planters and industrialists. Among other important provisions, the Laudo Alvear established new mechanisms to regulate sale contracts and to determine cane prices thus responding directly to sugarcane planters' demands. In the late 1920s the provincial government also protected the interests of sugarcane planters by assisting in the construction of two cooperative ingenios, Ingenio Marapa and Ingenio Nuñorco. For more on the sugarcane planters and politics during the 1920s, see Bravo, "Sector cañero."

Chapter 4: Sugar Labor

1. Harry Franck, *Working North from Patagonia* (New York: Century, 1921), 59.

2. The absence of a stable and disciplined labor force had presented a problem for the authorities and the propertied classes even before sugar's takeoff. Daniel Campi, "Captación forzada de mano de obra y trabajo asalariado en Tucumán, 1856–1896," *Anuario del IEHS*, no. 8 (1993): 49–51.

3. For example, in his 1882 report, Paul Groussac observed that further expansion of sugarcane land was severely limited by labor scarcity. *El Orden* reported often on the negative effects that labor shortages had on the industry and urged the authorities to intervene. Groussac, Alfredo Bousquet, Inocencio Liberani, Juan M. Terán, and Javier Frías, *Memoria histórica y descriptiva de la provincia de Tucumán* (Buenos Aires: Imprenta de M. Biedma, 1882), 539–40.

4. Police Code 1877, sec. 5, art. 52; Ana María Ostengo de Ahumada, *La legislación laboral en Tucumán: Recopilación ordenada de leyes, decretos y resoluciones sobre derecho del trabajo y seguridad social, 1839–1969*, 3 vols. (Tucumán: Facultad de Derecho y Ciencias Sociales, Instituto de Derecho del Trabajo Juan Bautista Alberdi, Universidad Nacional de Tucumán, 1969), 1:25.

5. Throughout the 1880s the number of individuals jailed for gambling increased during harvest time. On occasions, raids resulted in the incarceration of more than one hundred people at the same time.

6. Police Code 1877, sec. 5, arts. 47, 48, 49, 50, 52, 53, 57, 58, 79; Ostengo de Ahumada, *Legislación laboral*, 1:25–27.

7. Governor Ildefonso Muñecas, decree, San Miguel de Tucumán, May 14, 1879; Ramón Cordeiro, Carlos Dalmiro Viale, Horacio Sánchez Loria, and Ernesto del Moral, eds. *Compilación ordenada de leyes, decretos y mensajes del período constitucional de la Provincia de Tucumán que comienza en el año 1852,* 33 vols. (Tucumán: Prebisch y Violeto, 1915–19), 7:324–25.

8. Cordeiro et al., *Compilación ordenada,* 13:297–300.

9. The passing of the Servants' Law was accelerated by a labor code approved in Santiago del Estero that included provisions that could potentially limit workers' options to migrate to Tucumán.

10. According to Daniel Campi, several factors led to the abrogation of the Servants' Law, among them the financial losses that resulted from workers' flight, the use of the police to intervene in private affairs (which increased public expenses), the contradictions that existed between liberal principles and the law's coercive nature, pressures from small and medium planters (who could not compete with ingenios), and the constant pressure from the press in Buenos Aires. Campi, "Coacción y mercado de trabajo: Consideraciones en torno a Tucumán, Argentina: Segunda mitad del siglo XIX," in *Historia I: Projecte Social,* ed. Joseph Fontana (Barcelona: Crítica, 2004), 766–67.

11. Servants' Law, art. 5; Ostengo de Ahumada, *Legislación laboral,* 1:62–65.

12. Servants' Law, arts. 1, 2, 4, 5, 7, 8, 11, 12, 13, 14, 15, 16, 18, 19, 20, 21, 23, 24, 30, 37, 54, 71, 72; Ostengo de Ahumada, *Legislación laboral,* 1:62–65.

13. Cordeiro et al., *Compilación ordenada,* 7:248.

14. Ostengo de Ahumada, *Legislación laboral,* 1:55.

15. *El Orden* (San Miguel de Tucumán), December 11, 1885, 2.

16. Cordeiro et al., *Compilación ordenada,* 9:436.

17. The use of recruiters (*enganchadores*) was not exclusive to Tucumán's sugar industry. In Chile, for example, nitrate producers resorted to enganchadores to recruit workers in central Chile, Peru, and Bolivia. Similarly, highland workers were recruited to work on the coastal sugar plantations in Peru. In Guatemala the government intervened in labor recruitment through the *mandamiento* (labor draft) system. Michael Monteón, "The Enganche in the Chilean Nitrate Sector, 1880–1930," *Latin American Perspectives* 6, no. 3 (1979): 66–79; Michael J. Gonzales, "Capitalist Agriculture and Labour Contracting in Northern Peru, 1880–1905," *Journal of Latin American Studies* 12, no. 2 (1980): 291–315; David McCreery, "'An Odious Feudalism': Mandamiento Labor and Commercial Agriculture in Guatemala, 1858–1920," *Latin American Perspectives* 13, no. 1 (1986): 99–117.

18. AHT, Sección judicial del crimen, 1898, box 280, file 4.

19. Emile Daireaux, *Vida y costumbres en el Plata* (Buenos Aires: F. Lajouane, 1888), 439–40.

20. AHT, Sección judicial del crimen, 1898, box 280, file 4.

21. Juan Bialet Massé, *Informe sobre el estado de las clases obreras argentinas a comienzos del siglo,* 2 vols. (1904; repr., Buenos Aires: Hyspamérica, 1986), 1:224.

22. Cordeiro et al., *Compilación ordenada,* 10:341.

23. *El Orden,* December 1, 1894, 1; December 21, 1894, 1.

24. Campi has examined the evolution of sugar workers' wages between 1881 and 1893 and found that real wages in the sugar industry increased during the period, with the most significant increase experienced between 1888 and 1891. Campi, "La evolución del salario real del peón azucarero en Tucumán (Argentina) en un contexto de coacción y salario 'arcaico' (1881–1893)," *América Latina en la historia económica,* no. 22 (2004): 119–21.

25. *El Orden,* December 28, 1887, 1.

26. Mark Jefferson, *Peopling the Argentine Pampas* (New York: American Geographical Society, 1926), 34.

27. AHT, Sección judicial del crimen, 1895, box 108, file 1.

28. *El Orden,* July 30, 1891, 1.

29. *El Orden,* December 9, 1913, 2.

30. Tucumán. Exposición Nacional, *Album argentino: Provincia de Tucumán: Su vida, su trabajo, su progreso* (Tucumán: Tip. Lit. La Velocidad, 1910).

31. *El Orden,* January 5, 1893, 1.

32. AHT, Sección judicial del crimen, 1894, box 136, file 3.

33. Paulino Rodríguez Marquina, "Las clases obreras: La mano de obra, costumbres, vicios y virtudes de las clases obreras y medios para mejorar sus condiciones," *Tucumán literario* 17 (September 1894): 14.

34. Unfortunately, the evidence on workers' debts is scarce and unsystematic. Campi has found information on debts incurred by nineteen workers between 1858 and 1894. The average debt at the beginning of the period amounted to three months but increased over time to reach six months of wages. Campi, "Azúcar y trabajo: Coacción y mercado laboral, 1856–1896" (PhD diss., Universidad Complutense de Madrid, 2002), 275.

35. Julio Avila, "Medios prácticos para mejorar la situación de las clases obreras," in *Tucumán Intelectual: Producciones de los miembros de la Sociedad Sarmiento,* ed. Manuel Pérez (Tucumán: Imprenta La Argentina, 1904), 177–98.

36. The degree of coercion involved in recruitment and the use of debt as a mechanism to force workers into servitude has been widely debated by scholars in Latin America. For many decades the literature on labor in Latin America considered peonage as an oppressive system that relied exclusively on coercion to keep workers tied to a job. During the late 1970s scholars revised early notions

and portrayed peonage as a more voluntary system in which cash advances acted as a market incentive that eventually gave rise to free wage labor. Representative figures of the former group included Lesley Bird Simpson, Peter Klarén, and Frederick Katz, while the latter included Arnold Bauer, Alan Knight, and Michael Gonzales. See Arnold Bauer, "Rural Workers in Spanish America: Problems of Peonage and Oppression," *Hispanic American Historical Review* 59, no. 2 (1979): 34–63; Brian Loveman, "Critique of Arnold Bauer's 'Rural Workers in Spanish America: Problems of Peonage and Oppression,'" *Hispanic American Historical Review* 59, no. 3 (1979): 478–86. More recent contributions to the debate include Tom Brass, "The Latin American Enganche System: Some Revisionist Interpretations Revisited," *Slavery and Abolition* 11, no. 1 (1990): 74–103; Elizabeth Dore, "Debt Peonage in Granada, Nicaragua, 1870–1930," *Hispanic American Historical Review* 83, no. 3 (2003): 521–59.

37. *El Orden,* June 15, 1904, 1.

38. Jefferson, *Peopling the Argentine Pampas, 36.*

39. *El Orden,* June 13, 1890, 1.

40. Daniel Campi, "Captación y retención de la mano de obra por endeudamiento: El caso de Tucumán en la segunda mitad del siglo XIX," in *Estudios sobre la historia de la industria azucarera argentina,* 2 vols. (Jujuy: Ediciones del Gabinete, 1992), 1:130–47.

41. There are some inconsistencies between the figures provided by the national census (14,810 workers) and data from other official sources, such as the Anuario de la Provincia de Tucumán. Donna Guy's analysis, based on data from factories and provincial censuses, estimates the number of workers engaged in sugar activities in 1895 at twenty-three thousand. This figure is more likely to be accurate since a congressional report in 1897 estimated that during the harvest season sixty-two thousand workers were engaged in sugar-related activities. Guy, "The Rural Working Class in 19th-Century Argentina: Forced Plantation Labor in Tucumán," *Latin American Research Review* 13, no. 1 (1978): 135–45.

42. Argentina, Comisión Directiva del Censo, *Segundo censo de la República Argentina, Levantado el 10 de mayo de 1895,* 3 vols. (Buenos Aires: Taller Tipográfico de la Penitenciaría Nacional, 1898), 2:xxi.

43. In his 1894 report on the sugar industry, José Terry estimated that the number of workers from Santiago del Estero was somehow between fifteen and twenty thousand. In 1905, Juan Alsina maintained that twenty thousand workers came from Santiago and ten thousand from Catamarca and Córdoba. Terry, *Memoria presentada al Sr. Presidente de la República: Tucumán, Salta, Jujuy y Santiago* (Buenos Aires: Compañía Sud-Americana de Billetes de Banco, 1894); Alsina, *El obrero en la República Argentina.* 2 vols. Buenos Aires: Imprenta Calle Mexico, 1905.

44. Immigration accounts for population growth in the littoral provinces. In 1895, Capital, Buenos Aires, Santa Fe, and Entre Ríos concentrated 85 percent of Argentina's foreign population. Tucumán's share was only 1 percent.

45. Pierre Denis, *The Argentine Republic, Its Development and Progress,* trans. Joseph McCabe (New York: Scribner's, 1922), 76-77.

46. Mariana Feyling, "La inmigración francesa en Tucumán, 1830-1880 (master's thesis, Universidad Nacional de Tucumán, 2000).

47. Argentina, Comisión Directiva, *Segundo censo,* 2:527.

48. Ibid., 2:553.

49. AHT, Sección protocolos, series D, 1882, fols. 148-50.

50. AHT, Paulino Rodríguez Marquina, "Memoria descriptiva de Tucumán y de la industria azucarera: Su presente, su pasado y porvenir estadístico" (unpublished manuscript, 1889), 192.

51. This information corresponds to the sample taken from the 1895 census manuscript schedules for Cruz Alta. It is not possible to determine whether these individuals were involved in cane agriculture. Still the difference in the share of participation confirms the idea of lower participation of foreigners as fieldworkers. AGN, Comisión Directiva del Censo, Segundo censo de la República Argentina, unpublished census manuscripts, Boletines de población, vols. 1320-31, 1334-38, 1362.

52. AHT, Sección protocolos, series D, 1879, fols. 370-72.

53. Bialet Massé, *Informe,* 2:806.

54. Jefferson, *Peopling the Argentine Pampas,* 32.

55. Jorge Balán, "Migraciones, mano de obra y formación de un proletariado rural en Tucumán, Argentina, 1870-1914," *Demografía y economía* 10, no. 2 (1976): 231.

56. Almost 50 percent of Santiagueños settled in Cruz Alta. Catamarqueños instead revealed a more diversified settlement pattern, although they concentrated in sugar areas as well, with a large majority settling in Río Chico, Famaillá, and Monteros.

57. In 1910 the National Department of Labor commissioned Federico Figueroa to report on the sugar industry with instructions to pay special attention to the labor situation. The report indicated that while Catamarqueños preferred to work in ingenios, Santiagueños were mostly employed in field-related activities. Figueroa, "Los obreros de la industria azucarera en Tucumán: Informe de un comisionado: Informe presentado al Departamento de Trabajo presentado por el señor Federico Figueroa en desempeño de una comisión que se le había confiado," *Revista azucarera* (Buenos Aires), May 1910, 6.

58. AGN, Comisión Directiva, Segundo censo.

59. In 1905, Juan A. Alsina published a thorough report on the working class in Argentina. The result, a two-volume compendium, supplements the

information in Juan Bialet Massé's report. Alsina, *El obrero en la República Argentina,* 1:317.

60. This was not necessarily the situation in all ingenios. Juan Bialet Massé indicated that working conditions varied among ingenios. For example, the author contrasted the benevolence of Ingenio Esperanza's owners with the situation encountered in those ingenios that belonged to the CAT. Furthermore, labor conditions were also determined by other factors, such as the situation of the industry. Labor demands must have been more intense during the early years of the industry, when labor was more difficult to find and ingenios had larger demands for sugarcane. Bialet Massé, *Informe,* 2:827.

61. Usually one thousand kilograms.

62. Alsina, *Obrero,* 1:313.

63. Bialet Massé, *Informe,* 2:799.

64. Túbal C. García, *La industria azucarera argentina y las consecuencias de su protección* (Buenos Aires: Imprenta Mercatali, 1920), 171.

65. AHT, Sección judicial del crimen, 1899, box 240, file 3.

66. Provincia de Tucumán, *Album argentino.*

67. In contrast to other sugar economies, Tucumán's ingenio owners were not an absentee class but spent much time in the ingenio, in particular during the harvest season.

68. AHT, Sección protocolos, series A, 1879, fols. 376–78.

69. Ibid., series D, 1882, fols. 244–48.

70. Bialet Massé, *Informe,* 2:827–29. The attacks on the CAT could also be a result of the author's political position.

71. *El Orden,* June 1908 to July 18, 1910.

72. *Revista azucarera,* May 1910, 8.

73. Manuel Bernárdez, *La nación en marcha* (Buenos Aires: Talleres Heliográficos de Ortega y Radaelli, 1904), 16.

74. Bialet Massé, *Informe,* 2:795–96.

75. Franck, *Working North,* 60.

76. *Revista azucarera,* May 1910, 7.

77. Jefferson, *Peopling the Argentine Pampas,* 33.

78. Bialet Massé, *Informe,* 2:829–31.

79. AGN, Comisión Directiva, Segundo censo.

80. Paulino Rodríguez Marquina, *La mortalidad infantil en Tucumán* (Tucumán: Imprenta de La Razón, 1898), 55.

81. Bialet Massé, *Informe,* 2:771.

82. AGN, Comisión Directiva, Segundo censo.

83. Bialet Massé, *Informe,* 2:773.

84. Franck, *Working North,* 60.

85. Olga Paterlini de Koch, *Pueblos azucareros de Tucumán* (Tucumán: Editorial del Instituto Argentino de Investigaciones de Historia de la Arquitectura y del Urbanismo, 1987), 81.

86. Bernárdez, *Nación en marcha*, 5, 7, 11, 29.

87. Jules Huret, *De Buenos Aires al Gran Chaco*, 2 vols. (1900; repr., Buenos Aires: Hyspamérica, 1988), 1:202–3.

88. *El Orden*, June 8, 1886, 1.

89. Bialet Massé, *Informe*, 1:225–26.

90. Georges Clemenceau, *South America To-day* (New York: Putnam, 1911), 474–76.

91. *El Orden*, December 18, 1908, 1.

92. *El Orden*, November 14, 1894, 1.

93. *El Orden*, May 8, 1899, 1.

94. This situation persisted until child labor was regulated in the early twentieth century. In 1907 the Argentine congress approved a law that regulated the labor of women and children. Among other provisions, the law prohibited employers to hire children under ten years old or children who had not completed their elementary studies. Ana Teruel de Lagos, "Regulación legal del trabajo en haciendas, ingenios y plantaciones de caña de azúcar en la provincia de Jujuy: Siglo XIX a mediados del XX," in *Estudios sobre la industria*, ed. Daniel Campi, 1:139–49.

95. Argentina, *Segundo censo*, 2:545.

96. Lucía Vidal Sanz, "Las escuelas de los ingenios azucareros en Tucumán (1884–1916)," in *Estudios de historia social de Tucumán: Educación y política en los siglos XIX y XX*, ed. Luis Marcos Bonano (Tucumán: Facultad de Filosofía y Letras, Universidad Nacional de Tucumán, 2004), 55–58.

97. *El Orden*, December 9, 1908, 1; December 16, 1908, 2; December 18, 1908, 1.

98. *El Orden*, March 19, 1902, 1; June 20, 1902, 1; June 21, 1902, 1.

99. In 1892 the provincial authorities passed a resolution that regulated the disposal of waste in sugar areas. However, as noted by *El Orden* almost a decade later, ingenios failed to comply with regulations. *El Orden*, August 3, 1901, 1.

100. Tucumán, Comisión del Centenario, *Baedeker de la Provincia de Tucumán* (Tucumán: Talleres de la Razón, 1916), 86.

101. Bialet Massé, *Informe*, 1:226.

102. *El Orden*, January 29, 1903, 1; February 5, 1903, 1; February 6, 1903, 1.

103. For example, during his visit to the province in 1904, union leader Luis Lotito observed that alcohol played an important role in the lives of Tucumán's workers. Lotito, "El proletariado tucumano a comienzos del siglo, 1907" in *Sindicatos como los de antes*, ed. Torcuato di Tella (Buenos Aires: Editorial

Biblos, 1993), 21–36. Similar remarks were made regularly by the authorities and the press.

104. César Mur, *Registro estadístico de la Provincia de Tucumán correspondiente al año 1882* (Buenos Aires: Imprenta de Pablo Coni, 1884), 93.

105. Vicente Padilla, *El norte argentino: Tucumán, Salta, Jujuy, Santiago del Estero, Catamarca: Historia política, administrativa social, comercial e industrial de las provincias: Crónica de la época prehispana hasta nuestros días* (Buenos Aires: Imprenta Ferrari Hermanos, 1922).

106. Avila, "Medios prácticos," 190.

107. Cordeiro et al., *Compilación ordenada*, 16:300.

108. Flight, as a strategy of resistance, was endemic in plantation economies throughout Latin America. See, for example, Dore, "Debt Peonage"; Michael J. Gonzales, "Chinese Plantation Workers and Social Conflict in Peru in the Late Nineteenth Century," *Journal of Latin American Studies* 21, no. 3 (1989): 385–424; Catherine Legrand, "Informal Resistance on a Dominican Sugar Plantation during the Trujillo Dictatorship," *Hispanic American Historical Review* 75, no. 4 (1995): 555–96; Flavio dos Santos Gomes, "A 'Safe Haven': Runaway Slaves, Mocambos, and Borders in Colonial Amazonia, Brazil," *Hispanic American Historical Review* 82, no. 3 (2002): 469–98.

109. Thomas Hutchinson, *Buenos Ayres and the Argentine Gleanings, with Extracts from a Diary of Salado Exploration in 1862 and 1863* (London: Edward Stanford, 1865), 184.

110. Guy, "Rural Working Class," 142.

111. AHT, Sección judicial del crimen, 1899, box 240, file 3.

112. Ibid., 1899, box 220, file 5.

113. Ibid., 1891, box 133, file 16.

114. Bialet Massé, *Informe*, 1:232.

115. AHT, Sección judicial del crimen, 1889, box 100, file 10.

116. Ibid., 1892, box 163, file 7.

117. Cases of arson and destruction of machinery abound in other sugar economies as well. See, for example, Luis A. Figueroa, *Sugar, Slavery, and Freedom in Nineteenth-Century Puerto Rico* (Chapel Hill: University of North Carolina Press, 2005); Gonzales, "Chinese Plantation Workers"; Legrand, "Informal Resistance."

118. AHT, Sección judicial del crimen, 1885, box 86, file 13.

119. *El Orden*, September 1, 1884, 2.

120. AHT, Sección administrativa, Vol. 163, fols. 228–29.

121. *El Orden*, September 2, 1884, 2.

122. *El Orden*, September 9, 1884, 1.

123. *El Orden*, September 12, 1884, 2.

124. *El Orden,* October 1, 1889, 1.

125. *El Orden,* July 25, 1901, 1.

126. This was not the first trip that the union leader had made to the province. In 1902, Adrián Patroni visited Tucumán and held a series of conferences on democracy and socialism at the Centro Cosmopolita and the Casa de España. *El Orden,* May 5, 1902, 1.

127. María Celia Bravo, "Liberales, socialistas, iglesia y patrones frente a la situación de los trabajadores en Tucumán," in *La cuestión social en Argentina, 1870–1943,* ed. Juan Suriano (Buenos Aires: La Colmena, 2000), 31–61.

128. *El Orden,* June 11, 1904, 1.

129. James Scott, *Weapons of the Weak: Everyday Forms of Peasant Resistance* (New Haven: Yale University Press, 1985), 29.

130. Gustavo Rubinstein, *Los sindicatos azucareros en los orígenes del peronismo tucumano* (Tucumán: Universidad Nacional de Tucumán, 2006).

131. Lotito, "Proletariado tucumano," 21.

132. Bernárdez, *Nación en marcha,* 11.

Chapter 5: Sugar and the Province

1. Ramón Cordeiro, Carlos Dalmiro Viale, Horacio Sánchez Loria, and Ernesto del Moral, eds. *Compilación ordenada de leyes, decretos y mensajes del período constitucional de la Provincia de Tucumán que comienza en el año 1852,* 33 vols. (Tucumán: Prebisch y Violeto, 1915–19), 17:95–96.

2. Bartolomé Mitre, for example, used subsidies regularly in an attempt to gain provincial support. David Rock, *Argentina, 1516–1987: From Spanish Colonization to Alfonsín* (Berkeley: University of California Press, 1987), 125.

3. Arsenio Granillo, *Provincia de Tucumán,* Serie de artículos descriptivos y noticiosos (Tucumán: Imprenta de la Razón, 1872), 48.

4. Cordeiro et al., *Compilación ordenada,* 6:261.

5. According to article 67 in the 1853 national constitution the congress could distribute subsidies to supplement provincial incomes. In 1857 the confederation passed a law that provided for educational subsidies for the provinces. Juan Carlos Vedoya, *Cómo fue la enseñanza popular en la Argentina* (Buenos Aires: Plus Ultra, 1973), 44.

6. Ibid., 45.

7. Rock, *Argentina,* 130.

8. Vedoya, *Enseñanza popular,* 49–51.

9. Cordeiro et al., *Compilación ordenada,* 6:261.

10. Law 361, December 1872.

11. Law 432, December 1878.

12. Before the 1878 law, one cuadra was considered equivalent to the area cultivated with two hundred surcos, or furrows. Since there was no standard distance between furrows, the system allowed for significant differences among cultivators depending on the distance between surcos. By establishing that one cuadra was equal to 166 square *varas* (one vara equals 0.86 meter), the new provision created a standard cuadra, equal to 2.066 hectares.

13. Cordeiro et al., *Compilación ordenada*, 7:355–86.

14. Law 443, December 1880.

15. However, according to census commissioners, as late as 1895 the population was still using the old system, which had existed since colonial times. Argentina, Comisión Directiva del Censo, *Segundo censo Nacional de la República Argentina, levantado el 10 de Mayo de 1895* (Buenos Aires: Taller Tipográfico de la Penitenciaría Nacional, 1898), 3:xxv.

16. Cordeiro et al., *Compilación ordenada*, 7:532–33.

17. Law 465, December 1881.

18. Cordeiro et al., *Compilación ordenada*, 12:274–80.

19. Laws 559, 560, December 1887.

20. Law 597, February 1889.

21. Law 635, February 1893.

22. In 1890 that ingenio would have paid 1,500 pesos, whereas in 1893 the fee was 3,000 pesos. Adjusted for inflation, using 1903 as a base year, the latter amount was 3,296 pesos.

23. Furthermore, besides the direct impact on fiscal revenues, modifications in tax policies should be understood as part of a larger program of consolidation of the provincial state through the institutionalization of systems of collection that were accepted by society as legitimate. Oscar Oszlak, *La formación del estado argentino* (Buenos Aires: Editorial de Belgrano, 1982), 30–32.

24. Tucumán, *Memorias de la contaduría general correspondientes a los años 1892 y 1893 presentadas al Ministerio de Hacienda* (Tucumán: Tip. Lit. La Velocidad, 1894), 27.

25. Law 635, February 1893.

26. Between 1895 and 1900 the additional taxes on alfalfa, tobacco, and rice were eliminated.

27. *El Orden* (San Miguel de Tucumán), May 31, 1894, 2.

28. Cordeiro et al., *Compilación ordenada*, 18:392.

29. Donna Guy, *Argentine Sugar Politics: Tucumán and the Generation of Eighty* (Tempe: Center for Latin American Studies, Arizona State University, 1980), 93.

30. The choice to eliminate the tax that directly affected the industrial group over the one that affected the agricultural interests reveals also that industrialists had greater political clout than sugarcane farmers.

31. Law 782, March 1900.

32. For a 6 percent yield, one hundred kilograms of sugarcane produced six kilograms of sugar.

33. In the late 1890s, according to contemporary sources, the average output of one hectare of sugarcane was around forty thousand kilos. Thus, considering a 6 percent yield, as established by law, one hectare produced twenty-four hundred kilos of sugar. For this estimate I follow Antonio Correa's 1897 data on sugarcane output and sugar yields as they are the closest in time to the period under consideration. Argentina, Congreso Nacional, Cámara de Diputados, Comisión de Agricultura y Colonización, *Investigación parlamentaria sobre agricultura, ganadería, industrias derivadas y colonización: Ordenada por la Honorable Cámara de Diputados en resolución de 19 de junio de 1896*. Anexo G. Tucumán y Santiago del Estero por Antonio M. Correa. Revised and expanded by Emilio Lahitte (Buenos Aires: Tipografía de la Penitenciaría, 1898).

34. Law 859, October 1903; law 862, December 1903.

35. Law 884, June 1906.

36. Cordeiro et al., *Compilación ordenada*, 28:184–85.

37. Law 916, January 1907; law 922, June 1907.

38. Law 988, December 1908.

39. Tucumán, *Memorias de la contaduría general correspondiente al ejercicio de 1898 y 1899* (Tucumán: Imprenta La Velocidad, 1900), 139; Tucumán, *Anuario estadístico de la provincia de Tucumán*, published under the direction of Paulino Rodríguez Marquina (Tucumán: Imprenta La Velocidad, 1915), 19:151–53.

40. Some of the taxes in this category were meat and certain patentes. The highest bidder obtained the right to collect the tax and keep the difference between what was collected and what was paid to the government. The payment was made in twelve installments. Therefore, the bidder did not need to have all the money right away.

41. For example, provincial records and reports by census takers in 1895 show a significant disparity between the area under cultivation. While according to national sources Tucumán's area under cultivation extended over fifty-five thousand hectares, provincial returns list only forty thousand hectares.

42. Tucumán, *Anuario estadístico*, 1896, 2:10; Tucumán, *Anuario estadístico*, 1912, 16:139.

43. Cordeiro et al., *Compilación ordenada*, 28:242.

44. César Mur, *Registro estadístico de la Provincia de Tucumán, correspondiente al año 1882* (Buenos Aires: Imprenta de Pablo Coni, 1884), 159–160; Tucumán, *Anuario estadístico*, 1916, 20:163.

45. Similarly, investments in public works increased but they reveal significant oscillations in their share of total investments, which suggests that this sector was the most vulnerable to spending cuts.

46. Oszlak, *Estado argentino,* 15–16.

47. Cordeiro et al., *Compilación ordenada,* 9:13.

48. Law 172, March 1861.

49. Law 369, March 1873.

50. Cordeiro et al., *Compilación ordenada,* 6:200–3.

51. Ibid., 23:112.

52. Ibid., 6:574–76.

53. In 1881, Governor Miguel Nougués proposed to the provincial legislature the creation of cooperatives of parents and the implementation of instructional fees. Cordeiro et al., *Compilación ordenada,* 18:18.

54. Law 492, August 1883.

55. Cordeiro et al., *Compilación ordenada,* 9:165; Tucumán, *Anuario estadístico, 1912,* 16:142.

56. This problem affected other provinces as well, which further complicated Tucumán's situation. For example, in the 1880s and 1890s Santa Fe and Córdoba attracted several Tucumano teachers by offering them higher salaries.

57. Tucumán, *Anuario estadístico, 1896,* 2:20; Tucumán, *Anuario estadístico, 1912,* 16:97.

58. These figures include only public schools funded by the province. Tucumán, *Anuario estadístico, 1898,* 3:20; Tucumán, *Anuario estadístico, 1912,* 16:95–97.

59. For example, in 1898 almost 90 percent of the buildings used for public schools were listed as "private buildings," as opposed to "public buildings." Tucumán, *Anuario estadístico, 1898,* 3:20.

60. The school-age group included children from six to fourteen years old.

61. Mur, *Registro estadístico,* 159–60; Tucumán, *Anuario estadístico, 1916,* 20:163.

62. Argentina, *Boletín del Departamento Nacional de Agricultura: 1883* (Buenos Aires: Imprenta del Departamento Nacional de Agricultura, 1884), 40.

63. The consejo was created in 1887 to replace the ineffective Tribunal Médico (Medical Tribunal). The organization became the cornerstone of the health system in the province and had jurisdiction over health, hygiene, and pharmaceutical matters. Two years later, the responsibilities of the consejo were broadened, with the incorporation in its jurisdiction of the Oficina Química, in charge of the analysis of food, water, and toxic wastes in the province. The Laboratorio de Bacteriología, created in the 1900s, cooperated with the consejo and played an important role in particular during epidemics.

64. Paulino Rodríguez Marquina, *La mortalidad infantil en Tucumán* (Tucumán: Imprenta de la Razón, 1898), 135.

65. *El Orden,* June 26, 1885, 1.

66. *El Orden*, February 25, 1885, 1.

67. Superstition and common practices guided procedures performed by hábiles. For example, in order to prepare a woman for birth, they made her use dirty clothes because they were smoother, and, when the time came, the mother was asked to lie on a cover and was thrown into the air in order for the baby to "loosen up." According to Rodríguez Marquina, sometimes these women were drunk or sick, adding more danger to an already complicated situation. Rodríguez Marquina, *Mortalidad infantil*, 55.

68. Benigno Vallejo and Estergidio de la Vega, *Morbilidad y mortalidad de la primera infancia en Tucumán. Estudio presentado al Primer Congreso Nacional de Medicina por los delegados del Gobierno de la Provincia de Tucumán* (Tucumán: Talleres de la Provincia, 1917), 52.

69. *El Orden*, April 21, 1908, 2.

70. Vallejo and de la Vega, *Morbilidad y mortalidad*, 11–22.

71. Tucumán, *Anuario estadístico, 1900*, 8:73; Tucumán, *Anuario estadístico, 1914*, 18:69.

72. Tucumán, *Anuario estadístico, 1910*, 14:243.

73. Tucumán, *Guía ilustrada para el viajero* (Tucumán: Colombres y Piñero Editores, 1901), 41–42.

74. Tucumán, *Anuario estadístico, 1910*, 14:xlii; Carlos Díaz Alejandro, *Essays on the Economic History of Argentina* (New Haven: Yale University Press, 1970), 23.

75. Tucumán, *Anuario estadístico, 1910*, 14:lii–liii.

76. Roberto Pucci, "La población y el auge azucarero en Tucumán," in *Breves contribuciones del Instituto de Estudios Geográficos* 7 (1992), 16.

77. John Foster Fraser, *The Amazing Argentine: A New Land of Enterprise* (London: Cassell, 1914), 249–50.

78. For example, in 1882 the city counted four hundred kerosene lamps, mostly located in the plaza and downtown area. Six years later the number of street lamps had increased to almost one thousand, to serve an area of 152 square blocks. The most significant improvement in city lighting, however, was achieved in March 1889 with the inauguration of electrical services in the downtown area, although the city's suburbs remained illuminated with kerosene lamps until 1915. Tucumán, *Mensajes del poder ejecutivo al abrir las sesiones la legislatura de la provincia*, 10 vols. (Tucumán: Imprenta de la Razón, 1888), 4.

79. During the early 1900s urban San Miguel boasted three hundred kilometers of telephone lines, whereas the rest of the province had a total of four hundred kilometers. Tucumán, Comisión del Centenario, *Baedeker de la Provincia de Tucumán* (Tucumán: Talleres de la Razón, 1916), 47.

80. Tucumán, *Mensaje del PE*, 6.

81. Floods were not the only reason for water contamination. Industrial wastes from ingenios were an important source as well. As early as 1892 the provincial government had shown concern for the problem. In his trip to the province, Jules Huret observed the ingenios' careless disposal of contaminated materials and its effect on the rural population.

82. The system consisted of seven collectors in the San Javier area connected to the city by forty kilometers of metal pipes. In San Miguel, three service reservoirs and filters completed the facilities. Argentina, *Impresiones de la República Argentina en el siglo veinte: Su historia, gente, comercio, industria y riqueza* (London: Lloyd's Greater Britain Publishing Co., 1911).

83. Between 1900 and 1912 the share of health expenditures in the city budget rose from 5 to 22 percent. Tucumán, *Anuario estadístico, 1900,* 8:139–40; Tucumán, *Anuario estadístico, 1912,* 16:149–50.

84. *El Orden,* September 3, 1913, 1.

85. For example, in 1916 in the department of Famaillá only one out of forty-three patients who died had received professional assistance, despite the presence of three physicians in the area.

86. Fraser, *Amazing Argentine,* 250.

87. Tucumán, *Baedeker,* 11.

88. Tucumán, *Album general de la Provincia de Tucumán en el primer centenario de la independencia argentina* (Buenos Aires: Establecimiento Gráfico Rodríguez Giles, 1917).

89. Tucumán, *Guía ilustrada,* 110.

Conclusion

1. Harry Franck, *Working North from Patagonia* (New York: Century, 1921), 59.

2. During his term as Sarmiento's minister of education, Avellaneda had manipulated subsidies to obtain the support of the provinces, thus creating a new power structure that incorporated members of regional elites into the national alliance. David Rock, *State Building and Political Movements in Argentina, 1860–1916* (Stanford: Stanford University Press, 2002), 70.

3. Donna Guy, *Argentine Sugar Politics: Tucumán and the Generation of Eighty* (Tempe: Center for Latin American Studies, Arizona State University, 1980), 3.

4. As Fernando Rocchi has convincingly argued, at the same time that the agropastoral export economy expanded Argentina consolidated its national market and underwent a process of industrial growth. His study challenges the "canonical version" of Argentine industrialization, which situates the development of a national industry in the post-1930 depression and traces Argentina's

industrial development to the last quarter of the nineteenth century. During this period tariff policies were guided by a "pragmatic protectionism" that attempted to maintain a balance among different sectors in society. His findings indicate that the interests of the agrarian sector did not always dominate tariff policies, which depended on the success of lobbying groups. Rocchi, *Chimneys in the Desert: Industrialization in Argentina during the Export Boom Years, 1870–1930* (Stanford: Stanford University Press, 2006).

5. Emilio Schleh estimated that between 1875 and 1881 Tucumán imported sugar machinery for a total value of 2 million pesos. Schleh, *La industria azucarera argentina: Pasado y presente* (Buenos Aires: Ferrari Hermanos, 1930), 76.

6. Similarly, the wine industry in Mendoza participated in and from the economic bonanza that characterized turn of the century Argentina. As was the case with Tucumán, the national authorities assisted producers with infrastructure, tariffs, and regulations to protect local wine production from foreign competition. The Banco Nacional gave Mendocino producers access to credit. In 1885 the first railroad line arrived in Mendoza and facilitated communications with the market in Buenos Aires. High tariffs and other regulations such as the 1904 Wine Law encouraged the expansion of Mendoza's wine industry by protecting it from foreign and artificial wines. Jorge Balán, "Una cuestión regional en la Argentina: Burguesías provinciales y el mercado nacional en el desarrollo agroexportador," *Desarrollo económico* 18, no. 69 (1978): 73–79.

7. Stuart Schwartz, *Sugar Plantations in the Formation of the Brazilian Society, Bahia, 1550–1835* (New York: Cambridge University Press, 1985).

8. B. J. Barickman, *A Bahian Counterpoint: Sugar, Tobacco, Cassava, and Slavery in the Recôncavo, 1780–1860* (Stanford: Stanford University Press, 1998).

9. Peter Eisenberg, *The Sugar Industry in Pernambuco: Modernization without Change, 1840–1910* (Berkeley: University of California Press, 1974).

10. Ibid., 107.

11. Kit Sims Taylor, *Sugar and the Underdevelopment of Northeastern Brazil, 1500–1970* (Gainesville: University Presses of Florida, 1978).

12. Rebecca Scott, "The Transformation of Sugar Production in Cuba after Emancipation, 1880–1900: Planters, Colonos and Former Slaves," in *Crisis and Change in the International Sugar Economy, 1860–1914,* ed. Albert, Bill and Adrian Graves (Norwich, UK: ISC Press, 1984), 111–19.

13. Alan Dye, *Cuban Sugar in the Age of Mass Production: Technology and the Economics of the Sugar Central, 1899–1929* (Stanford: Stanford University Press, 1998).

14. Fe Iglesias García, *Del ingenio al central* (San Juan: Editorial de la Universidad de Puerto Rico, 1998).

15. The literature on Brazil and Cuba sugar economies is vast. Besides those cited above, other traditional studies include, but are not limited to, Anton Allahar, *Class, Politics, and Sugar in Colonial Cuba* (Lewiston, NY: Edwin Mellen Press, 1990); César Ayala, *American Sugar Kingdom: The Plantation Economy of the Spanish Caribbean, 1898–1934* (Chapel Hill: University of North Carolina Press, 1999); Gerald Cardoso, *Negro Slavery in the Sugar Plantations of Veracruz and Pernambuco, 1550–1680: A Comparative Study* (Washington, DC: University Press of America, 1983); David Denslow, *Sugar Production in Northeastern Brazil and Cuba, 1858–1908* (New York: Garland, 1987); Ramiro Guerra y Sánchez, *Sugar and Society in the Caribbean: An Economic History of Cuban Agriculture* (New Haven: Yale University Press, 1964); Fernando Ortiz, *Cuban Counterpoint: Tobacco and Sugar* (New York: Knopf, 1947); Antonio Santamaría García, *Sin azúcar no hay país: La industria azucarera y la economía cubana (1919–1939)* (Seville: Consejo Superior de Investigaciones Científicas, Universidad de Sevilla, 2001).

16. Schwartz, *Sugar Plantations,* 303.

17. Barickman, *Bahian Counterpoint,* 119.

18. Ayala, *American Sugar,* 121. For the sugar industry in Puerto Rico, see Ayala, *American Sugar;* Humberto García Muñiz, "La plantación que no se repite: Las historias azucareras de la República Dominicana y Puerto Rico, 1870–1930," *Revista de Indias* 65, no. 233 (2005): 172–91; Teresita Martínez Vergne, *Capitalism in Colonial Puerto Rico: Central San Vicente in the Late Nineteenth Century* (Gainesville: University Press of Florida, 1992); Andrés A. Ramos Mattei, "The Plantations of the Southern Coast of Puerto Rico, 1880–1910," *Social and Economic Studies* 37, nos. 1–2 (1988): 365–404; Francisco A. Scarano, *Sugar and Slavery in Puerto Rico: The Plantation Economy of Ponce, 1800–1850* (Madison: University of Wisconsin Press, 1984).

19. In his traditional study of Cuban sugar, Ramiro Guerra depicted the group of colonos as the basis for the consolidation of a rural middle class in Cuba. This view has been rebutted by such authors as Juan Alier and Antonio Santamaría García. Santamaría García and Luis Miguel García Mora, "Colonos: Agricultores cañeros, ¿Clase media rural en Cuba? 1880–1898," *Revista de Indias* 58, no. 212 (1998): 131–61. Unlike Cuba, studies have shown that colonos in the Caguas district in Puerto Rico developed stronger lines of alliance to defend their interests and the island's colonial status. José A. Solá, "The Technological Transformation of the Sugar Industry and American Protectionism in the Emergence of the Colonos in Caguas, Puerto Rico, 1898–1928" (PhD diss., University of Connecticut, 2004).

20. For the sugar industry in Peru, see Bill Albert, *An Essay on the Peruvian Sugar Industry, 1880–1922: And the Letters of Ronald Gordon, Administrator of the British Sugar Company in the Cañete Valley, 1914–1919* (Norwich, UK:

School of Social Studies, University of East Anglia, 1976); Daniel Campi and Patricia Juarez-Dappe, "Despegue y auge azucarero en Perú y Argentina: Semejanzas y contrastes," *Illes i imperis,* no. 9 (December 2006): 79–115; Michael J. Gonzales, *Plantation Agriculture and Social Control in Northern Peru, 1875–1933* (Austin: University of Texas Press, 1985); Peter Klarén, *Modernization, Dislocation, and Aprismo: Origins of the Peruvian Aprista Party, 1870–1932* (Austin: Institute of Latin American Studies, University of Texas, 1973); Pablo Macera, *La plantaciones azucareras en el Perú, 1821–1875* (Lima: Centro Peruano de Historia Económica, 1974); Jean Piel, *Capitalismo agrario en el Perú,* trans. Francis Eherran (Buenos Aires: Universidad Nacional de Salta; Lima: Instituto Francés de Estudios Andinos, 1995).

21. For the sugar industry in Mexico, see Horacio Crespo, *Historia del azúcar en México* (Mexico City: Fondo de Cultura Económica, 1988); María Teresa Huerta, "Empresarios y ferrocarriles en Morelos, 1875–1900," *Siglo XIX* 5, no. 14 (1996): 69–87; Gisela Landázury Benítez and Verónica Vázquez Mantecón, *Azúcar y estado (1750–1880)* (Mexico City: Fondo de Cultura Económica, 1988); Roberto Melville, *Crecimiento y rebelión: El desarrollo económico de las haciendas azucareras en Morelos, 1880–1910* (Mexico City: Centro de Investigaciones de Desarrollo Rural, 1979); Ernest Sánchez Santiró, "Evolución productiva de la agroindustria azucarera de Morelos durante el siglo XIX: Una propuesta de periodización," *América latina en la historia económica* 26 (July-December 2006): 111–27; Doménico Síndico, "Modernization in Nineteenth-Century Sugar Haciendas: The Case of Morelos: From Formal to Real Subsumption of Labor to Capital," *Latin American Perspectives* 7, no. 4 (1980): 83–99; Arturo Warman, *We Come to Object: The Peasants of Morelos and the National State,* trans. Stephen K. Ault (Baltimore: Johns Hopkins University Press, 1980).

22. Arturo Warman, "The Cauldron of the Revolution: Agrarian Capitalism and the Sugar Industry in Morelos, Mexico, 1880–1910," in *Crisis and Change in the International Sugar Economy, 1860–1914,* ed. Bill Albert and Adrian Graves (Norwich, UK: ISC Press, 1984), 167.

23. Scholars disagree on whether the expansion of the area under sugarcane cultivation was done over "terrenos del temporal," which belonged to the haciendas, or over the native communities' lands. Crespo, *Historia del azúcar,* 96–98.

24. Peter Klarén, "The Sugar Industry in Peru," *Revista de Indias* 65, no. 233 (2005): 40.

25. Warman, "Cauldron of the Revolution," 165–80.

26. Eisenberg, *Sugar Industry,* 180–215.

27. Jorge Balán, "Una cuestión regional en la Argentina: Burguesías provinciales y el mercado nacional en el desarrollo agroexportador," *Desarrollo*

económico 18, no. 69 (1978): 58; Marcos Giménez Zapiola, "El interior argentino y el 'desarrollo hacia afuera': El caso de Tucumán," in *El régimen oligárquico: Materiales para el estudio de la realidad argentina hasta 1930,* comp. Giménez (Buenos Aires: Amorrortu Editores, 1975), 109.

Glossary

agricultor	Farmer.
arroba	A unit of weight equal to approximately eleven and a half kilograms.
basculero	Sugarcane scale operator.
cantina	Canteen.
cañero	Sugarcane planter who owned or rented his or her land.
colonia	Ingenio lands under the care of colonos.
colono	Sugarcane planter who leased out an ingenio's lands.
conchabo	Formal bonding of workers.
contribución directa	Tax on real estate or amount involved in capital transactions.
cuadra	A unit of land equal to 2.066 hectares.
ingenio	Sugar mill.
jornalero	Day laborer.
libreta	Notebook in which workers' debts were registered.
papeleta	Certificate of employment.
patente	Tax on commercial, industrial, professional, and agricultural activities.
peón	Farmhand.
tarea	Daily labor quota.
trapiche	Wooden sugar mill.
zafra	Sugarcane harvest.

Bibliography

Archives

AGN Archivo General de la Nación, Buenos Aires

Comisión Directiva del Censo. Primer censo de la República Argentina. Unpublished census manuscript. Boletines de población, vols. 441–49, 465.

———. Segundo censo de la República Argentina. Unpublished census manuscript. Boletines de población, vols. 1320–31, 1334–38, 1362.

———. Segundo censo de la República Argentina: Censo económico y social. Unpublished census manuscript. Sección agricultura, bulletin 27, vol. 3, fols. 46–133.

AHT Archivo Histórico de la Provincia de Tucumán

Rodríguez Marquina, Paulino. "Memoria descriptiva de Tucumán y de la industria azucarera. Su presente, su pasado y porvenir estadístico." 2 vols. Unpublished manuscript, 1889.

———. "Registro estadístico de Tucumán." Unpublished manuscript, 1889.

Sección judicial civil, series A, 1880–95.

Sección judicial del crimen, 1880–95.

Sección protocolos, series A, C, D, 1862–90.

Government Publications

Argentina

Agricultural and Pastoral Census of the Nation: Stock-Breeding and Agriculture in 1908. Buenos Aires: Argentine Meteorological Office, 1909.

Anuario estadístico de la República Argentina, correspondiente al año 1897. 2 vols. Buenos Aires: Compañía Sud-Americana de Billetes de Banco, 1898.

Estadística gráfica: Progreso de la República Argentina en la exposición de Chicago. Buenos Aires: Taller Tipográfico de la Penitenciaría Nacional, 1892.

Impresiones de la República Argentina en el siglo veinte: Su historia, gente, comercio, industria y riqueza. London: Lloyd's Greater Britain Publishing Co., 1911.

Comisión Directiva del Censo. *Primer censo de la República Argentina, verificado en los días 15, 16, y 17 de septiembre de 1869.* Buenos Aires: El Porvenir, 1872.

———. *Segundo censo de la República Argentina, levantado el 10 de mayo de 1895.* 3 vols. Buenos Aires: Taller Tipográfico de la Penitenciaría Nacional, 1898.

Comisión Nacional del Censo. *Tercer censo nacional, levantado el 1 de junio de 1914 ordenado por la Ley no. 9108 bajo la presidencia del dr. Roque Saenz Peña, ejecutado durante la presidencia del dr. Victorino de la Plaza,* 10 vols. Buenos Aires: Talleres gráficos de L. J. Rosso, 1916–19.

Congreso Nacional. Cámara de Diputados. Comisión de Agricultura y Colonización. *Investigación parlamentaria sobre agricultura, ganadería, industrias derivadas y colonización, ordenada por la Honorable Cámara de Diputados en resolución de 19 de junio de 1896.* Anexo G. Tucumán y Santiago del Estero por Antonio M Correa. Revised and expanded by Emilio Lahitte. Buenos Aires: Tipografía de la Penitenciaría Nacional, 1898.

Departamento Nacional de Agricultura. *Boletín del Departamento Nacional de Agricultura.* 10 vols. Buenos Aires: Imprenta del Departamento Nacional de Agricultura, 1878–96.

———. *Informe del Departamento Nacional de Agricultura.* Presentado por Juan Terán. Buenos Aires: Imprenta del Departamento Nacional de Agricultura, 1875.

Tucumán

Album general de la Provincia de Tucumán en el primer centenario de la independencia argentina. Buenos Aires: Establecimiento Gráfico Rodríguez Giles, 1917.

Anuario estadístico de la Provincia de Tucumán. Published under the direction of Paulino Rodríguez Marquina. 20 vols. Tucumán: Imprenta La Velocidad, 1895–1916.

Boletín Estadístico de la Provincia de Tucumán correspondiente al primer semestre de 1894. Publicado bajo la dirección del jefe de la Oficina de Estadística doctor Felipe Bravo. Córdoba: Tip. Lit. La Minerva de A Villafañe, 1894.

Celebración nacional del centenario de la independencia en Tucumán, 1916. Publicación hecha por el gobierno de la Provincia de Tucumán. Tucumán: Imprenta de La Razón, 1917.

Censo de la capital de Tucumán, 1913: Población, habitación, industria y comercio, levantado el día 1 de agosto con referencia a la noche del 31 de julio. Bajo la administración del Dr Ernesto Padilla por Paulino Rodríguez Marquina, director de la Oficina de Estadística y del Trabajo. Buenos Aires: Compañía Sud-Americana de Billetes de Banco, 1914.

Contaduría general: Estado administrativo hasta el 31 de marzo de 1890, correspondiente al año económico de 1889. Tucumán: Imprenta de Gil Blas, 1890.

Guía ilustrada para el viajero. Tucumán: Colombres y Piñero Editores, 1901.

Memoria del Departamento Ejecutivo correspondiente al año 1897. Buenos Aires. Compañía Sud-Americana de Billetes de Banco, 1898.

Memoria del Ministerio de Hacienda e Instrucción Pública correspondiente al año 1895, presentada a las Honorables Cámaras Legislativas en 1896. Tucumán: Imprenta La Velocidad, 1897.

Memoria del Ministerio de Hacienda e Instrucción Pública presentada a las Honorables Cámaras Legislativas en 1901. Tucumán: Imprenta La Velocidad, 1902.

Memorias de la contaduría general. 13 vols. Tucumán: Imprenta La Velocidad, 1892–1915.

Mensajes del PE al abrir la Legislatura de la Provincia. 15 vols. Tucumán: Imprenta de La Razón, 1880–1901.

Comisión del Centenario. *Baedeker de la Provincia de Tucumán.* Tucumán: Talleres de la Razón, 1916.

Departamento de Hacienda. *Ley de presupuesto para el año 1889.* Tucumán: Tipografía y Encuadernación La Razón, 1889.

Exposición Nacional. *Album argentino: Provincia de Tucumán: Su vida, su trabajo, su progreso.* Tucumán: Tip. Lit. la Velocidad, 1910.

Newspapers and Journals

Buenos Ayres Herald, 1897
La Nación (Buenos Aires), 1892–95
El Orden (San Miguel de Tucumán), 1883–1915
Revista Azucarera (Buenos Aires), 1894–1914

Other Primary Sources

Alsina, Juan. *El obrero en la República Argentina.* 2 vols. Buenos Aires: Imprenta Calle Mexico, 1905.

Alurralde, Pedro. "La Crisis Azucarera." *Anales de la Facultad de Derecho y Ciencias Sociales* 1 (1902): 360.

Avila, Julio. *La ciudad arribeña: Tucumán, 1810–1816.* San Miguel, Tucumán: Biblioteca América, 1920.

———. "Medios prácticos para mejorar la situación de las clases obreras." In *Tucumán Intelectual: Producciones de los miembros de la Sociedad Sarmiento,* edited by Manuel Pérez, 177–98. Tucumán: Imprenta La Argentina, 1904.

Bernárdez, Manuel. *La nación en marcha.* Buenos Aires: Talleres Heliográficos de Ortega y Radaelli, 1904.

Bialet Massé, Juan. *Informe sobre el estado de las clases obreras argentinas a comienzos del siglo.* 2 vols. 1904. Reprint, Buenos Aires: Hyspamérica, 1986.

Borea, Domingo. *El desenvolvimiento económico rural en las Provincias de Tucumán y Santiago del Estero.* Buenos Aires: Imprenta Calle Mexico, 1917.

Bousquet, Alfredo. *Estudio sobre el sistema rentístico de la Provincia de Tucumán de 1820 a 1876.* Tucumán: Imprenta de La Razón, 1878.

Burmeister, Hermann. *Descripción de Tucumán.* 1858. Reprint, Buenos Aires: Imprenta y Casa Editora de Coni Hermanos, 1916.

Cámara Azucarera Regional de Tucumán. *Cincuentenario del Centro Azucarero Argentino: Desarrollo de la industria en medio siglo: Trabajo preparado por el Gerente-Secretario del Centro Azucarero Argentino, Sr. Emilio Schleh.* Buenos Aires: Imprenta Ferrari Hermanos, 1944.

Capria, José. *Contribución al estudio del cultivo de la caña de azúcar.* Buenos Aires: Imprenta de Pablo Gadola, 1915.

Castilla Portugal, Manuel. *La República Argentina: Su historia, geográfia, industria y costumbres.* Barcelona: Librería de Antonio J. Bastinos, 1897.

Centro Azucarero Nacional. *La industria azucarera argentina.* Buenos Aires: Imprenta Ferrari Hermanos, 1926.

Clemenceau, Georges. *South America To-day.* New York: Putnam, 1911.

Comisión de Industriales. *El problema azucarero (1914-1915).* Buenos Aires: A de Martino. Sarmiento 1289, 1915.

Concolorcorvo. *El Lazarillo: A Guide for Inexperienced Travelers between Buenos Aires and Lima, 1773.* Translated by Walter D. Kline. Bloomington: Indiana University Press, 1965.

Cordeiro, Ramón, Carlos Dalmiro Viale, Horacio Sánchez Loria, and Ernesto del Moral, eds. *Compilación ordenada de leyes, decretos y mensajes del período constitucional de la Provincia de Tucumán que comienza en el año 1852.* 33 vols. Tucumán: Prebisch y Violeto, 1915-19.

Daireaux, Emile. *Vida y costumbres en el Plata.* Buenos Aires: F. Lajouane, 1888.

Denis, Pierre. *The Argentine Republic, Its Development and Progress.* Translated by Joseph McCabe. New York: Scribner's, 1922.

Ferrocarril Central de Córdoba. *Album comercial, industrial, agropecuario.* Buenos Aires: Imprenta de Jose Tragant, 1920.

Franck, Harry A. *Working North from Patagonia.* New York: Century, 1921.

Fraser, John Foster. *The Amazing Argentine: A New Land of Enterprise.* London: Cassell, 1914.

Freyre, Ricardo Jaimes. *Tucumán en 1810: Noticia histórica y documentos inéditos.* Tucumán: Imprenta de La Razón, 1909.

García, Túbal C. *La industria azucarera argentina y las consecuencias de su protección.* Buenos Aires: Imprenta Mercatali, 1920.

Granillo, Arsenio. *Provincia de Tucumán,* serie de artículos descriptivos y noticiosos. Tucumán: Imprenta de la Razón, 1872.

Groussac, Paul, Alfredo Bousquet, Inocencio Liberani, Juan M. Terán, and Javier Frías. *Memoria histórica y descriptiva de la provincia de Tucumán.* Buenos Aires: Imprenta de M. Biedma, 1882.

Guzmán, Alfredo. *Réplica de los señores Guzman y Cia al sindicato Union Azucarera Argentina.* Tucumán: Talleres de El Norte, Calle Muñecas, Num. 283, 1896.

Huret, Jules. *De Buenos Aires al Gran Chaco.* 2 vols. 1900. Reprint, Buenos Aires: Hyspamérica, 1988.

Hutchinson, Thomas. *Buenos Ayres and Argentine Gleanings, with Extracts from a Diary of Salado Exploration in 1862 and 1863.* London: Edward Stanford, 1865.

Jefferson, Mark. *Peopling the Argentine Pampas.* New York: American Geographical Society, 1926.

Lahitte, Emilio. *La industria azucarera: Apuntes de actualidad.* Buenos Aires: Imprenta Europea de M. A. Rosas, 1902.

Lotito, Luis. "El proletariado tucumano a comienzos del siglo, 1907." In *Sindicatos como los de antes. . . .* Edited by Torcuato di Tella. Buenos Aires: Editorial Biblos, 1993.

Lozano, Pedro. *Historia de la conquista del Paraguay, Río de la Plata y Tucumán.* 5 vols. Buenos Aires: Casa Editora "Imprenta Popular," 1873–75.

Mabragaña, Heraclio, ed. *Los mensajes: Historia del desenvolvimiento de la nación argentina, redactada cronológicamente por sus gobernantes, 1810–1910.* 6 vols. Buenos Aires: Talleres Gráficos de la Compañía General de Fósforos, 1910.

Marbais du Graty, Alfredo. *La confederación argentina.* Translated from the French by Sara Elena Bruchez. 1858. Reprint, Buenos Aires: Comisión Nacional de Monumentos y Museos Históricos, 1968.

Moneta, Pompeyo. *Informe sobre la practicabilidad de la prolongación del Ferrocarril Central Argentino desde Córdoba hasta Jujuy.* Buenos Aires: Tipografía "La Tribuna," 1867.

Mulhall, Michael G., and Edward T. Mulhall. *Handbook of the River Plate, comprising Buenos Ayres, the Upper Provinces, Banda Oriental, and Paraguay.* Buenos Aires: *Standard* Printing Office, 1875.

———. *Handbook of the River Plate, comprising the Argentine Republic, Uruguay, and Paraguay, with railway map.* London: Kegan Paul, Trench, 1892.

———. *Handbook of the River Plate, comprising the Argentine Republic, Uruguay, and Paraguay, with six maps.* 5th ed. London: Trübner, 1885.

———. *The River Plate Hand-book, Guide, Directory and Almanac for 1863*, comprising the City and Province of Buenos Ayres, the other Argentina provinces, and Montevideo. Buenos Aires: Editors of the *Standard*, 1863.

Mur, César. *Registro estadístico de la Provincia de Tucumán, correspondiente al año 1882*. Buenos Aires: Imprenta de Pablo Coni, 1884.

Pacottet, P., and G. Ancizar. *Informe sobre Tucumán. Extracto del Boletín del Ministerio de Agricultura*. Buenos Aires: Talleres de la Dirección Meteorológica Argentina, 1913.

Padilla, Vicente. *El norte argentino: Tucumán, Salta, Jujuy, Santiago del Estero, Catamarca: Historia política, administrativa, social, comercial e industrial de las provincias: Crónica de la época prehispana hasta nuestros días*. Buenos Aires: Imprenta Ferrari Hermanos, 1922.

Pages, Pedro. *La industria azucarera en el norte de la República*. Buenos Aires: Imprenta del Departamento Nacional de Agricultura, 1888.

Parish, Woodbine. *Buenos Aires y las provincias del Río de la Plata, desde su descubrimiento y conquista por los españoles*. Translated by Justo Maeso. 1853. Reprint, Buenos Aires: Librería Hachette, 1958.

Paz, José María. *Contribución al estudio del cultivo y elaboración de la caña de azúcar en la Provincia de Tucumán*. Buenos Aires: Imprenta y Litografía Oscar Mengen, 1921.

Quesada, Vicente. *Memorias de un viejo: Escenas de costumbres de la República Argentina*. Buenos Aires: Jacobo Peuser, 1889.

Quintero, Eduardo. *Ocho días en Tucumán: Apuntes de viaje*. Buenos Aires: Imprenta de M. Biedma, 1877.

Rickart, Ignacio. *Mineral and Other Resources in the Argentine Republic in 1869*. London: Longmans, Green, 1870.

Rodríguez Marquina, Paulino. "Las clases obreras: La mano de obra, costumbres, vicios y virtudes de las clases obreras y medios para mejorar sus condiciones." *Tucumán literario* 17 (September 1894).

———. *La mortalidad infantil en Tucumán*. Tucumán: Imprenta de La Razón, 1898.

———. *La provincia de Tucumán. Breves apuntes*. Tucumán: Tip. y Encuadernación de *El Orden*, 1890.

Salvatierra, D. F. *Ingenio "La Florida" de la Compañía Azucarera Tucumana: Monografías industriales*. Buenos Aires: Imprenta y Casa Editora de Coni Hermanos, 1900.

Terry, José. *Memoria presentada al Sr. Presidente de la República: Tucumán, Salta, Jujuy y Santiago*. Buenos Aires: Compañía Sud-Americana de Billetes de Banco, 1894.

Unión Azucarera. *La Unión Azucarera Argentina y los Señores Guzman y Cia.* Buenos Aires: Imprenta y Encuadernación de J. Schürer-Stolle, 1896.

Vallejo, Benigno, and Estergidio de la Vega. *Morbilidad y mortalidad de la primera infancia en Tucumán. Estudio presentado al Primer Congreso Nacional de Medicina por los delegados del Gobierno de la Provincia de Tucumán.* Tucumán: Talleres de la Provincia, 1917.

Wauters, Carlos. *El riego en Tucumán a través de los siglos, desde la fundación de la capital hasta la sanción de la Ley Vigente, 1868–1897.* Tucumán: Talleres de la Provincia, 1904.

Secondary Sources

Adelman, Jeremy. "Agricultural Credit in the Province of Buenos Aires, Argentina, 1890–1914." *Journal of Latin American Studies* 22, no. 1 (1990): 69–87.

———. *Frontier Development: Land, Labor, and Capital on the Wheatlands of Argentina and Canada, 1890–1914.* New York: Oxford University Press, 1994.

———. *Republic of Capital: Buenos Aires and the Legal Transformation of the Atlantic World.* Stanford: Stanford University Press, 1999.

Albert, Bill. *An Essay on the Peruvian Sugar Industry, 1880–1922: And the Letters of Ronald Gordon, Administrator of the British Sugar Company in the Cañete Valley, 1914–1919.* Norwich, UK: School of Social Studies, University of East Anglia, 1976.

Albert, Bill, and Adrian Graves, eds. *Crisis and Change in the International Sugar Economy, 1860–1914.* Norwich, UK: ISC Press, 1984.

———, eds. *The World Sugar Economy in War and Depression, 1914–1940.* London: Routledge, 1988.

Allahar, Anton. *Class, Politics, and Sugar in Colonial Cuba.* Lewiston, NY: Edwin Mellen, 1990.

———. "The Cuban Sugar Planters (1790–1820)." *Americas* 41, no. 1 (1984): 37–57.

Assadourián, Carlos Sempat. *El sistema de la economía colonial: Mercado interno, regiones y espacio económico.* Lima: Instituto de Estudios Peruanos, 1982.

Ayala, César. *American Sugar Kingdom: The Plantation Economy of the Spanish Caribbean, 1898–1934.* Chapel Hill: University of North Carolina Press, 1999.

Balán, Jorge. "Una cuestión regional en la Argentina: Burguesías provinciales y el mercado nacional en el desarrollo agroexportador." *Desarrollo económico* 18, no. 69 (1978): 49–87.

———. "Migraciones, mano de obra y formación de un proletariado rural en Tucumán, Argentina, 1870–1914." *Demografía y economía* 10, no. 2 (1976): 201–34.

Balán, Jorge, and Nancy López. "Burguesías y gobiernos provinciales en la Argentina: La política impositiva de Tucumán y Mendoza entre 1873 y 1914." *Desarrollo económico* 17, no. 67 (1977): 391–433.

Barickman, B. J. *A Bahian Counterpoint: Sugar, Tobacco, Cassava, and Slavery in the Recôncavo, 1780–1860.* Stanford: Stanford University Press, 1998.

———. "Persistence and Decline: Slave Labour and Sugar Production in the Bahian Recôncavo, 1850–1888," *Journal of Latin American Studies* 28, no. 3 (1996): 581–633.

———. "Revisiting the 'Casa-Grande': Plantation and Cane-Farming Households in Early Nineteenth-Century Bahia." *Hispanic American Historical Review* 84, no. 4 (2004): 619–59.

Barrett, Ward. *The Sugar Hacienda of the Marqueses del Valle.* Minneapolis: University of Minnesota Press, 1970.

Bascary, Ana María. *Familia y vida cotidiana: Tucumán a fines de la colonia.* Tucumán: Universidad Nacional de Tucumán, 1999.

Bauer, Arnold. "Rural Workers in Spanish America: Problems of Peonage and Oppression." *Hispanic American Historical Review* 59, no. 2 (1979): 34–63.

Bazán, Armando Raúl. *Historia del noroeste argentino.* Buenos Aires: Editorial Plus Ultra, 1986.

———. *El noroeste y la Argentina contemporánea.* Buenos Aires: Editorial Plus Ultra, 1992.

Bergad, Laird. *Cuban Rural Society in the Nineteenth Century: The Social and Economic History of Monoculture in Matanzas.* Princeton: Princeton University Press, 1990.

———. "The Economic Viability of Sugar Production Based on Slave Labor in Cuba, 1859–1878." *Latin American Research Review* 24, no. 1 (1989), 95–113.

Bliss, Horacio William. *Del virreinato a Rosas: Ensayo de historia económica argentina, 1776–1829.* Tucumán: Editorial Richardet, 1958.

Botana, Natalio. *El orden conservador: La política argentina entre 1880 y 1916.* Buenos Aires: Editorial Sudamericana, 1977.

Botana, Natalio, and Ezequiel Gallo. *De la república posible a la república verdadera (1880–1910).* Buenos Aires: Ariel, 1997.

Brass, Tom. "The Latin American Enganche System: Some Revisionist Interpretations Revisited." *Slavery and Abolition* 11, no. 1 (1990): 74–103.

Bravo, Augusto. *La industria azucarera en Tucumán: Sus problemas sanitarios y sociales.* Tucumán: Universidad Nacional de Tucumán, 1966.

Bravo, María Celia. "El campesinado tucumano: De labradores a cañeros; De la diversificación agraria hacia el monocultivo." *Población y sociedad,* no. 5 (October 1998): 83–132.

———. "Especialización azucarera, agua y política en Tucumán." *Travesía*, no. 1 (1998): 17–39.

———. "Las leyes 'machete' y la ruptura del frente azucarero tucumano." In *Estudios sobre la historia de la industria azucarera argentina*, edited by Daniel Campi, 2 vols., 97–139. Jujuy: Ediciones del Gabinete, 1992.

———. "Liberales, socialistas, iglesia y patrones frente a la situación de los trabajadores en Tucumán." In *La cuestión social en Argentina, 1870–1943*, edited by Juan Suriano, 31–61. Buenos Aires: Editoria La Colmena, 2000.

———. "Sector cañero y política en Tucumán, 1895–1930." PhD diss., Universidad Nacional de Tucumán, 2000.

Brennan, James. *Labor Wars in Córdoba, 1955–1976: Ideology, Work, and Labor Politics in an Argentine Industrial City.* Cambridge, MA: Harvard University Press, 1994.

Brennan, James, and Ofelia Pianetto, eds. *Region and Nation: Politics, Economy, and Society in Twentieth-Century Argentina.* New York: St. Martin's, 2000.

Brown, Jonathan C. *A Socioeconomic History of Argentina, 1776–1860.* Cambridge: Cambridge University Press, 1979.

Burgin, Miron. *The Economic Aspects of Argentine Federalism, 1820–1852.* Cambridge, MA: Harvard University Press, 1946.

Campi, Daniel. "Azúcar y trabajo: Coacción y mercado laboral, 1856–1896." PhD diss., Universidad Complutense de Madrid, 2002.

———. "Captación forzada de mano de obra y trabajo asalariado en Tucumán, 1856–1896." *Anuario del IEHS*, no. 8 (1993): 49–51.

———. "Coacción y mercado de trabajo: Consideraciones en torno a Tucumán, Argentina: Segunda mitad del siglo XIX." In *Historia I: Projecte Social*, edited by Joseph Fontana, 760–68. Barcelona: Crítica, 2004.

———, ed. *Estudios sobre la historia de la industria azucarera argentina.* 2 vols. Jujuy: Ediciones del Gabinete, 1992.

———. "La evolución del salario real del peón azucarero en Tucumán (Argentina) en un contexto de coacción y salario 'arcaico' (1881–1893)." *América Latina en la historia económica*, no. 22 (2004): 105–28.

Campi, Daniel, and Patricia Juarez-Dappe. "Despegue y auge azucarero en Perú y Argentina: Semejanzas y contrastes." *Illes i imperis*, no. 9 (December 2006): 79–115.

Cardoso, Gerald. *Negro Slavery in the Sugar Plantations of Veracruz and Pernambuco, 1550–1680: A Comparative Study.* Washington, DC: University Press of America, 1983.

Carrington, Selwyn. *The Sugar Industry and the Abolition of the Slave Trade.* Gainesville: University Press of Florida, 2002.

Chalmin, Ph. G. "The Important Trends in Sugar Diplomacy before 1914." In *Crisis and Change in the International Sugar Economy, 1860-1914,* edited by Bill Albert and Adrian Graves, 9-21. Norwich, UK: ISC Press, 1984.

Chamosa, Oscar. "Archetypes of Nationhood: Folk Culture, Sugar Industry, and the Birth of Cultural Nationalism in Argentina, 1895-1945." PhD diss., University of North Carolina, Chapel Hill, 2003.

Chiaramonte, José Carlos. *Nacionalismo y liberalismo económicos en Argentina, 1860-1880.* Buenos Aires: Solar/Hachette, 1971.

Conti, Viviana. "Articulación económica de los Andes centromeridionales, siglo XIX," *Anuario de estudios americanos,* no. 46 (1989): 423-53.

Cornblit, Oscar, Ezequiel Gallo, and Alfredo O'Connell. "La generación del 80 y su proyecto: Antecedentes y consecuencias." *Desarrollo económico* 1, no. 4 (1962): 5-45.

Cortés Conde, Roberto. *La economía argentina en el largo plazo.* Buenos Aires: Editorial Sudamericana, 1997.

———. *The First Stages of Modernization in Spanish America.* New York: Harper and Row, 1974.

———. *El progreso argentino, 1880-1914.* Buenos Aires: Editorial Sudamericana, 1979.

———. *Trends of Real Wages in Argentina.* Working paper 26. Cambridge: Centre for Latin American Studies, University of Cambridge, 1976.

Cortés Conde, Roberto, and Shane Hunt, eds. *The Latin American Economies: Growth and the Export Sector, 1880-1930.* New York: Holmes and Meier, 1985.

Crespo, Horacio. *Historia del azúcar en México.* Mexico City: Fondo de Cultura Económica, 1988.

Cuccorese, Horacio Juan. *Historia de los ferrocarriles en la Argentina.* Buenos Aires: Ediciones Macchi, 1984.

Cushner, Nicholas. *Jesuit Ranches and the Agrarian Development of Colonial Argentina, 1650-1767.* Albany: State University of New York Press, 1983.

Daunton, Martin. *Trusting Leviathan: The Politics of Taxation in Britain, 1799-1914.* Cambridge: Cambridge University Press, 2001.

Deerr, Noël. *The History of Sugar.* 2 vols. London: Chapman and Hall, 1949-50.

De la Fuente, Ariel. *Children of Facundo: Caudillo and Gaucho Insurgency during the Argentine State-Formation Process (La Rioja, 1853-1870).* Durham: Duke University Press, 2000.

Delich, Francisco. *Tierra y conciencia campesina en Tucumán.* Buenos Aires: Ediciones Signo, 1970.

Denslow, David. *Sugar Production in Northeastern Brazil and Cuba, 1858-1908.* New York: Garland, 1987.

Díaz Alejandro, Carlos. *Essays on the Economic History of the Argentine Republic*. New Haven: Yale University Press, 1970.

Di Tella, Guido, and D. C. M. Platt, eds. *The Political Economy of Argentina, 1880–1916*. Basingstoke: Macmillan, 1986.

Dore, Elizabeth. "Debt Peonage in Granada, Nicaragua, 1870–1930." *Hispanic American Historical Review* 83, no. 3 (2003): 521–59.

Dos Santos Gomes, Flavio. "A 'Safe Haven': Runaway Slaves, Mocambos, and Borders in Colonial Amazonia, Brazil." *Hispanic American Historical Review* 82, no. 3 (2002): 469–98.

Dunn, Richard. *Sugar and Slaves: The Rise of the Planter Class in the English West Indies, 1624–1713*. New York: Norton, 1973.

Dye, Alan. *Cuban Sugar in the Age of Mass Production: Technology and the Economics of the Sugar Central, 1899–1929*. Stanford: Stanford University Press, 1998.

Eisenberg, Peter. *The Sugar Industry in Pernambuco: Modernization without Change, 1840–1910*. Berkeley: University of California Press, 1974.

Ely, Roland T. *Cuando reinaba su majestad el azúcar*. Havana: Imagen Contemporánea, 1963.

Engerman, Stanley. "Contract Labor, Sugar, and Technology in the Nineteenth Century." *Journal of Economic History* 43, no. 3 (1983): 635–59.

FAO. *The World Sugar Economy in Figures, 1880–1959*. Rome: Food and Agriculture Organization of the United Nations, 1961.

Fernández Murga, Patricia. "La tierra en Tucumán en la primera mitad del siglo XIX: Propiedad, formas de acceso y de tenencia: El derecho y la realidad: Compraventas y compradores." Master's thesis, Universidad Internacional de La Rábida, 1996.

Ferns, H. S. *Britain and Argentina in the Nineteenth Century*. Oxford: Clarendon Press, 1960.

Ferrer, Aldo. *La economía argentina: Las etapas de su desarrollo y problemas actuales*. Mexico City: Fondo de Cultura Económica, 1973.

Feyling, Mariana. "La inmigración francesa en Tucumán, 1830–1880." Master's thesis, Universidad Nacional de Tucumán, 2000.

Figueroa, Luis A. *Sugar, Slavery, and Freedom in Nineteenth-Century Puerto Rico*. Chapel Hill: University of North Carolina Press, 2005.

Fodor, Jorge, and Arturo O'Connell. "La Argentina y la economía atlántica en la primera mitad del siglo XX." *Desarrollo económico* 13, no. 49 (1973): 3–65.

Gallo, Ezequiel. *La pampa gringa: La colonización agrícola en Santa Fe (1870–1895)*. Buenos Aires: Editorial Sudamericana, 1984.

Gallo, Ezequiel, and Roberto Cortés Conde. *Argentina: La república conservadora*. Buenos Aires: Editorial Paidós, 1972.

Galloway, J. H. "The Last Years of Slavery on the Sugar Plantations of Northeastern Brazil." *Hispanic American Historical Review* 51, no. 4 (1971): 586–605.

———. *The Sugar Cane Industry: An Historical Geography from Its Origins to 1914.* Cambridge: Cambridge University Press, 1989.

García Muñiz, Humberto. "La plantación que no se repite: Las historias azucareras de la República Dominicana y Puerto Rico, 1870–1930." *Revista de Indias* 65, no. 233 (2005):172–91.

García Soriano, Manuel. "La condición social del trabajador en Tucumán durante el siglo XIX." *Revisión histórica,* no. 1 (May 1960): 7–46.

Garzón Maceda, Ceferino. *Economía del Tucumán: Economía natural y economía monetaria, rentas eclesiásticas.* Córdoba, Arg.: Universidad Nacional de Córdoba, 1965.

Giarraca, Norma. *Los campesinos cañeros: Multiocupación y organización.* Buenos Aires: Facultad de Ciencias Sociales, Universidad de Buenos Aires, 1991.

Giberti, Horacio. *El desarrollo agrario argentino: Estudio de la región pampeana.* Buenos Aires: Editorial Universitaria de Buenos Aires, 1964.

Giménez Zapiola, Marcos. "El interior argentino y el 'desarrollo hacia afuera': El caso de Tucumán." In *El régimen oligárquico: Materiales para el estudio de la realidad argentina hasta 1930,* compiled by Giménez, 72–115. Buenos Aires: Amorrortu Editores, 1975.

Girbal de Blacha, Noemí. "Estado, modernización azucarera y comportamiento empresario en la Argentina (1876–1914)." In *Estudios sobre la historia de la industria azucarera,* 2 vols., edited by Daniel Campi, 1:17–59. Jujuy: Ediciones del Gabinete, 1992.

Gómez Guerra, Juan Manuel. *Camajuaní: La Plantación Azucarera en el siglo XIX.* Cuba: Editorial Santa Clara, 2001.

Gonzales, Michael J. "Capitalist Agriculture and Labour Contracting in Northern Peru, 1880–1905." *Journal of Latin American Studies* 12, no. 2 (1980): 291–315.

———. "Chinese Plantation Workers and Social Conflict in Peru in the Late Nineteenth Century," *Journal of Latin American Studies* 21, no. 3 (1989): 385–424.

———. *Plantation Agriculture and Social Control in Northern Peru, 1875–1933.* Austin: University of Texas Press, 1985.

González Rodríguez, Adolfo Luis. *La encomienda en Tucumán.* Seville: Artes Gráficas Padura, 1984.

Goveia, Elsa. *Slave and Society in the British Leeward Islands at the End of the Eighteenth Century.* Westport, CT: Greenwood, 1980.

Greenberg, Daniel. "The Dictatorship of the Chimneys: Sugar, Politics and Agrarian Unrest in Tucumán, Argentina, 1914-1930." PhD diss., University of Washington, 1985.

Guerra y Sánchez, Ramiro. *Sugar and Society in the Caribbean: An Economic History of Cuban Agriculture.* New Haven: Yale University Press, 1964.

Guy, Donna. *Argentine Sugar Politics: Tucumán and the Generation of Eighty.* Tempe: Center for Latin American Studies, Arizona State University, 1980.

———. "Refinería Argentina, 1888-1930: Límites de la tecnología azucarera en una economía periférica." *Desarrollo económico* 28, no. 111 (1988): 353-73.

———. "The Rural Working Class in 19th-Century Argentina: Forced Plantation Labor in Tucumán." *Latin American Research Review* 13, no. 1 (1978): 135-45.

———. "Women, Peonage, and Industrialization: Argentina, 1810-1914." *Latin American Research Review* 16, no. 3 (1981): 65-89.

Halperín-Donghi, Tulio. "Gastos militares y economía regional: El Ejército del Norte (1810-1817)." *Desarrollo económico* 11, no. 41 (1971): 87-99.

———. *Una nación para el desierto argentino.* Buenos Aires: Centro Editor de América Latina, 1982.

———. *Politics, Economics and Society in Argentina in the Revolutionary Period.* Cambridge: Cambridge University Press, 1975.

Hattingh, Alistair. "Cuyo and Goliath: The Province of San Juan and the Argentine Federal Government, 1930-1943." PhD diss., University of California, Santa Barbara, 2003.

Healey, Mark. "The Ruins of the New Argentina: Peronism, Architecture, and the Remaking of San Juan after the 1944 Earthquake." PhD diss., Duke University, 2000.

Holloway, Thomas. *Immigrants on the Land: Coffee and Society in São Paulo, 1886-1934.* Chapel Hill: University of North Carolina Press, 1980.

Hora, Roy. *Los terratenientes de la pampa argentina: Una historia social y política, 1860-1945.* Buenos Aires: Siglo Veintiuno de Argentina Editores, 2002.

Huerta, María Teresa. "Empresarios y ferrocarriles en Morelos, 1875-1900." *Siglo XIX* 5, no. 14 (1996): 69-87.

Iglesias García, Fe. *Del ingenio al central.* San Juan: Editorial de la Universidad de Puerto Rico, 1998.

Jones, David. "Shifting Patterns of Sugar Cane Production in Northwest Argentina." PhD diss., Michigan State University, 1975.

Juarez-Dappe, Patricia. "*Cañeros* and *Colonos:* Cane Planters in Tucumán, 1876-1895." *Journal of Latin American Studies* 38, no. 1 (2006): 123-47.

Kantarovsky, Pablo. *300 años de lugares y edificios, San Miguel de Tucumán, 1685-1985.* Tucumán: Municipalidad de la Ciudad de San Miguel de Tucumán, 1985.

Kirchner, John. *Sugar and Seasonal Labor Migration: The Case of Tucumán, Argentina.* Research paper 192. Chicago: Department of Geography, University of Chicago, 1980.

Klarén, Peter. *Modernization, Dislocation, and Aprismo: Origins of the Peruvian Aprista Party, 1870–1932.* Austin: Institute of Latin American Studies, University of Texas, 1973.

———. "The Sugar Industry in Peru." *Revista de Indias* 65, no. 233 (2005): 33–48.

Knight, Alan. "Mexican Peonage: What Was It and Why Was It?" *Journal of Latin American Studies* 18, no. 1 (1986): 41–74.

Knight, Franklin W. "Origins of Wealth and the Sugar Revolution in Cuba, 1750–1850." *Hispanic American Historical Review* 57, no. 2 (1977): 231–53.

Lagos, Marcelo. "The Organization of Jujuy's Sugar Ingenios in a Regional Context (1870–1940)." In *Region and Nation: Politics, Economy, and Society in Twentieth-Century Argentina,* edited by James Brennan and Ofelia Pianetto, 103–29. New York: St Martin's, 2000.

Laks, J. *La verdad sobre la cuestión azucarera.* Buenos Aires: Editorial Documentos, 1960.

Landázury Benítez, Gisela, and Verónica Vázquez Mantecón. *Azúcar y estado (1750–1880).* Mexico City: Fondo de Cultura Económica, 1988.

Langer, Erick. "Espacios coloniales y economías nacionales: Bolivia y el norte argentino (1810–1930)." *Siglo XIX* 2, no. 4 (1987): 135–60.

Langer, Erick, and Viviana E. Conti. "Circuitos comerciales y cambio económico en los Andes centromeridionales (1830–1930)." *Desarrollo económico* 31, no. 121 (1991): 91–111.

La Rosa Corzo, Gabino. *Runaway Slave Settlements in Cuba: Resistance and Repression.* Chapel Hill: University of North Carolina Press, 2003.

Legrand, Catherine. "Informal Resistance on a Dominican Sugar Plantation during the Trujillo Dictatorship." *Hispanic American Historical Review* 75, no. 4 (1995): 555–96.

León, Carlos. *El desarrollo agrario de Tucumán en el período de transición de la agricultura diversificada al monocultivo cañero.* Buenos Aires: Programa Interdisciplinario de Estudios Agrarios, 1999.

———. "El desarrollo agrario de Tucumán en el período de transición de la economía de capitalismo incipiente a la expansión azucarera." *Desarrollo económico* 33, no. 130 (1993): 217–36.

Lewis, Colin. *British Railways in Argentina, 1857–1914: A Case Study of Foreign Investment.* Atlantic Highlands, NJ: Humanities Press, 1983.

———. "The Political Economy of State-Making: The Argentine, 1852–1955." In *Studies in the Formation of the Nation-State in Latin America,* edited by James Dunkerley, 169–81. London: Institute of Latin American Studies, 2002.

Lizondo, Mary Ann. "The Impact of the Sugar Industry on the Middle Class of an Argentine City: San Miguel de Tucumán, 1869–1895." PhD diss., George Washington University, 1982.

Lizondo Borda, Manuel. *Historia de Tucumán (siglo XIX).* Tucumán: Universidad Nacional de Tucumán, 1948.

López, Mario Justo. *Ferrocarriles, deuda y crisis: Historia de los ferrocarriles en la Argentina de 1887 a 1896.* Buenos Aires: Editorial de Belgrano, 2000.

López de Albornoz, Cristina. *Los dueños de la tierra: Economía, sociedad y poder; Tucumán, 1770–1820.* Tucumán: Facultad de Filosofía y Letras, Universidad Nacional de Tucumán, 2003.

Loveman, Brian. "Critique of Arnorld Bauer's 'Rural Workers in Spanish America: Problems of Peonage and Oppression.'" *Hispanic American Historical Review* 59, no. 3 (1979): 478–86.

Luiggi, Alice Houston. *65 Valiants.* Gainesville: University of Florida Press, 1965.

Macera, Pablo. *La plantaciones azucareras en el Perú, 1821–1875.* Lima: Centro Peruano de Historia Económica, 1974.

Martínez Vergne, Teresita. *Capitalism in Colonial Puerto Rico: Central San Vicente in the Late Nineteenth Century.* Gainesville: University Press of Florida, 1992.

———. "New Patterns for Puerto Rico's Sugar Workers: Abolition and Centralization at San Vicente, 1873–1892." *Hispanic American Historical Review* 68, no. 1 (1988): 45–74.

Martos, Sofía. "The Balancing Act: Ethnicity, Commerce, and Politics among Syrian and Lebanese Immigrants in Argentina, 1890–1955." PhD diss., University of California, Los Angeles, 2007.

McCreery, David. "'An Odious Feudalism': Mandamiento Labor and Commercial Agriculture in Guatemala, 1858–1920." *Latin American Perspectives* 13, no. 1 (1986): 99–117.

McDonald, Roderick. *The Economy and Material Culture of Slaves: Goods and Chattels on the Sugar Plantations of Jamaica and Louisiana.* Baton Rouge: Louisiana State University Press, 1993.

McGreevey, William Paul. *An Economic History of Colombia, 1845–1930.* Cambridge: Cambridge University Press, 1971.

Melville, Roberto. *Crecimiento y rebelión: El desarrollo económico de las haciendas azucareras en Morelos, 1880–1910.* Mexico City: Centro de Investigaciones de Desarrollo Rural, 1979.

Micele, Antonio. *La industria azucarera en la República argentina.* Buenos Aires: Talleres Gráficos de la Cia. Gral. Fabril Financiera, 1936.

Mintz, Sidney. *Sweetness and Power: The Place of Sugar in Modern History.* New York: Penguin, 1988.

Mitre, Antonio. *El monedero de los Andes: Región económica y moneda boliviana en el siglo XIX*. La Paz: Hisbol, 1986.

Moitt, Bernard, ed. *Sugar, Slavery, and Society: Perspectives on the Caribbean, India, the Mascarenes, and the United States*. Gainesville: University Press of Florida, 2004.

Monteón, Michael. "The Enganche in the Chilean Nitrate Sector, 1880–1930." *Latin American Perspectives* 6, no. 3 (1979): 66–79.

Moreno Fraginals, Manuel. *The Sugarmill: The Socioeconomic Complex of Sugar in Cuba, 1760–1860*. New York: Monthly Review Press, 1974.

Morton, F. W. O. "Growth and Innovation: The Bahian Sugar Industry, 1790–1860." *North/South* 5, no. 10 (1980): 37–54.

Müller-Bergh, Klaus. "Comercio interno y economía regional en Hispanoamérica colonial: Aproximación cuantitativa a la historia económica de San Miguel de Tucumán, 1784–1809," *Jahrbuch für Geschichte von Staat, Wirtschaft und Gesellschaft Lateinamerikas,* no. 24 (1987): 265–334.

Nougués, Miguel Alfredo. *Los fundadores, los propulsores, los realizadores de San Pablo*. Buenos Aires: Club de Lectores, 1976.

Ortiz, Fernando. *Cuban Counterpoint: Tobacco and Sugar*. New York: Knopf, 1947.

Ostengo de Ahumada, Ana María. *La legislación laboral en Tucumán: Recopilación ordenada de leyes, decretos y resoluciones sobre derecho del trabajo y seguridad social, 1839–1969*. 3 vols. Tucumán: Facultad de Derecho y Ciencias Sociales, Instituto de Derecho del Trabajo Juan Bautista Alberdi, Universidad Nacional de Tucumán, 1969.

Oszlak, Oscar. *La formación del estado argentino*. Buenos Aires: Editorial de Belgrano, 1982.

Otonello, Tulio Santiago. "El ferrocarril y su influencia en el desarrollo y posterior decaimiento de la Villa de Medinas." In *Ensayos sobre la ciudad,* edited by Alba Omil, 40–67. Tucumán: Ediciones del Rectorado, Universidad Nacional de Tucumán, 1995.

Panettieri, José. *Los trabajadores*. Buenos Aires: Centro Editor de América Latina, 1982.

Paterlini de Koch, Olga. *Pueblos azucareros de Tucumán*. Tucumán: Editorial del Instituto Argentino de Investigaciones de Historia de la Arquitectura y del Urbanismo, 1987.

Paz, Gustavo. "Province and Nation in Northern Argentina: Peasants, Elite, and the State, Jujuy, 1790–1880." PhD diss., Emory University, 1999.

Piel, Jean. *Capitalismo agrario en el Perú*. Translated by Francis Eherran. Buenos Aires: Universidad Nacional de Salta; Lima: Instituto Francés de Estudios Andinos, 1995.

Pineda, Yovanna. "The Firm in Early Argentine Industrialization, 1890–1930: A Study of Fifty-five Joint-Stock Companies' Owners, Finance Sources, Productivity, and Profits." PhD diss., University of California, Los Angeles, 2002.

Prinsen Geerligs, Hedrick. *Cane Sugar and Its Manufacture.* London: Norman Rodger, 1909.

———. *The World's Cane Sugar Industry, Past and Present.* Manchester: Norman Rodger, 1912.

Pucci, Roberto. "Azúcar y proteccionismo en Argentina, 1870–1920." In *Estudios sobre la historia de la industria azucarera argentina,* 2 vols., edited by Daniel Campi, 1:43–69. Jujuy: Ediciones del Gabinete, 1992.

———. *La élite azucarera y la formación del sector cañero en Tucumán (1880–1920).* Buenos Aires: Centro Editor de América Latina, 1984.

———. "La población y el auge azucarero en Tucumán," in *Breves contribuciones del Instituto de Estudios Geográficos* 7:1 (1992): 7–44.

———. "La revolución industrial azucarera en Cuba, Brasil y Argentina: Tecnología y cambio social, ca. 1870–1930." *América latina en la historia económica,* 16 (July–December 2001): 123–49.

Ramos Mattei, Andrés A. "The Plantations of the Southern Coast of Puerto Rico, 1880–1910." *Social and Economic Studies* 37, nos. 1–2 (1988): 365–404.

Ricci, Teodoro. *Evolución de la ciudad de San Miguel de Tucumán.* Tucumán: Universidad Nacional de Tucumán, 1967.

Rocchi, Fernando. *Chimneys in the Desert: Industrialization in Argentina during the Export Boom Years, 1870–1930.* Stanford: Stanford University Press, 2006.

Rock, David. *Argentina, 1516–1987: From Spanish Colonization to Alfonsín.* Berkeley: University of California Press, 1987.

———. "Argentina in 1914: The Pampas, the Interior, Buenos Aires." In *Argentina since Independence,* edited by Leslie Bethell, 113–39. Cambridge: Cambridge University Press, 1993.

———. *Politics in Argentina, 1890–1930: The Rise and Fall of Radicalism.* Cambridge: Cambridge University Press, 1975.

———. *State Building and Political Movements in Argentina, 1860–1916.* Stanford: Stanford University Press, 2002.

Romero, Luis Alberto. *A History of Argentina in the Twentieth Century.* Translated by James Brennan. University Park: Pennsylvania State University Press, 2003.

Roseberry, William, Lowell Gudmundson, and Mario Samper Kutschbach, eds. *Coffee, Society, and Power in Latin America.* Baltimore: Johns Hopkins University Press, 1995.

Rosenzvaig, Eduardo. *La cepa: Arqueología de una cultura azucarera.* Tucumán: Editorial Letra Buena, 1995.

———. *Historia social de Tucumán y del azúcar.* 2 vols. Tucumán: Universidad Nacional de Tucumán, 1986.

Rosenzvaig, Eduardo, and Luis Bonano. *De la manufactura a la revolución industrial: El azúcar en el norte argentino.* Tucumán: Universidad Nacional de Tucumán, 1992.

Rubinstein, Gustavo. *Los sindicatos azucareros en los orígenes del peronismo tucumano.* Tucumán: Universidad Nacional del Tucumán, 2006.

Sábato, Hilda. *Agrarian Capitalism and the World Market: Buenos Aires in the Pastoral Age.* Albuquerque: University of New Mexico Press, 1990.

———. *The Many and the Few: Political Participation in Republican Buenos Aires.* Stanford: Stanford University Press, 2001.

Sábato, Jorge F. *La clase dominante en la Argentina moderna: Formación y características.* Buenos Aires: Grupo Editor Latinoamericano, 1988.

Saksonoff Velarde, Atilio. "Historia de las instituciones bancarias de la provincia." In *Primer Congreso de Historia de los Pueblos de la Provincia de Tucumán.* Tucumán: Imprenta del Ministerio de Gobierno, 1953.

Sánchez Román, José Antonio. *La dulce crisis: Estado, empresarios e industria azucarera en Tucumán, Argentina (1853–1914).* Seville: Diputación de Sevilla, Universidad de Sevilla; Madrid: Consejo Superior de Investigaciones Científicas, Escuela de Estudios Hispano-Americanos, 2005.

Sánchez Santiró, Ernest. "Evolución productiva de la agroindustria azucarera de Morelos durante el siglo XIX: Una propuesta de periodización." *América latina en la historia económica* 26 (July-December 2006): 111–27.

Santamaría, Daniel. *Azúcar y sociedad en el noroeste argentino.* Buenos Aires: Ediciones del Instituto de Desarrollo Económico y Social, 1986.

———. *Las huelgas azucareras de Tucumán, 1923.* Buenos Aires: Centro Editor de América Latina, 1984.

Santamaría García, Antonio. "Reformas coloniales, economía y especialización productiva en Puerto Rico y Cuba, 1760–1850." *Revista de Indias* 65, no. 235 (2005): 709–28.

———. *Sin azúcar no hay país: La industria azucarera y la economía cubana (1919–1939).* Seville: Consejo Superior de Investigaciones Científicas, Universidad de Sevilla, 2001.

Santamaría García, Antonio, and Alejandro García Alvarez. "Azucar en América." *Revista de Indias* 65, no. 233 (2005): 9–31.

Santamaría García, Antonio, and Luis Miguel García Mora. "Colonos: Agricultores cañeros, ¿Clase media rural en Cuba?" *Revista de Indias* 58, no. 212 (1998): 131–61.

Santillán de Andres, Selva Elvira, and Teodoro Ricardo Ricci. *Geografía de Tucumán.* Tucumán: Universidad Nacional de Tucumán, 1980.

———. *La región de la cuenca de Tapia-Trancas.* Tucumán: Departamento de Geografía, Universidad Nacional de Tucumán, 1966.

Scalabrini Ortiz, Raúl. *Historia de los ferrocarriles argentinos.* Buenos Aires: Editorial Devenir, 1958

Scarano, Francisco A. *Sugar and Slavery in Puerto Rico: The Plantation Economy of Ponce, 1800–1850.* Madison: University of Wisconsin Press, 1984.

Schickendantz, Emilio, and Emilio Rebuelto. *Los ferrocarriles en la Argentina, 1857–1910.* Buenos Aires: Fundación Museo Ferroviario, 1994.

Schleh, Emilio. *Compilación legal sobre el azúcar.* Buenos Aires: Ferrari Hermanos, 9 vols. 1939–1950.

———. *La industria azucarera argentina: Pasado y presente.* Buenos Aires: Ferrari Hermanos, 1930.

———. *La industria azucarera en su primer centenario, 1821–1921.* Buenos Aires: Ferrari Hermanos, 1921.

———. *Noticias históricas sobre el azúcar en la Argentina.* Buenos Aires: Ferrari Hermanos, 1945.

Schwartz, Stuart. *Sugar Plantations in the Formation of the Brazilian Society: Bahia, 1550–1835.* New York: Cambridge University Press, 1985.

———. *Tropical Babylons: Sugar and the Making of the Atlantic World, 1450–1680.* Chapel Hill: University of North Carolina Press, 2004.

Scobie, James. *Argentina: A City and a Nation.* 2nd ed. New York: Oxford University Press, 1971.

———. *Buenos Aires: Plaza to Suburb, 1870–1910.* New York: Oxford University Press, 1974.

———. *Revolution on the Pampas: A Social History of Argentine Wheat, 1860–1910.* Austin: University of Texas Press, 1968.

———. *Secondary Cities of Argentina: The Social History of Corrientes, Salta, and Mendoza, 1850–1910.* Completed and edited by Samuel Baily. Stanford: Stanford University Press, 1988.

Scott, James. *Weapons of the Weak: Everyday Forms of Peasant Resistance.* New Haven: Yale University Press, 1985.

Scott, Rebecca. "The Transformation of Sugar Production in Cuba after Emancipation, 1880–1900: Planters, Colonos and Former Slaves." In *Crisis and Change in the International Sugar Economy, 1860–1914,* edited by Bill Albert and Adrian Graves, 111–19. Norwich, UK: ISC Press, 1984.

Sheridan, Richard B. *Sugar and Slavery: An Economic History of the British West Indies, 1623–1775.* Baltimore: Johns Hopkins University Press, 1973.

Síndico, Doménico E. "Modernization in Nineteenth-Century Sugar Haciendas: The Case of Morelos: From Formal to Real Subsumption of Labor to Capital." *Latin American Perspectives* 7, no. 4 (1980): 83–99.

Solá, José A. "The Technological Transformation of the Sugar Industry and American Protectionism in the Emergence of the Colonos in Caguas, Puerto Rico, 1898–1928." PhD diss., University of Connecticut, 2004.

Stein, Stanley J. *Vassouras, a Brazilian Coffee County, 1850–1900.* Cambridge, MA: Harvard University Press, 1957.

Stinchcombe, Arthur. *Sugar Island Slavery in the Age of Enlightenment: The Political Economy of the Caribbean World.* Princeton: Princeton University Press, 1995.

Supplee, Joan. "Provincial Elites and the Economic Transformation of Mendoza, Argentina, 1880–1914." PhD diss., University of Texas, Austin, 1988.

Szuchman, Mark. *Mobility and Integration in Urban Argentina: Córdoba in the Liberal Era.* Austin: University of Texas Press, 1980.

Tandeter, Enrique. *Coercion and Market: Silver Mining in Colonial Potosí, 1692–1826.* Translated by Richard Warren. Albuquerque: University of New Mexico Press, 1993.

Taylor, Kit Sims. *Sugar and the Underdevelopment of Northeastern Brazil, 1500–1970.* Gainesville: University Presses of Florida, 1978.

Teruel de Lagos, Ana. "Regulación legal del trabajo en haciendas, ingenios y plantaciones de caña de azúcar en la provincia de Jujuy: Siglo XIX a mediados del XX." In *Estudios sobre la historia de la industria azucarera*, edited by Daniel Campi, 139–79. Jujuy: Ediciones del Gabinete, 1992.

Thompson, E. P. "Time, Work-Discipline, and Industrial Capitalism." In *Past and Present,* no. 38 (1967): 56–97.

Tío Vallejo, Gabriela. *Antiguo régimen y liberalismo: Tucumán, 1770–1830.* San Miguel de Tucumán: Facultad de Filosofía y Letras, Universidad Nacional de Tucumán, 2001.

Tomich, Dale. *Slavery in the Circuit of Sugar: Martinique and the World Economy, 1830–1848.* Baltimore: Johns Hopkins University Press, 1990.

———. "World Slavery and Caribbean Capitalism: The Cuban Sugar Industry, 1760–1868." *Theory and Society* 20, no. 3 (1991): 297–319.

Topik, Steven, and Allen Wells, eds. *The Second Conquest of Latin America: Coffee, Henequen, and Oil during the Export Boom, 1850–1930.* Austin: University of Texas Press, 1998.

Usandivaras de Garneri, Brigida, and Segundo Ferreyra. *Trancas: Monografía histórica de la formación, desenvolvimiento y decadencia del antiguo pueblo de Trancas.* Tucumán: Ediciones Universidad Nacional de Tucumán, 1951.

Van Young, Eric. *Hacienda and Market in Eighteenth-Century Mexico: The Rural Economy of the Guadalajara Region, 1675–1820.* Berkeley: University of California Press, 1981.

Vedoya, Juan Carlos. *Cómo fue la enseñanza popular en la Argentina.* Buenos Aires: Plus Ultra, 1973.

Vidal Sanz, Lucía. "Las escuelas de los ingenios azucareros en Tucumán (1884–1916)." In *Estudios de historia social de Tucumán: Educación y política en los siglos XIX y XX,* edited by Luis Marcos Bonano, 55–58. Tucumán: Facultad de Filosofía y Letras, Universidad Nacional de Tucumán, 2004.

Warman, Arturo. "The Cauldron of the Revolution: Agrarian Capitalism and the Sugar Industry in Morelos, Mexico, 1880–1910." In *Crisis and Change in the International Sugar Economy, 1860–1914,* edited by Bill Albert and Adrian Graves, 165–80. Norwich, UK: ISC Press, 1984.

———. *We Come to Object: The Peasants of Morelos and the National State.* Translated by Stephen K. Ault. Baltimore: Johns Hopkins University Press, 1980.

Whigham, Thomas. *The Politics of River Trade: Tradition and Development in the Upper Plata, 1780–1870.* Albuquerque: University of New Mexico Press, 1991.

Williams, Eric. *Capitalism and Slavery.* New York: Russel and Russel, 1944.

Wolford, Wendy. "Of Land and Labor: Agrarian Reform on the Sugarcane Plantations of Northeast Brazil." *Latin American Perspectives* 31, no. 2 (2004): 147–70.

Wright, Winthrop. *British-Owned Railways in Argentina: Their Effect on Economic Nationalism, 1854–1948.* Austin: Institute of Latin American Studies, University of Texas Press, 1974.

Yarrington, Doug. *A Coffee Frontier: Land, Society, and Politics in Duaca, Venezuela, 1830–1936.* Pittsburgh: University of Pittsburgh Press, 1997.

Zanetti Lecuona, Oscar, and Alejandro García. *Sugar and Railroads: A Cuban History, 1837–1959.* Chapel Hill: University of North Carolina Press, 1998.

Index

A page number in italic type indicates an illustration on that page. The letter *n* following a page number indicates an endnote on that page. The number following the *n* indicates the note number(s).

Aduana Seca, 158n10
Aguirre, Baltasar, 35–36
Alberdi, Salvador de, 11
Alsina, Juan, 190n43, 191n59
Alvear, Marcelo T. de, 187n145
Argentina: Argentine Confederation and, 143–44; economic development of, 1–2, 144–45, 158n14, 200n4; Franco-Prussian War and, 162n46; immigration and, 170n101; population of, 155n3, 175n43; public education and, 130–31; regions and provinces of (map), 3; state formation in, 158n15; sugar industry and, 145–46; Tucumán sugar and, 4
Argentine Agricultural and Pastoral Census, 51
Avellaneda, Nicolás, 5–6, 144, 200n2

Balán, Jorge, 99
Bernárdez, Manuel, 118
Bialet Massé, Juan, 99, 101, 104, 105, 114, 178n71
Boletín nacional de agricultura, 58
Bolivia, 18, 163n54. See also Upper Peru
Bousquet, Alfredo, 159n17
Bravo, Maria Celia, 175n44, 186n129
Brazil, sugar industry in, 173n17; Latin America and, 147–48; literature on, 202n15
Burmeister, Hermann, 8

Campi, Daniel, 97, 188n10, 189n24, 189n34
cañeros, *49;* capital requirements and, 61–62; disputes with ingenios and, 79–84, 185nn114–118; diverse socioeconomic backgrounds of, 60–61; families

and, 75, 96, 100–101; heterogeneity and, 60–74, 148; importance of, 58; landownership and use and, 55, 72; living conditions of, *64,* 72–74; local press and, 83–84, 186n141; output of, 197n33; outsiders as, 63–64, 85; partnership durations and, 62–63; previously unused lands and, 62; sale contracts and, 75–79; small and medium producers as, 61, 149; sugarcane economics and, 56–58. *See also* ingenios and planters
Capital Department, population and work force, 21–23, 164n64
Catamarca, 92–93
census data, 5, 49–51, 64–65, 153–54. *See also* manuscript schedules
Colombres, Obispo José Eusebio, 34
colonos, 68–72; contracts and, 69–70; credit and, 71, 183n77, 184n109; in Cuba, 148; labor provision and, 71–72; in Puerto Rico, 148; sale of crops and, 70–71; soil care and maintenance and, 70; in Tucumán and other areas, 182n59
Compañia Azucarera Tucumana (CAT), 46, 176n50, 177n51
Consejo de Higiene, 135, 198n63
Conti, Viviana, 157n4
contribución directa, 12
Correa, Antonio, 56, 57–58, 186n130
Cuba, sugar industry in, 147; colonos and, 148, 202n19; literature on, 202n15; railroads and, 168n95
Cuyo region, 155n2

Denis, Pierre, 74, 98

education, public, 129–32; Argentina and,
130–31; Education Law of 1883 and,
131–32; education levels and, 133–34;
infrastructure and, 132–33; Junta Central and, 130; as labor policy, 130–31;
teachers and, 132; in Tucumán, 131–34
Escuela de Ayudantes, 132
Escuela Normal, 132
Escuela Pedagógica Sarmiento, *134*
Estación Experimental Agrícola, 46–47

Fawcett, Preston, and Company, 99
Ferrocarril Buenos Aires y Rosario, 27–28
Ferrocarril Central Argentino, 24–25, 26,
27, 166n84, 166n86
Ferrocarril Central Norte, 5, 26–27; 1866
survey of, 24–25; sugar industry and, 39
Ferrocarril del Sud, 25–26, 166n86
Ferrocarril Noroeste Argentino, 26
Ferrocarril San Cristóbal, 27–28
Figueroa, Federico, 191n57
Franck, Harry, 2, 104; on the sugar indus-
try, *33*, 143; on sugar labor force, 87
Fraser, John Foster, 38–39; on San Miguel,
137; on sugar industry expansion, 53

Gallo, Santiago, 91
Giménez Zapiola, Marcos, 175n44
Granillo, Arsenio, 18, 36, 60; on San
Miguel floods, 24
Groussac, Paul, 18; on growth of sugar
industry, 39, 187n3; on new sugar tech-
nology, 60; on sugarcane economics,
57; on tax policies, 160n20
Guerra, Ramiro, 202n19
Guy, Donna, 6, 126, 145, 174n34, 190n41
Guzmán, Alfredo, 40

Hamilton, Alberto García, 180n19
health care, 134–38; disease control and,
136–37; government commitment to,
134–35; infant mortality and, 135; malnutrition and, 136; in San Miguel, 139–40
Hileret, Clodomiro, 40–41
Hora, Roy, 173n15
Hospital Mixto, 135, *138*
hurto de servicios, 13–14
Hutchinson, Thomas, 112

Ingenio Aguilares, 45
Ingenio Bella Vista, 42, 70, 80, 94, *100*,
102; bonuses and, 104; hospital at, *97*,
109; workers' rations and, 104; work
ethic and, 102
Ingenio Concepción, 39–40
Ingenio Contreras, 43
Ingenio Cruz Alta, 78, 115
Ingenio Esperanza, 37, 39, *40*, 103, 184n90;
child labor and, 104; living conditions
of, 108; workers' rations and, 104
Ingenio La Florida, 45, 46, 61, 69
Ingenio La Providencia, 94, 105, 106,
184n91
Ingenio Lules, 40–41, 68, 136
Ingenio Mercedes, 1910, 57, 71, 83, 103;
bonuses and, 104; CAT and, 176n50;
workers' rations and, 104
ingenios: land use and, 56; outside growers
and, 56–58; popular criticism of, 59;
sugarcane area and (map), *42*
Ingenio San Antonio, 45
ingenios and planters, 75–84; cash
advances, 78; conflicts and, 79–84;
contracts and, 75–76, 79–84; freshness
and planting procedures and, 77–78;
market instability and, 76; product
delivery and, 76–77; provincial government and, 82; railroads and, 77; size
of landholdings and, 58–59; taxation
and, 121–24; water rights and, 80–82,
185n121; weighing crops and, 77, 82–83
Ingenio San Miguel, strike of 1904 and, 96,
116–17
Irrigation Code of 1897 (Tucumán), 81–82,
186n129

Java sugarcane variety, 46–47
Jefferson, Mark, 94, 99, 105
Jesuits, 14, 18, 34, 43, 161n30
Jujuy, sugar industry in, 43–44, 176n46,
179n2

labor, sugar industry and, 13–14, *93*,
149–50; administrators and, 102–3;
alcohol and, 111, 113, 193n103; cash
advances and, 96; child labor and,
89–90, 193n94; chronic shortages

of, 96–97, 187n2; coercion and, 92,
189n36; corporal punishment and, 94;
dangers and, 103; employers' authority
and, 94; families and, 101, 104; field
and factory work and, 98–106; flight
and, 112–13, 194n108; housing and,
96, 106–8; immigration and, 98–101,
191n51, 191nn56–57; independent
contractors and, 91–92, 188n17;
indigenous workers and, 90–91; interprovincial competition and, 92–93;
organized resistance and, 116–18;
papeletas and, 13, 88–89, 160n22; payment systems and, 103–4; Police Code
of 1856 and, 13–14, 88; Police Code of
1877 and, 88–89; sabotage and, 114;
schools and medical facilities and,
96, 97, 109; seasonality and, 87–88;
seasonal workers and, 100; Servants'
Law of 1888 and, 89–90, 94, 95, 96,
116, 188nn9–10; strike of 1904 and, 96,
116–17; sugar community and, 106–18;
theft and, 113–14; vagrancy and, 13, 88,
160n22; violence and, 114–18; workforce discipline and, 93–95; workforce
size and, 97, 190n41, 190n43; working
conditions and, 101–4, 117–18
Lahitte, Emilio, 58
Langer, Erick D., 157n4
Latin America, sugar production and, 150;
impact of railroads on, 168n95
Lotito, Luis, 118, 193n103

Maeso, Justo, 161n37
malaria, 136–37
manuscript schedules, 49–51, 64–65, 72,
161n34. *See also* census data
Marbais, Alfred, 17
Martínez Muñecas, Domingo, 90
May Revolution, 11
Medina, Abraham, 28, 94–95
Medinas, 167n88
Méndez brothers, 36, 40, 58, 121; Fawcett,
Preston, and Company and, 99
Mendoza, economy of, 2
Mexico, sugar industry and, 149; literature
on, 203n21
Mitre, Bartolomé, 25, 144, 195n2

Moneta, Pompeyo, 24, 166nn81–82
Mulhall, E. T., 21, 57

National University of Tucumán (UNT),
132, *133*
Nougués family, 21, 28–29, 98, 198n53;
residence of, *107*

Oficina Química, 135, 198n63
Orden, El, 79; on planter-ingenio relations,
80; on planters, 59, 60, 83–84; on
Saavedra Lamas Law, 31; on sugarcane
prices, 76; on sugar concentration, 48;
on sugar towns, 109; on treatment of
workers, 94

papeletas, 13, 160n22
Parish, Woodbine, 161n37
patentes, 12, 121–29
Patroni, Adrián, 116, 195n126
Pellegrini, Carlos, 53
Peru, sugar industry in, 149; literature on,
202n20
Peruvian space, 157n4
Potosí, 9
public education. *See* education, public
public health. *See* health care
Pucci, Roberto, 175n44
Puerto Rico, sugar industry and, 148;
literature on, 202n18

Quesada, Vicente, 23
Quinteros, Lídoro, 61, 123

railroads, 25–31; construction of, 166n84;
privatization and, 167n90; sugar
industry in Latin America and, 28–29,
168n95; sugar industry in Tucumán
and, 28, 168n93; track gauges and,
167n89; in Tucumán (map), 27. *See also*
specific railroads
Rickart, Ignacio: on labor shortage, 14;
on sugar technology, 36; on Tucumán
prosperity, 14, 25
Río Sali, 186nn122–23
Rivadavia, Bernardino, 160n22
Roca, Julio A., 5–6, 90
Rocchi, Fernando, 200n4

Rodríguez Marquina, Paulino, 68, 95; on immigration, 99; on infant mortality, 135; on the sugar industry, 72
Rosas, Juan Manuel de, 120, 160n22
rural areas, 1870s, 15

Saavedra Lamas Law, 30–31
Sábato, Jorge, 173n15
Salta, sugar industry and, 43–44
Sánchez Román, José Antonio, 38, 164n59, 168n93; on protective tariffs, 171n109
San Germés, Pedro, 43
San Miguel de Tucumán, 138–41, 143; Burmeister on, 8; cart manufacture and, 10; as cultural center, 140–41; development of, 23–24; early history of, 9–10, 138–39, 158nn5–6; foreigners in, 98; Fraser on, 137; government palace in, 141; immigration and, 22–23; infrastructure of, 138–39, 199nn78–79; public health and, 139–40, 200nn81–82; Río de la Plata viceroyalty and, 10–11; sugar and, 2; Upper Peru and, 10
Santiago del Estero, 43, 92–93
Sarmiento, Domingo Faustino, 120, 144
Schleh, Emilio, 201n5
Sempat Assadourián, Carlos, 157n4
sharecroppers, 65; contracts and, 67; size of landholding and, 68
silver, Upper Peru and, 8–9
sugarcane, 64–65, 180n6; Java variety of, 46–47, 177nn53–54; mosaic virus and, 5; transporting, 29
sugar industry, 37; 1895 crisis and, 45; banking and, 179n5, 181n31; beginnings of, 33–39; bounties and, 30–31; Brazil and, 147–48, 173n17, 202n15; Brussels Treaty and, 30; colonias and, 68–72; Cuba and, 147–48, 168n95, 202n15, 202n19; cultivated hectares, 1895 (table), 65; diversity and, 37–39; firm organization and, 46; growth of, 33–34, 37, 39–48, 171n2; instability and, 44–45; investment and, 38–39, 173n15; Jesuits and, 34; Jujuy and, 43–44; labor and (see under labor, sugar industry and); land-holding patterns and, 64–74, 84, 149; land leases and,

65–67; land-use patterns and, 50; Latin America and, 44–45, 150; local economies and, 45–46; markets and, 38–39, 170nn104–5; Mexico and, 149, 203n21; modernization, product quality and, 41–42; modern technology and, 34–36, 39–40, 201n5; national government and, 145–46; organization of production and, 55–59; other provinces and, 42–44; outside growers and, 56–59, 72, 123; Peru and, 149, 202n20; plantation size, technology and, 36; production quotas and, 175n44; profitability and, 34, 172n5; Puerto Rico and, 148; quality standards and, 170n103; railroads and, 28–29, 163n53; raw material demand and supply and, 42–43, 46; Salta and, 43–44; sharecropping and, 67–68; tariff protection and, 29–30, 171n107, 171n109; taxation, 121–24; technology and, 34–37, 172n6; traditional methods and, 34–35; Tucumán and, 41, 141–43, 151; vulnerability and, 85. See also ingenios; ingenios and planters; planters (cañeros); specific industry elements
sugar towns, 106–12, 118; alcohol and gambling in, 111; company stores and, 109–10; ingenios and, 106, 111–12; public baths in, 110; schools and, 109

tariffs, 28–31, 169nn97–98, 171nn106–7. See also Saavedra Lamas Law
taxation: 1878 legislation and, 121–22, 137; 1880 legislation and, 122; 1881 legislation and, 123; 1887 legislation and, 123; 1889 legislation and, 124; 1895 legislation and, 125–27; 1897 production tax and bounty, 170n102; 1900–16 legislation and, 127–28; collection of, 12; contribución directa and, 12; ingenios and, 121–22; national subsidies and, 119–20; patentes and, 12, 124–26, 197n40; public education and, 120–21; sugar industry and, 121–24
tenants, 65; contracts and, 65–66; size of landholding and, 68
Terán, Juan, 15–16, 58, 72
Terry, José, 190n43

tobacco, 17, 20, 37–38, 54, 162n41
Tornquist, Ernesto, 41–42
Trancas, 165n66, 165n70
Tucumán, 31–32; 1853 commission report on, 17, 18, 20; before the sugar boom, 16–25; capital and, 21, 164n59; carts, *19*, 20, *71*, 163n50, 163n53, 167n88; cottage industries and, 52–53; early years in, 8–16; economic development of, 3; economy of, 2, 8, 162n41; ecosystem of, 161n29; general subsidies and, 119–20; grain crops in, 16, 48–49, 162n39; health expenditures and, 137; immigration and, 22–23, 98; Irrigation Code of 1897 in, 81–82; labor legislation and, 12–14, 159n16; land-holding system in, 14–16; land-use patterns in, 49–52; large landowners and, 50–51; local consumption and, 20; manufacturing in, 19–20; May Revolution and, 11; medium-sized land owners and, 50; migrants and, 23; national educational subventions and, 120–21; national patterns and, 158n15; occupational structure and, 52–53; pastoral sector and, 18; per capita output value and, 166n81; Police Code of 1856 and, 13–14; public education and, 131–32; public health and, 134–38; railroads and tariffs and, 25–31; small landowners and, 51; sugarcane and, 17, 197n33; sugar expansion and, 48–54; sugar industry and, 4, 41, 129–30, 141–42, 146–47, 151–52; tax policies and, 12, 119–29, 137, 159n16, 159n17, 159n19; tobacco and, 17; trade and, 20–21; visitors on, 23–24. *See also* education, public; health care; taxation

Unión General de Trabajadores (UGT), 116–17, 118
Upper Peru, 8–9, 157n3. *See also* Peruvian space
Urquiza, Justo José de, 35, 120

vagrancy, 13

water rights, 80–82
women, labor force and, 22, 53, 100, 105, 164n65, 165n68, 165nn67; census data and, 178n71; family survival and, 178n74

Yrigoyen, Hipólito, 5–6